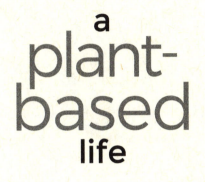

a
plant-
based
life

a plant-based life

Your Complete Guide to Great Food, Radiant Health, Boundless Energy, and a Better Body

Micaela Cook Karlsen

AMERICAN MANAGEMENT ASSOCIATION
New York • Atlanta • Brussels • Chicago • Mexico City • San Francisco
Shanghai • Tokyo • Toronto • Washington, D.C.

Bulk discounts available. For details visit: www.amacombooks.org/go/specialsales
Or contact special sales: Phone: 800-250-5308 | Email: specialsls@amanet.org
View all the AMACOM titles at: www.amacombooks.org
American Management Association: www.amanet.org

This publication is designed to provide accurate and authoritative information in regard to the subject matter covered. It is sold with the understanding that the publisher is not engaged in rendering legal, accounting, or other professional service. If legal advice or other expert assistance is required, the services of a competent professional person should be sought.

Library of Congress Cataloging-in-Publication Data

Names: Karlsen, Micaela Cook, author.
Title: A plant-based life : your complete guide to great food, radiant
  health, boundless energy, and a better body / Micaela Cook Karlsen ;
  foreword by T. Colin Campbell.
Description: New York : Amacom, [2016] | Includes bibliographical references
  and index.
Identifiers: LCCN 2016001353| ISBN 9780814437070 (pbk.) | ISBN 9780814437087
  (ebook)
Subjects: LCSH: Vegetarian cooking. | Vegetarianism. | LCGFT: Cookbooks.
Classification: LCC TX837 .K256 2016 | DDC 641.5/636--dc23 LC record available at http://lccn.loc.gov/2016001353

ABOUT AMA

American Management Association (www.amanet.org) is a world leader in talent development, advancing the skills of individuals to drive business success. Our mission is to support the goals of individuals and organizations through a complete range of products and services, including classroom and virtual seminars, webcasts, webinars, podcasts, conferences, corporate and government solutions, business books, and research. AMA's approach to improving performance combines experiential learning—learning through doing—with opportunities for ongoing professional growth at every step of one's career journey.

10 9 8 7 6 5 4 3 2 1

For my many Ms and one D.

"What you seek is seeking you"

—RUMI

CONTENTS

TREATS

ONGOING SUPPORT RESOURCES   291

FOREWORD

by T. Colin Campbell

Adopting diets mostly or entirely composed of intact, whole plants—vegetables, fruits, grains, legumes, nuts—has been a challenge for decades, if not for centuries, given the natural human tendency to seek more calorie-dense foods. Animal-based diets have long been preferred by most people, becoming firmly entrenched in the cultural fabric of societies able to afford these foods. At the same time, taste preferences have, over time, become fixed to the point that we can now call them addictions. In recent decades, this has been exacerbated by the increased use of refined carbohydrates—especially sugars and refined flours—primarily for the purpose of responding to what we might refer to as "snack attacks" by creating sweet-tasting convenience foods, which are also loaded with fat and salt.

The scientific evidence in favor of a whole food, plant-based diet has become impressive in recent years, suggesting to many people an urgency in making a dietary change, for a variety of personal and public reasons. However, because of the seeming intransigence of dietary tradition, change can be quite difficult. *A Plant-Based Life*, by Micaela Karlsen, addresses this challenge with a personal and professional focus that readers will find both useful and compelling.

Among those of us involved in the scientific and clinical development of data on the benefits of whole food, plant-based diets, there is good consensus that we need to find ways to make change possible. It is not a lack of reliable evidence favoring this way of eating but a question of behavior change, as the professionals like to call it. How can people navigate change for themselves and their families and friends? On a societal scale, there are powerful institutions that will resist this change using all the resources under their control and at their command, however reasonable or unreasonable their efforts may be. The answer, it seems to me, is to go directly to the consumer and offer them some ideas that make easier their transition to a better lifestyle. Readers will find such ideas, and more, in this book, making the path to a plant-based life desirable as well as achievable.

PREFACE

AT AGE 17, I made a decision to stop eating meat. My reasons then weren't anything like my reasons now. There was just a vague feeling that moved me to stop. It could have been related to the fact that some of my friends didn't eat meat, or it could have been some innate instinct for health, but for whatever reason, I just didn't want meat anymore. Becoming a vegetarian was gradual over months, but by the time I had turned 18 and was in my senior year of high school, I had stopped eating meat completely and began to think more specifically about my health. I was highly allergic to dust and dust mites, so much so that I was a candidate for weekly allergy shots. The shots helped but, it seemed, only up to a point. I have memories of waking up on the morning of my shots with dry lips and a sore throat from breathing through my mouth all night. I would sit up in bed feeling everything in the world start sliding downwards. My nose ran, the room spun, and it was all I could do to stumble into the shower, where the hot water gave me 15 wonderful minutes of normal breathing. Add skin problems, sleep deprivation due to insomnia, typical concern over my weight, and it's amazing that I was still a good student.

The diet I ate as a vegetarian in high school involved lots of white bread, skim milk and cereal, cans of green beans for lunch, and orange juice. I organized my choices around an attempt to lose weight by eating a low-fat diet. I did lose weight, but I was always hungry. Constantly looking ahead to my next meal, while at the same time trying to concentrate on calculus or my after-school job, I limped along in a state of deprivation that seemed justified because it allowed me to maintain a healthy weight—or at least a weight at which I didn't feel self-conscious. Moving into my freshman year of college soon ended my dedication to a low-fat diet as the all-you-can-eat buffets provided more than enough extra calories for me to gain the "freshman 15."

During my junior year, one of my best friends, Meghan Murphy, took a popular course at Cornell, *NS:200 Vegetarian Nutrition*, taught by Dr. T. Colin Campbell, the university's Professor Emeritus in nutritional biology, and later the coauthor of *The China Study* (2005), the first and most comprehensive account of the research on plant-based diets and health, as well as author of *Whole* (2013). Through Meghan, the evidence-based, scientific information about diet and disease began to seep into my thinking. Having already read John Robbins's *Diet for a New America*, and eaten a vegetarian diet for several years, it was no big mental leap to cut out dairy and think of myself as a vegan. Physically, my cravings for cheese remained in full force for a few years (in contrast to giving up meat), but intellectually a totally plant-based diet made sense.

By the time I began working for Dr. Campbell's foundation in my mid-twenties, I'd been eating what I considered a vegan diet for several years, had much improved my allergies and skin, and had settled into something close to my ideal weight—and minus the deprivation. Being so closely involved with information about whole food, plant-based (WFPB) nutrition, I was able to further refine my understanding of what "whole food" meant. It took me at least another six months to a year to move into a truly whole food, 100 percent plant-based diet, but it's now been almost a decade of this gradual shift, and I couldn't be more pleased. Once I started eating a truly whole food, plant-based diet, I felt comfortable in my body for the first time since I was a child. I still have challenges when I'm in certain food environments and I have to strategize around them to make sure that I don't get pulled back down the addictive rabbit hole of fatty foods. But I am able to maintain my dietary lifestyle successfully because of specific strategies that are discussed in this book, and these strategies can work for everyone.

The people whose stories are shared in *A Plant-Based Life*, who provide supporting evidence for the research and examples of certain principles we'll cover, can also serve as inspiration to you. Many who were motivated have struggled. They have overcome their backgrounds, their childhood eating patterns, unsupportive family members or spouses, and challenges with their children, but they have achieved permanence in following a dietary lifestyle that is quite unusual in the current environment, and they have attained good health that they can enjoy for many years. I was one of those people, and it took me years of trial and error to arrive at a peaceful and successful place with my eating and my diet. I'm grateful for what I've learned, and now I'd like to help you skip some of that difficulty.

a
plant-
based
life

INTRODUCTION

T HE SECRET'S OUT, AND everyone's trying it. Eating a whole food, plant-based diet not only can prevent and reverse chronic disease, it's delicious, beautiful, environmentally sustainable, compassion-ate—it's the prescription you've always wanted, the one that actually makes you feel better than you ever thought you could with only positive side-effects.

Once it's a habit, plant-based eating can be easy, not to mention tasty. But reformatting your patterns and old way of interacting with food takes skill and strategy; like any habit, sustaining it requires some ongoing main-tenance. It's not something that happens to you; you have to choose to make it happen. Our busy schedules, long commutes, and the sheer volume of food choices we have make the modern food environment a relentless challenge to healthy eating. *A Plant-Based Life* is a resource to help you understand, navigate, and conquer these challenges at your own pace so you can enjoy a life of dietary ease and health. It will also help you stay connected to other people while you're on this journey.

You may have picked up this book because you're just beginning your journey of eating plant-based food. You may have picked it up because you've been eating some version of a whole food, plant-based diet for some time and you've hit a roadblock or a plateau.

1

You may not actually want to eat a vegetarian, vegan, or largely plant-based diet but are just looking for strategies to help you incorporate more vegetables and fruits into your life.

If any of those things are true, you are in the right place.

Even for motivated eaters who may care deeply about their health, our environment, or the suffering of animals, it can be difficult to stick with your intentions about what you want to put in your mouth. You may have streaks of great success interrupted by periods of "falling off the wagon." You may feel satisfied with your overall diet but wish to ferret out those few habits that prevent you from losing the final five pounds so many other plant-based eaters seem to lose so easily.

You may be facing a serious illness, confronted by the reality that changing your diet is essential—but you have no idea where to begin.

You may have read other books on nutrition or factory farming that provided motivation to give it a try, but you're dubious about whether or not you can stick with it.

This book is written to be an effective and compassionate how-to manual for anyone who wants to know more about what a whole food plant-based diet is, how to transform his or her own diet, and how to ensure success in sticking with it.

It's hard to explain to someone who's never tried it just how *good* you can feel eating whole, plant foods. Personally, I think that feeling good is one of the reasons it's so much easier to stick with it than other behaviors we feel we "should" do for our health. People who eat some version of a plant-based diet already will be familiar with the improved energy and clarity of mind, but it doesn't stop there. You may want to lose weight and achieve a healthy weight without counting calories, and you can. Plant-based diets have also been demonstrated to reverse (that's right—reverse, not just prevent) type 2 diabetes[1] and heart disease,[2] stop the progression of MS,[3] and reduce the risk for cancer.[4] These are the major causes of preventable death and disability in the Western world!

But this isn't just about physical health. You may want to eat in alignment with your values, and you can. You may want to create a sustainable future for our planet, and you can. The power of plant-based eating is that you can make a real and appreciable difference in your own life, which at the same time makes a difference in our world.

Most people embarking on a whole food, plant-based diet for the first time will have questions and concerns about plant-based nutrition. We will cover these questions and concerns carefully, tackling these topics from an evidence-based perspective.

Evidence-based thinking means allowing the available scientific research to direct your conclusions, with your mind open to changing your position if the evidence supports it. Evidence may include personal experiences and case studies, but it should be founded on population-based or intervention research studies that track the response of groups to different conditions. It is the most objective and trustworthy way of gathering "food for the mind."

Here are some of the questions and concerns that people often express:

- Will I get enough protein without eating animal foods?
- Don't carbs make you fat?
- What about B_{12}?
- What about vitamin D?
- Don't I need to take fish oil supplements for omega-3s?
- What is gluten-free all about?
- I ate a vegetarian diet in the past and I was so tired. I'm not sure if it's good for me.
- I think my body needs meat, or needs dairy.
- What about raw food? Is a raw diet healthier?
- How do I know what to believe about nutrition? There's a new diet every week.

You may also be concerned about any of the numerous roadblocks you will encounter in making healthy choices and you're not alone in this. We're going to address each of these concerns and lead you through the steps you can take to overcome the obstacles. You may relate to some of the following:

- I know eating a whole food, plant-based diet is a good thing. How do I stay motivated?
- What am I actually eating for breakfast, lunch, and dinner? How do I do this diet?
- What ingredients do I buy? What do I cook?
- How can I get my family on board?
- What do I feed my kids?

- I feel insecure when friends and family question me about what I'm doing. I'm not sure what to say, and I start to doubt my decision.
- I can't say no; temptation gets me every time and I eat food I don't want to be eating.
- I get so hungry when I'm out of the house that I end up buying unhealthy, prepared food.
- I'm addicted to fat, sugar, and salt.
- Every time I get close to breaking the addictions, I give in to cravings and I'm back to square one.
- There are reasons other than hunger that I turn to eating (emotional eating or overeating).
- No one in my immediate circle is supportive of my diet.
- I live in a place where healthy food is hard to find or actually get to, or where it's very expensive.
- I'm too busy to cook.
- I won't be able to go to normal restaurants with my friends now that I eat this way.
- I feel intimidated thinking about giving up so many foods I love.

I have heard these beliefs from people many times. These are the places where people get stuck, but there is a path through each one of them and the reward far outweighs the challenge. Even if you have tried eating a plant-based diet in the past and struggled or met with only mixed success, you definitely *can* succeed—if you commit to success and use the strategies we'll discuss here. You have an incredible opportunity to change your life. Change is initially uncomfortable, but so, so worth it. You'll be repaid many times over in long-term ease and comfort in your body.

HOW TO USE THIS BOOK

J ANET HAS ALWAYS BEEN an inspiration to me around cooking. "I love food!" she has declared. Some of my favorite lasagna experiences are thanks to Janet; she makes an ever-varying recipe, sometimes using zucchini for the noodles, sometimes rice pasta, and sometimes just layering various vegetables and herbs in a delicious approximation of lasagna that I have only wondered how to replicate. I've settled for being grateful to have such a talented friend.

Janet has such a "right relationship"—to use her words—with eating that I am often caught up in a poetic appreciation of her cooking. "I belong to a local farm, and last night I picked up some chard," she once told me. "This chard, it's grown in a hoop house—it's just the sweetest, tenderest, most delectable chard you can imagine. The closer it is to the point of picking, the more exciting it is, the more nourishing and comforting it is."

I don't actually love chard, but I love Janet, and hearing her thoughts about it made me love the chard in that moment, too.

Of my many friends who eat a whole food, plant-based diet, Janet's delight in it is inspiring, especially when you consider her background. As a child, her family food environment revolved around Sunday dinners of exquisite torture. The weekly ritual, aptly named "Prison Dinner" by her parents, efficiently precluded any possibility of undiscovered misdeeds going unpunished, as all the children were fed special food the parents had reserved in the back of the refrigerator to grow moldy, thus systematically penalizing all uncaught misbehavior. After decades of healing, experimenting, learning, testing, getting help, and trying various eating patterns, Janet's diet is worlds away from what she ate as a child, as it is from the steak and hamburger she ate regularly in her twenties, and food is now a source of joy and inspiration. Today, those childhood horrors no longer seem to affect her except in shaping her tolerance of other people's food choices. She has health and vitality, alignment with her personal values, and a lot of friends who love to eat her cooking.

How is Janet able to do it, and how can you do it as well? Wavering commitment to a dietary goal is something many of us have shared at one point or another in our lives. The inspiration to eat a healthier diet might have come from a health crisis, influence or pressure from friends and family, innate curiosity, desire for greater fulfillment, or as an expression of your principles. Whatever the source of your urge, there are two certainties. First, you have to start somewhere, with some kind of motivation to make an improvement. And second, it's going to take more than your initial burst of enthusiasm to keep it going. Making permanent lifestyle change requires experimentation, adjustments, and continual recommitment. This is how you integrate new information and make it your own.

If you're ready to take time out of your busy schedule to improve your diet, it's worthwhile to get a heads up on how to maximize your return on investment in reading this book. We'll begin by discussing the book's structure and approach, what to expect, and how to get the most out of it, all to the purpose of making it easy and possible for you to successfully sustain plant-based eating as a lifestyle. We'll then move on to a self-assessment that will help you to determine which approach to a plant-based diet is best for you, and a discussion of SMART goals and accountability that will help you create a support structure for your new habits. Let's start with the big picture. This book is organized in two parts. Part 1 leads you through a program of five steps to transition you to radiant health, renewed energy, and a better body. Each step addresses a different aspect of dietary behavior change and guides you in taking concrete next actions toward a plant-based diet. These next actions lead to three suggested paths for change at the close of each step: a gradual change, called *Easing In*; a more moderate pace, called *Rev It Up*; and a 100 percent transition path, called *Total Transformation*. You will have the choice to move at the pace that feels right to you.

Following the five steps of change, Part 2 offers the Recipe and Resources sections of the book—essential cooking and how-to information and additional opportunities for connection and engagement to help you stay plugged into a plant-based lifestyle. There are 100 delicious, plant-based recipes from my heroes, mentors, and friends, as well as reading lists, recommended programs and conferences, social media sites, and more. These resources will help you stay connected, keep going, and make plant-based eating a lifetime habit.

The five steps of this program—finding your motivating force, adding plant-based food to your diet, choosing health over habit, making your food environment match your biology, and making your diet socially sustainable—are founded on some of the key elements that research has identified as being important in transitioning your diet and maintaining it afterwards (see Figure 1). The more of these elements you possess, the more likely you are to succeed.

All of the elements in the figure enhance each other and act in concert. We'll cover the why, the what, and the how of each of these in depth in the

Figure 1: **YOUR PATH TO CHANGE**

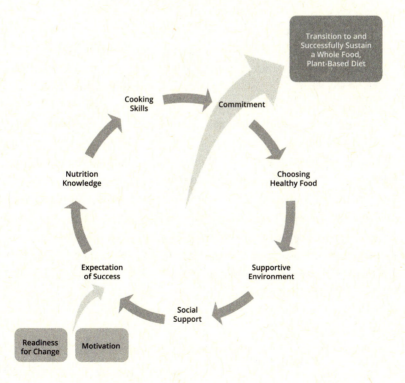

five steps ahead, but let's begin with an overview of where you'll find guidance on each of these elements in the book.

You need an expectation of success, which means the more belief you have in your ability to control your diet,[1] and the more you know that the outcome is possible for you, the more likely you are to succeed.[2] And success definitely is possible! Stories like Janet's, and the others that follow, will keep reminding you of the attainability of a plant-based lifestyle. The conceptual model outlining how to successfully transition to and maintain a plant-based diet is presented in Figure 1 so you can start thinking about the big picture of your life and how well it supports your dietary goals. The journey begins with a readiness in you for change and a motivation to eat a plant-based diet.[3] As discussed in Step One, that motivation may come from a variety of sources, and it's well worth your time to enhance those impulses, crystallize your vision, and make a point to stay engaged with your reasons for eating this way.

You then need both knowledge of nutrition so that you can evaluate dietary options and make decisions based on credible information and cooking skills so that you can actually prepare the food. These will enable you to add in more and more whole, plant-based foods, which we'll discuss in Step Two.

The greater your commitment, especially at the beginning, the more you'll be able to choose healthy food to satisfy your hunger. This will allow you to reset your taste preferences and break free of cravings.[4] Step Three will show you how to let go of the processed and animal-based foods and successfully withdraw from food addictions.

Finally, for lasting and sustainable change, you need a supportive physical environment[5] and plenty of social support.[6] Step Four will guide you on a thorough examination of your home, work, travel, and other environments and provide strategies for making each place supportive of your dietary intentions so that you don't have to stop and think about what you'll be eating and you won't have to rely on your willpower.

Step Five will help you create a socially supportive environment by maintaining healthy and nurturing relationships with friends and family, cultivating new friendships with people who share a plant-based diet, and building a like-minded community. The social environment is often a make-or-break point for many people in maintaining a plant-based lifestyle in the long-term.

You may be wondering, "Do I need *all* of these elements?" or "Is this worth doing if I'm starting with nothing?" Don't worry. First of all, it's not overwhelming when we break it down piece by piece and develop each element one at a time. Second, you *can* succeed despite lacking most of these elements. But our purpose is for you to have the easiest experience possible, and the more elements you cultivate and grow, the easier it will be. There's plenty of time for you to move at your own pace. Unless you have a life-threatening condition, there is no rush. If you do have a serious medical reason for eating differently, you may need to make a dramatic change quickly; if so, be sure to communicate with your doctor about changing your diet.

This book's comprehensive approach to shifting your diet allows you to examine each part of your life and to determine how it either helps or hinders your intentions regarding what you eat. Researchers now pinpoint a whole slew of factors, collectively termed "the built environment," as the underlying framework enabling our poor diets. The built environment refers to any part of the world we interact with that is created by people— land use and transportation, buildings, food supply, etc.— anything that humans bring into existence. A major component of the built environment is the availability of food—what is sold and where it's sold; the elements of convenience; price; and how access to it changes depending on income, race, region, and other factors.[7]

Some researchers actually attribute the major part of our problems with obesity to the built environment,[8] a perspective that has emerged in recent years as a counterpoint to the traditional view that held individuals accountable for their weight problems even though many of the factors that enable and promote overweight are caused by circumstances almost entirely outside of a person's personal control.[9] These circumstances, which include advertising; access to fast food and processed food in supermarkets; situational cues like specific social contexts, larger portion sizes, modeling from other people or public figures; and a host of other triggers, have an ability to influence food purchasing and consumption in ways people are not even aware of.[10] Collectively, these factors automatically steer us toward diets heavily based on calorie-rich animal foods that almost all contain added fat, sugar, and salt. We'll talk about this more in Step Three, but artificially created foods like these stimulate addictive pathways in the brain, and achieving a healthy diet isn't as simple as "eating in moderation."[11]

Countering this stacked deck requires you to make a personal decision to live differently and to create a new environment that supports your goals. Though many of the circumstances that enable and promote this condition *are* due to factors almost entirely outside of our personal control, as a culture we tend to hold individuals personally accountable for their diet choices. This causes most of us a lot of frustration when we try to change what we eat and it's not really working. It's almost as if we need to take more than full responsibility for our diets if we want to make a real change, because the larger environment steers you largely in one direction—constantly eating animal-based and rich, energy-dense foods with added sugar, fat, and salt.

Unfortunately, the impulse to change is not always enough on its own. Janet has developed the habits and created the support structure she needs to maintain consistent success in what she eats, and as a result she's having a completely different experience in her body, her mind, and her life from most people her age—one without fear of a heart attack, without guilt about eating too much or losing self-control at a buffet, without allergies, and without the frustration of not sticking with her intentions. This doesn't happen without design. She and the other people whose stories are shared in the pages ahead are successful for specific reasons.

Wherever you start, and whatever your goals may be, you can use the five steps once or over and over again to arrive at your next level of healthy eating. Sometimes change occurs quickly, but in my own experience and through observing other people who have made a plant-based transition, *lasting* change arrives only when the new behavior becomes a habit, often after several rounds of readjustment and recommitment. Although I have met many people who went plant-based immediately and absolutely, I've met many more (and been one of them myself) who had to take a very active role in the transition for a fairly long period of time before the new behaviors became habitual.

Studying habits and their role in eating behavior is still kind of a fresh idea in research. So far, we know that intentions, the active components of decision making, can be crucial at the beginning of a new behavior, but the more we develop habits, the less our intentions actually matter.[12] This is particularly relevant to eating behavior, because the more "automaticity" (not thinking about what we're doing) we exhibit when choosing what to eat, the less we have to use our willpower, and the more likely we will be to have the energy to make healthy choices.[13] We'll get into this in more detail in Step Four, but avoiding the use of willpower as much as possible is vital to making a plant-based diet easy to sustain.

Habits are also triggered by our environment, and breaking habits is hard when you're accustomed to behaving in a certain way in a certain context. You can probably relate to automatically munching on chips and dip at a party without thinking about it, arriving at your office without noticing how you drove yourself there, or ordering your favorite dessert at a restaurant after seeing the dessert tray, though you had planned not to get dessert before you got to the restaurant.

The good news is that breaking old habits becomes easier in a new environment, so part of your work will be to create an environment around you that steers you toward the eating behaviors you want. And not only changing the circumstances around your eating, but simply repeating a behavior helps to form new habits, so the more repetition the better. This five-step program for beginning or improving your plant-based diet will guide you in forming new habits so that eating plant-based is easy and ingrained in your behavior—and you won't have to stop to think about it!

WHAT TO EXPECT

As previously mentioned, each of the five steps addresses part of the conceptual model, and the next actions for each step are presented with varying degrees of intensity: *Easing In* moves at a gradual pace, *Rev It Up* goes a bit faster, and *Total Transformation* takes you through a complete transition very quickly. Depending on your readiness, you may follow any of the three suggested time frames shown in Figure 2. However, you should set time goals for yourself based on your intuition. You can also take yourself through the five-step program more than once—first to make some major changes, and again to pursue refinements.

Tuning in to the right pace for you makes the process work. Moving ahead more gradually will still take you toward the same end goal; while it will take more time, there's no rush. As my friend Meghan used to say,

Figure 2: **SUGGESTED TIMELINE FOR TRANSITIONING TO A PLANT-BASED DIET**

WEEK	1	2	3	4	5	6	7	8	9	10	11	12
Easing In	Step 1		Step 2			Step 3			Step 4		Step 5 and Keep Going	
Rev It Up	Step 1	Step 2			Step 3		Step 4		Step 5 and Keep Going			
Total Transformation	Step 1	Step 2	Step 3	Step 4	Step 5 and Keep Going							

"Life is a long time." But if you dramatically overreach compared to your capacity to handle change in the moment, it can be easy to lose momentum.

You are most likely to succeed when you challenge yourself with kindness and in manageable chunks. Research has found that making a moderate number of changes is associated more strongly with achieving permanent lifestyle changes, compared to making just one change or a whole bunch of changes at once.[14] The theory is that engaging in a transition through involvement with two or three goals keeps you more connected to the process and more likely to succeed than trying to make a single change. At the same time, if you try to take on too many goals at once, they can overwhelm you. In keeping with this principle, the next actions for each of the three paths in the program are based on just a few themes. These themes underlie all the suggested goals, which you can pursue to the degree you are ready for:

- Increasing the amount of whole, plant-based foods you eat
- Decreasing the amount of animal-based and processed foods you eat
- Creating an environment that supports your success

We'll talk about the specifics of what each of these goals looks like in the chapters to come—mixed with stories of people who've created a sustainable, plant-based lifestyle. Remember, you are in control of the pace and you set your own goals within this framework. It will be important as we continue for you to set multiple, specific goals of your own to stay engaged in the process, but equally important that you not exceed your capacity for change by overreaching. As you continue reading, take the opportunity to self-reflect and let yourself be drawn toward one path or the other.

HOW TO GET THE MOST OUT OF THIS BOOK

Engagement leads to action, and action is what you'll need to change the way you eat. You will get the biggest payoff from reading this book if you engage 100 percent and participate fully. This book contains a number of exercises that offer valuable opportunity for self-reflection and goal setting. If you are just planning to read, I urge you to make a small commitment to get involved and at minimum complete the exercises. If you are already

12

planning on implementing the material, I challenge you to do so unreservedly. You have no idea what might be awaiting you. At the very least, as you begin to eat a plant-based diet you may find you have improved energy and an improved understanding of your own patterns. At most, you may find your whole life transformed.

While you envision the possibilities for your new, more plant-based lifestyle, assessing your readiness to make shifts provides a useful framework for setting goals. Diet can be an emotional topic. How you eat both interacts with and is affected by a variety of dynamics—not only your own health but also your past preferences, your identity and family history, your culture, your lifestyle, your friends, and the list goes on. It can get messy when you shake things up, but wherever you start, and wherever you want to go, it's all completely okay. The more you eat a whole food, plant-based diet, the better you'll feel and the healthier you'll be.

SELF-ASSESSMENT: HOW MUCH CHANGE AM I READY FOR?

This self-assessment will help you determine how quickly, and on which path, you want to move ahead. Your score doesn't mean you have to stick to that path throughout the process; it simply serves as a tool to help you consider how much you want to change your diet and reflect on what the right level of challenge is. As mentioned earlier, you can follow this program more than once. You can even jump between paths as you build momentum or encounter a reason to slow down. What makes it simple is that *the goals of the program are the same at every step of the way:* to help you move toward an increase in whole, plant-based foods in your eating habits, a decrease in animal-based and processed foods, and an improvement in the supportiveness of your environment. You will create your own specific goals that fit with your larger vision for your diet and your life, and the framework of the program will focus your efforts and steer you steadily forward to delicious, beautiful, and health-promoting food choices.

Self-Assessment #1: I would rank my overall level of motivation for changing my diet as:

1. I'm not sure if there's anything there.
2. I feel a slight flutter of motivation.

13

3. I feel motivated but I feel other emotions, too.

4. I am very willing and motivated.

5. I absolutely must change my diet: There is no other way for me.

Self-Assessment # 2: At the thought of eating a whole food, plant-based diet, I feel:

1. Alarmed

2. Skeptical

3. Indifferent

4. Interested

5. Excited

Self-Assessment #3: At the thought of not eating some of my favorite animal-based foods, I feel:

1. There's no way I could give up my favorite foods.

2. Oh . . . maybe . . . I don't know.

3. Do I feel anything?

4. I'm ready.

5. I don't want to eat that stuff anyway.

Self-Assessment #4: My willingness to try cooking and eating new foods is best described as:

1. I'll eat foods I already like but that's it.

2. New foods and I don't have the best relationship.

3. I could go either way.

4. Sure; I'll try anything.

5. I love trying new foods; I'm hoping to eat in a totally different way.

Self-Assessment #5: My openness to rearranging my schedule and routines to support different habits is:

1. I'm skeptical. I don't think I could really change my routine.

2. I could make some small changes.

3. I'm definitely ready to make some changes.

4. I'm pretty sure I can make almost anything work.

5. Nothing could stand in my way. Change has to happen!

14

Now, using the number associated with each of the statements that most closely matched your feelings, total your scores and let's see where you're at. There is a spectrum of readiness, and few people fall at either extreme. We all have moments of fluctuation on a day-to-day basis as well, and this natural rhythm to your change is normal. Whether you're just starting out or considering making more subtle, plant-based refinements to your diet, as you build momentum you will probably find your motivation increasing. It's likely you will feel noticeably better fairly quickly, which may also increase your willingness to make changes.

- **If your score is between 5 and 14:** Try *Easing In*: The start of a great new direction for you.
- **If your score is between 15 and 21:** You can *Rev It Up*: You're ready to step it up a notch.
- **If your score is between 22 and 25:** Go for *Total Transformation*: Sounds like you're ready for some major changes.

Remember, this assessment provides you with an opportunity to reflect and tune in to what feels like the right pace for you. You may start moving more quickly later on, but how you feel now is important, and it can be helpful to consider your feelings about these questions when you choose your initial tempo.

SMART GOALS AND ACCOUNTABILITY

Step One of this program will help you define your big vision and overall goals—what you want your diet, your lifestyle, and your health to be. Crystallizing that vision will lay the groundwork for you to set specific goals and move forward. The next actions for each of the three paths offer ideas for your goals, each of which are relevant to the information in each step.

In creating your own specific goals, the best approach is to follow the SMART goals model, a method widely used by clinicians and health educators to make goal setting more effective. The SMART acronym stands for: **S**pecific, **M**easurable, **A**ctionable, **R**elevant, and **T**ime-limited.

- *Specific* means you know exactly what the action is. "Eating better" doesn't create a clear picture of what you'll be doing, whereas "Eating three salads a week" is a specific and obvious activity.

15

- *Measureable* means you can tell quickly whether you've met the goal or not. If your goal is eating three salads, and if you eat only one salad, you know you haven't met your goal. If your goal were just to "eat better," you'd have no criteria for telling whether you have achieved it or not.
- *Actionable* means you can take action on the goal immediately. Eating three salads is something you can clearly put into practice right away, but "eating better" is something you cannot do until you know what it looks like.
- *Relevant* means that your SMART goal supports your larger vision and overall goals in your life. Eating three salads a week is relevant if your vision is to eat a whole food, plant-based diet.
- *Time-limited* means you allot yourself a designated amount of time in which to complete the goal, with a set deadline. In this case, planning to eat three salads in the coming week means you will have completed your goal in the next seven days.

There is one more important element to maximize your likelihood of successfully changing your diet—human connection. When you embark on any kind of change, it's essential that you do so in connection with other people if you want the change to be lasting. Particularly because eating is a social behavior, dietary isolation can dampen the desire to continue for many people who were initially bursting with enthusiasm. We'll discuss the power of community more in Step Five, including how and where to find a plant-based community if you don't already have one, but at this point you no doubt have some fresh and inspired ideas about your life and your eating that need to be shared with someone who can support that vision and provide some structure that you can lean on during the transition. You might call this person a support buddy, an accountability partner, a coach, or just a good friend, but whatever you call them they have to have a few particular qualities:

- They have to be someone you know, and to whom you can talk regularly (in person, over the phone, or through email) so they can personally respond to you. The goal here is to get live, personal feedback.
- They do not have to eat a plant-based diet (though that would be preferable), but they do need to be open to and accepting of your intentions with the diet and have a genuine interest in helping you reach your goals.

16

- They must be organized and reliable enough that you can depend on them to check in with you about the goals you've set, how you've met them, and what might be getting in your way. You need to feel a sense of accountability and that person's expectation that you will follow through on what you plan to do.

So right now, while you're thinking about this, make a list of the people you connect with for support and accountability. You don't need to convince them to eat a plant-based diet. This is about you and about finding the right person to support your needs. Does anyone stand out? Starting with your top pick, reach out and share what you're about to do. You can even approach more than one person if that feels right. Here's one possible way of approaching the person:

> *I want to ask your help with something. I've been feeling like I really want to make some changes to the way I eat. I want to eat a more plant-based diet, and I don't want to go through this transition in isolation. I'm reading a book that suggests finding someone I can share my goals with, who can help keep me accountable, check in on me, and help me celebrate successes! Would you be willing to do something like this? I think it could make a difference for me in being able to stick with this change.*

The arrangement you create with this person will depend on what works for each of you in your lives, but you'll get the most out of the arrangement if you follow two steps:

1. Review what SMART goals are with your support buddy. Make sure he or she understands the elements your goals need to include, and then share and review each of them with him or her when you set them to make sure they are specific, measurable, actionable, relevant to your larger goals, and time-limited.
2. Ask your support buddy to initiate contact with you after the period of time you've given yourself for each goal: to celebrate, if you've achieved that goal, or to help you process what happened and then readjust, if you haven't.

Your arrangement could mean scheduling a phone call or visit with your support buddy at the end of a week or after a deadline has passed. It could mean your support buddy emails you at a specified time to ask you how it went. The critical piece is that once you have made the plan, you know that

17

your next point of contact is either scheduled or that your support buddy will be reaching out to you. This structure gently upholds your deadlines and allows you to focus on actually following through with your target.

It's time to move into Step One, Finding Your Motivating Force. We're going to ramp up your excitement by discussing some of the exciting, beautiful, and delicious benefits to eating a plant-based diet; we will help you crystallize your larger vision for your diet; and, finally, we will dive into the strategies to stay connected to your vision and motivation. You're well on your way.

1

5 STEPS TO GREAT FOOD AND RADIANT HEALTH

making a plant-based diet easy and sustainable

FIND YOUR MOTIVATING FORCE
gathering food for the mind

❧

"**YOU NAME IT, I** pretty much had it," Gary told me, as he leaned back and mused about his old life. "I'd had one bypass surgery and was facing another. I was really heavy—like 70 pounds heavier than now. I felt sluggish all the time and I was on these fiber drinks because I was so constipated. Plus, I was taking pills for my blood pressure and my cholesterol. My doctor said I was prediabetic. I didn't sleep well but I wasn't really ever awake either. I felt like it was the beginning of the end of my life, even though I was supposed to be looking forward to my retirement."

Even with all these symptoms, it wasn't until the birth of Gary's grandson, a stern warning from his doctor, and the realization that he controlled his own health that he developed the impulse to try a plant-based path. Now, he says, his motivation grows stronger every day, as he keeps feeling better and better—especially when he thinks about all the medication he no longer takes. But it took a health crisis and the pressure to stay well for his grandchildren to get him started.

The motivation to change your diet because of a health issue doesn't always wait until you're older. My friend Pulin became a vegetarian at age eight and gave up all animal products at age seventeen. This translated to a tan-colored diet composed largely of peanut butter sandwiches, soymilk, and cereal, and it expanded to include the vegan junk food so readily available in the big cities he lived in as young adult. Pulin didn't regret his decision to go vegan, but the diet he was following pushed his cholesterol to 265 and his triglycerides to 795, even while he avoided animal foods. His doctor warned him that those were the first steps to an eventual heart attack, and he found himself facing taking statins in his early thirties.

Pulin was scared, but he turned his fear into action. After replacing the processed fake meats with whole plants and letting go of the vegan mayonnaise and fatty salad dressings, he found that his new diet was working.

A few weeks after we spoke, I got a text from Pulin that read: "Cholesterol 175, triglycerides 111." I felt so happy for him, knowing he had just set a new course for his life that avoided the slew of problems that Gary had faced. These sorts of results are common when people are motivated to switch to a whole food, plant-based diet, and they are possible for everyone. Provided, that is, that you are motivated, informed, and engaged.

In Step One, we will take a look at what you need to cultivate motivation, examine the health benefits of plant-based diets (which really serves to strengthen your motivation!), and discuss how to stay in touch with that feeling on a daily basis.

THE MOTIVATION EQUATION

Gary's and Pulin's stories emphasize the positive effects that plant-based eating can bring. Reading these stories can deepen your expectation of your own success. Keeping in mind or reminding yourself of the health benefits that can be derived from plant-based eating can also strengthen the value you ascribe to the diet.

Educators at the What Kids Can Do organization,[1] a cutting-edge nonprofit based in Providence, Rhode Island, that develops materials to improve educational outcomes for children, use a concept they call the Motivation Equation. This equation links motivation with expectation and value. It's readily applied to adults and nutrition and is as follows:

Motivation = Value × Expectation of Success.

Motivation is the impulse moving you toward a goal, but you can't be motivated without both *valuing* the results and also *expecting* that those results are possible for you—and each one of these two elements increases the impact of the other.

22

Expectation of success creates belief in the potential outcome, and it comes from two sources: your emotions and your intellect. The stories in this book of people who've achieved good health and lasting dietary change will help you relate to dietary success on an emotional level. At the same time, knowing the scientific basis for the health benefits of plant-based diets will frame the nutrition recommendations and make it possible for you to understand how and why you can take charge of your health. Together, these two components work in concert to keep you motivated and charged. If you revisit Figure 1 on page 7, you'll see that not only do you need to be ready for change, you also need several other elements that we'll address here in Step One: *motivation, expectation of success, nutrition knowledge*, which we'll introduce in this step, and *commitment*.

We know you're interested and that you have some level of motivation, but you must also value success, and you'll find that even easier after reading about some of the documented health benefits that a plant-based diet can bring.

THE HEALTH BENEFITS OF A PLANT-BASED DIET

The scientific evidence that demonstrates and supports the benefits of a plant-based diet is growing all the time, and the most dramatic aspect is that the effects not only prevent people from getting sick but, for certain serious conditions, the food they eat can also make them well.

Making people well is not something that medication for chronic disease has ever accomplished, and perhaps it never will. This is not for lack of effort on the part of drug developers or doctors, but the medications for chronic disease manage symptoms rather than treat the cause of the illness. Many studies suggest that when you look at the rates of adherence for medication, they are pretty dismal—many patients struggle to take their prescriptions as directed, and quitting altogether is common![2] And who can blame them? Often, medications have side effects that make them feel worse, not better.[3]

In contrast, many people who switch to a whole food, plant-based diet are highly motivated to continue because suddenly, perhaps for the first time in a long while, they feel good! For heart disease and type 2 diabetes, there are countless examples of individuals who, by changing their diet, have been able to reduce or discontinue their medications under their doctor's supervision. These outcomes are consistent with what has been demonstrated in the peer-reviewed research data on people who eat plant-based diets over the long-term,[4] as well as intervention studies in which participants are assigned to a plant-based eating plan and their results are compared with other diets.[5] This information has begun to permeate the field of medicine, as increasingly more physicians now support plant-based diets as the foundation of medical treatment for a variety of chronic diseases.[6]

The feelings of sustained energy and longer-lasting satiety (feeling full after a meal) are only the beginning of the many benefits of a plant-based diet. While you no doubt have your own reasons for reading this book, in the next few pages we're going to cover some of the demonstrated health benefits for the prevention and/or reversal of four major chronic health problems that people in developed countries currently face: weight issues (which impact many conditions and diseases), type 2 diabetes, cardiovascular disease (heart disease), and cancer. For each, we'll take a look at the typical outcomes for plant-based eaters, delve into some background as to what is going wrong when these conditions develop, and explain how a plant-based diet can remove the source of the problem. This information will not only provide you with a deeper understanding of the positive effects of this diet, but may also serve to inform your conversations with your family, friends, and doctors. The results speak for themselves!

Weight Issues

How would you like to eat until you felt full every time you were hungry, maintain a healthy weight, and never have to worry about counting calories? That is what can be gained by eating a plant-based diet. Plant-based eaters, both vegetarians (who eat no meat), and vegans (who eat no animal foods at all), are more likely to be at their normal weight compared to omnivores.[7] They're also more likely to gain *less* weight over time[8]—the nemesis of many aging adults.

Both overweight children[9] and adults[10] also lose weight more easily eating a plant-based diet than other types of diets, and this is true even without controlling portion size. In an exciting experiment published by researchers at the University of South Carolina, five different diet groups of overweight adults were given guidelines for the kinds of foods to eat, but without any portion control. In other words, they could eat as much as they wanted—they could eat until they were satisfied—and the individuals in

24

the vegan group lost more weight compared to pesco-vegetarians (plant foods plus fish), semi-vegetarians (reduced animal food), and omnivores (plants and animals)![11]

The total energy you use on a daily basis is primarily determined by three factors: your basal metabolism, which reflects the minimum level of energy you need to keep your body alive while at rest—breathing, eating, digesting, keeping your heart and other organs working, maintaining your immune system, and performing countless other jobs; your level of physical activity; and adaptive thermogenesis (how much of the food you eat is converted to heat and released). Of course, it's possible to eat less than the minimum level of energy you need to stay alive; that's called *negative energy balance,* and it's what happens when you lose weight because you are using energy that your body has previously stored as fat.

WHAT'S GOING WRONG?

You create those fat stores when the energy you take in (in the form of food) is greater than the energy you use. This is called *positive energy balance,* and it's no secret that this constitutes a major problem for many people. Currently in the United States it's less common to be at a healthy weight than it is to be overweight. Two-thirds of all Americans are overweight and half of those are obese;[12] sadly, almost one-third of children in the United States are overweight, with an additional 16 percent being obese;[13] globally this disturbing trend continues in many other countries.[14]

Beyond the immediate personal discomforts, physical and emotional, that can come with being overweight, excess pounds also put you at greater risk for a host of chronic diseases, especially the three we'll cover next—type 2 diabetes, cardiovascular disease, and cancer. Most adults in the United States continue to gain weight as they age, averaging almost half a pound per year after age 20.[15] If left unchecked, this pattern increases the risk of developing metabolic syndrome (MetS), type 2 diabetes (T2D), heart disease, cancer, sleeping problems, kidney disease, depression, asthma, and osteoarthritis.[16]

Gaining weight is easy in the modern world because the majority of the foods we're consuming are very *energy-dense,* meaning that when compared to the amount of space they take up in the stomach, they pack a lot of calories. We'll discuss this further in Step Three, but suffice it to say that animal foods like meat, cheese, eggs, and butter; processed foods like soda,

25

cookies, chips, candy, white flour products; and sugary or oily snacks (like the colorful spread of packaged "foods" you might see for sale in a gas station or the middle aisles of a grocery store) make it easier than ever to eat more calories than you need, usually without realizing it. Table 1 shows the energy-density of 100 grams each of a sampling of various foods, and how much exercise a 175-pound person would need to perform to burn them off.[17] This is the source of the disappointing results of research studies that attempt to produce weight loss with physical activity but without changing diet; if you were to choose either changing your diet or exercising more, you would get a much bigger bang for your buck by choosing to eat different foods than by trying to exercise off what you've eaten.[18]

Don't get me wrong—exercise is important and brings a lot of health benefits, like reduced risk of other diseases,[19] but when it comes to achieving a healthy weight, you can't do it without adjusting your diet. It's just too easy to eat larger portions of foods that are more energy dense, even without realizing it, and the delicate balance of *homeostasis* (the steady-state of dynamic equilibrium) that our bodies work so hard to maintain can be

Table 1: **TIME NEEDED TO BURN 100 GRAMS OF VARIOUS FOODS FOR A 175-POUND PERSON**

FOOD (100 GRAMS)	CALORIES	YOU'D NEED TO BIKE FOR:	YOU'D NEED TO RUN FOR:	YOU'D NEED TO WALK FOR:
Oil / added fat	884	1 hr, 30 min	1 hr, 36 min	3 hr, 12 min
Parmesan cheese	392	40 min	43 min	1 hr, 25 min
Sugar	387	39 min	42 min	1 hr, 24 min
Chicken nuggets	260	26 min	28 min	56 min
Ground beef	243	25 min	26 min	52 min
Chickpeas	164	16 min	18 min	36 min
Bananas	89	9 min	10 min	20 min
Sweet potatoes	76	8 min	9 min	17 min
Carrots	41	4 min	5 min	9 min
Lettuce	16	2 min	2 min	4 min

thrown off in a heartbeat. Since one pound of fat contains about 3,500 calories, you need only 10 unburned calories per day to gain a pound over the course of a year. Most adults are eating several hundred calories more than they need, which provides that excess weight, even after the body's automatic adjustments to try to burn the extra energy. Over time, this leads to a steady weight gain in adulthood.[20]

Although not everything we eat comes in 100 gram quantities, Table 1 illustrates how much *more* exercise is required to burn off energy-dense foods—884 calories of fat is about seven tablespoons, which sounds like a lot but can easily be worked into a meal if you're not paying attention by choosing fatty foods, sautéing food in oil, buttering your bread, and eating almost any typical dessert.

HOW CAN A PLANT-BASED DIET HELP?

While most adults gain weight as they age, this is not part of healthy aging, and it doesn't have to happen to you! The foods that make up a plant-based diet (whole grains, legumes [peas, beans, and lentils, for example], fruits, vegetables, and limited amounts of nuts and seeds) are dense in vitamins and minerals but contain plenty of fiber (mostly indigestible complex carbohydrates—what many people call "roughage"). Because for the most part we don't digest fiber, it doesn't add any calories to the diet. This is why you can fill up eating whole plant foods and still consume fewer calories.

Fiber provides bulk as well as slows the emptying of your stomach. This helps you feel full longer, causing you to want to eat less. Fiber also makes it physically impossible to overeat, because the added bulk activates the "stretch receptors" in the stomach. These receptors signal the brain that you've had enough. Animal foods contain no fiber (meat and dairy), and processed foods have either had fiber removed (white flour) or had energy added in the form of fat and sugar without an increase in fiber (French fries). So a meal of a cheeseburger, white bun, and fries packs a lot of calories but it doesn't fill you the way a meal of brown rice, vegetables, and beans does, even though the plant meal has a lot less energy! Most people starting to eat a whole food, plant-based diet for the first time find that excess weight just slides away, even without increasing their level of exercise. This is not only true for people who are already plant-based, but also for those who step it up a notch and take out the added fat as well.

27

Type 2 Diabetes and Cardiovascular Disease

A plant-based diet is the only treatment that has been shown to reverse our top culprits of disability and mortality. More plant food consumption predicts lower blood pressure,[21] improved blood lipids, lower risk of developing type 2 diabetes,[22] and a lower risk of death from cardiovascular disease (CVD).[23] But it doesn't stop there. Physicians who prescribe plant-based diets as treatment get results unmatched by medication. A word of warning here: It's very important to talk to your doctor before changing your diet if you are taking any medication, especially if it is a medicine that lowers your blood pressure or controls your blood sugar. Dr. Neal Barnard, from the Physicians Committee for Responsible Medicine, in collaboration with George Washington University School of Medicine, has conducted studies of type 2 diabetics and found that medication changes are frequently required after switching to a low-fat, vegan diet. The effect of totally plant-based eating is so rapid that your blood sugar can drop to dangerously low levels if you are taking medication at the same time.

Imagine being told it would best to go home and prepare for the end because there was nothing more that doctors could do for you. And if your advanced stage heart disease was being treated only with statins, stents, medications, or surgery, you would probably be right to do so! Fortunately, the work of two notable physicians, Dr. Caldwell Esselstyn at the Cleveland Clinic and Dr. Dean Ornish at the University of California, has demonstrated the efficacy of reversing damage to arteries from the Western diet by switching patients to a low-fat, vegan diet.[24] In fact, at the time Dr. Esselstyn began his work with diet, most of his patients had been given no other options by their doctors but to get their affairs in order.

WHAT'S GOING WRONG?

CVD is the number one killer among chronic diseases in the United States[25] and mortality from diabetes trails closely behind at number seven;[26] these two diseases annually claim 610,000 and roughly 70,000 lives, respectively.[27] These are not just statistics. A diagnosis of either one often comes with restrictions on physical activity, fear of overexertion, and stress from the prescribed treatments. The combination of these two diseases presents further cause for concern, as both risk of stroke and mortality from heart disease are two to four times greater among adult diabetics.[28] That means a lot of people have elevated risk for CVD—11.3 percent of adults in the

United States are estimated to have diabetes and 35 percent are estimated to have prediabetes; these figures jump to 50 percent and 26.9 percent, respectively, of adults over age 65.[29]

Cardiovascular disease is a general term that covers a range of problems in different parts of the body relating to the heart and all the blood vessels. One problem, a *stroke,* is brain cell damage from lack of oxygen due to reduced or blocked blood flow in the brain. Another problem, erectile dysfunction, or impotence as many people call it, is usually one of the first signs of heart disease—the tiniest blood vessels are the first to go[30] (men experiencing this problem might want to take extra note of the fact that the condition is reversible).

Type 2 diabetes, a closely related problem, is a condition in which our ability to use glucose (sugar), the simplest form of carbohydrate, for fuel is disrupted. Normally, the beta cells of the pancreas produce insulin, which is often compared to the key that unlocks the door to our cells so energy can be brought inside. Insulin ushers the glucose into our cells from the bloodstream, making it possible for us to use the glucose in our blood.

Type 2 diabetes used to be called "adult-onset diabetes," but the term is no longer used because so many children have it. Type 2 diabetes is a common and rapidly growing problem due to diet and lifestyle. In diabetics, the pancreas still makes insulin but either it's not enough or the cells do not recognize it. This is a state called *insulin resistance.* If your cells are insulin resistant, at first the pancreas will try to produce extra insulin to catch up with your mounting blood sugar levels. This may work for a while, but if your cells aren't allowing the insulin to work, the pancreas can wear out, start producing less insulin, and the sugar you eat will stay in the bloodstream at even higher levels.[31] If your cells can't access the fuel, you'll have trouble producing the energy you need, which leads to fatigue and a variety of problems. Eventually, the complications that develop can range from depression to amputations to death.

Both conditions are caused by eating a diet high in animal foods and low in plant foods,[32] diets high in total fat, saturated fat, and refined carbohydrates. The saturated fat increases the body's own production of cholesterol past the point at which the body can keep up and eliminate it. The body tries to deal with the problem by storing the cholesterol in little pockets here and there, wherever it can. Plaque forms as remnants of low-density-lipoprotein (LDL, or "bad") cholesterol are sucked through the cells lining the arteries and consumed by immune cells called *macrophages,* whose central job is this "cleanup" of LDL remnants. Once these macrophages ingest

29

the LDL, they become *foam cells* (so called because they are filled with whitish cholesterol that looks like foam) and they die. The accumulation of dead cells builds up under the surface of the endothelial cells that line the blood vessels. At some point, this thin lining wears away due to the pressure of pumping blood. When this happens, the rupture causes a blood clot, which can then cause a stroke or heart attack. A rupture is more likely than a gradual blockage due to plaque buildup, which is why the first symptom of heart disease for many patients is a fatal heart attack. Type 2 diabetics are at an even greater risk for CVD because of a condition known as *diabetic dyslipidemia*—essentially they tend to have even more of these LDL remnants, which promotes the process of plaque formation even faster.[33]

Excess fat and sugar consumption both raise blood triglycerides (the fat present in our blood), which can clog the insulin receptor cells that are supposed to enable insulin to work, thus promoting insulin resistance. The body is then even less equipped to handle the sudden rush of blood sugar that takes place when you consume pastry, white flour, cookies, or sugary drinks. This leads to elevated blood sugar levels over time, and eventually to diabetes.

HOW CAN A PLANT-BASED DIET HELP?

Whole food, plant-based diets are naturally low in all of the components known to promote plaque formation in the blood vessels or cause insulin receptor cell failure. These include trans fat, saturated fat, refined carbohydrates, dairy products, and red meat. At the same time, whole food, plant-based diets are naturally rich in all the nutrients and foods that have been associated with decreased risk—more fruits and vegetables, whole grains, legumes, and nuts. Not only can they help us avoid developing CVD and type 2 diabetes, but they also make excellent health and wellness possible as we age.

When people with advanced stage heart disease start eating a low-fat, whole food, plant-based diet, the results are remarkable. Within weeks, most patients can notice an improvement of certain symptoms they had been experiencing—such as shortness of breath and angina (chest pain). Over time, they can also expect that the damage done to their arteries by their former diet will gradually be repaired. Dr. Neal Barnard's pioneering work in treating type 2 diabetes with plant-based diets has now been documented in multiple studies. Within a time frame of weeks or months, type 2 diabetics are able to reduce or eliminate medication.[34] Just think

30

of the improved quality of life and cost savings, as well as the blessing of not being ill!

Cancer

Although cancer is a more complex disease than being overweight or having diabetes or heart disease, the evidence is strong that whole food, plant-based eating is the best protection and the best dietary choice to complement cancer treatment. Researchers have estimated that the major of portion of cancers are lifestyle related—another way of saying *preventable*—with a substantial portion preventable directly by diet.[35] Red meat and dairy products, not just smoking and alcohol consumption, are independently associated with cancer risk, and plant-eaters have lower rates of cancer even with very small increases in animal food intake.[36] The China Project, a research survey of 6,500 adults in 65 counties in China conducted by Dr. T. Colin Campbell and his collaborators from Oxford University and the Chinese government, found there was no threshold of animal food consumption that was not associated with increased risk for cancer mortality and other chronic disease in a comprehensive survey of dietary and lifestyle risk factors in China.[37] This means the more plants we eat, the better.

WHAT'S GOING WRONG?

There are many potential mechanisms that indicate the effect of animal foods on cancer risk, but one of the most striking and interesting, as it relates directly to plant-based patterns, is the seeming effect of animal protein on promoting cancer development. First, cancer is initiated—meaning that a genetic mutation occurs. If the immune system doesn't catch this mutation and repair it, it may reproduce and continue on to the promotion stage, in which cancerous cells and eventually a tumor, grow.

One of protein's major roles is cell growth and repair, but cancer occurs when cell growth is unchecked and the normal signals for cell death are overridden. Dr. Campbell's experiments in the laboratory demonstrated decades ago that increased levels of animal protein, but not plant protein, had the ability to promote the growth of cancer—and, perhaps even more interesting, he showed that decreasing the level of animal protein in the diet could *reverse* the growth of cancer after it had been initiated. His team replicated these experiments many times and in many ways.

The critical threshold in rats (who need about the same amount of protein as humans) at which excess animal protein starts to promote cancer growth seemed to be about 10 percent. At 5 percent of total calories, protein had no effects on rats who were predisposed to cancer, meaning they had been previously exposed to chemical toxins or viruses. At 20 percent of total calories, precancerous cells formed and grew more quickly than at 5 percent. When the researchers switched the diet back and forth between 5 percent and 20 percent and then back to 5 percent protein calories, they saw the cancer cells first stay dormant, then grow, and then recede.[38] Most of us, especially those of us eating animal food, are eating much more than 10 percent protein.

Similar findings on the risk associated with higher protein consumption were demonstrated in an exciting 2013 study from the National Nutrition and Health Examination Survey (NHANES). Their analysis of protein consumption among adults in the United States showed that a higher intake of protein among adults under 65 was associated with higher rates of cancer and higher overall mortality.[39] The researchers found that this association was most likely due to the animal protein, but not to the plant protein these individuals consumed. This analysis was paired with a series of animal experiments and demonstrated multiple pathways by which protein might promote the growth of cancer, confirming earlier experimental work.

HOW CAN A PLANT-BASED DIET HELP?

These kinds of results are important, because crossing above the range of 10 percent protein consumption is well within the range of what most people are eating; the average protein intake is between 11 and 22 percent. Contrast this to cancer research on chemical carcinogens and environmental toxins; these are usually considered a demonstrated danger at levels much higher than humans normally encounter them.

Eating a whole food, plant-based diet will naturally give you beween 10 and 12 percent of your calories from protein without even trying! There is no need to make a point of "getting enough protein in your diet"—it happens easily and naturally, making this a risk factor well within your realm of control. Physicians are beginning to recommend plant-based diets to complement cancer treatment;[40] there have already been some encouraging findings regarding the use of diet as the treatment itself. Dr. Dean Ornish has demonstrated in a well-known and remarkable randomized controlled intervention trial that a low-fat vegan diet is able to delay or even eliminate the need for treatment of prostate cancer among patients who are undergoing active surveillance, known as the "watch and wait" approach.[41] After two years, 27 percent of the control group, but only 5 percent of the plant-based group, had undergone conventional prostate cancer treatment. While this didn't work for every patient, for those whom it did, imagine the relief at avoiding chemotherapy, radiation, and surgery!

So What About Other Nutrition News?

This all sounds pretty good, right? Straightforward health benefits with no negative side effects. Live better, live longer, and let the diseases of modern society pass you by. While this is clearly good news, there many pieces of what is apparently equally good news in the media. Not a day passes by without a blog or website turning up new news about nutrition and health—though not all of it makes sense.

You can find declarations in the news that popcorn is healthier than vegetables, claims that butter should be added to coffee, and evidence that acai berries by themselves can do everything from promoting weight loss to preventing cancer to slowing aging. These wildly varying assertions and others cover almost every type of nutrient, food, and food group. They even extend to a variety of fad diets that may or may not have scientific evidence behind them. The health benefits of plant-based diets discussed earlier in this chapter are based on repeated, peer-reviewed, scientific studies, not just one or two papers. (I encourage you to check the references of this book if you are interested in reading the original sources for all this information.) That isn't necessarily the case for all the health claims found on the Internet

While it's easy to make a case for almost any position based on a single study taken out of context, solid theories require many repeatable results from different study designs, examining the same questions in different populations, similar findings produced by various investigators, and consistency no matter who is funding the research. What virtually all nutrition researchers agree on is that an overall dietary pattern that emphasizes fruits, vegetables, whole grains, legumes, nuts, and seeds and that limits food high in saturated fat and refined carbohydrates (such as sugar, white flour, and sugar-sweetened beverages) will reduce risk for chronic disease and support positive health outcomes. Though not all scientists are interested in totally plant-based diets per se, experts do agree that these are shared components of healthy dietary patterns. Notably, these elements are common to all traditional diets where rates of chronic disease are very low.

33

These include the traditional diets of the Mediterranean cultures,[42] the Okinawans in Japan[43] (a hotspot of centenarians), and the indigenous Tarahumara, a population from Mexico with virtually no heart disease among those eating a traditional diet.[44]

The great thing about focusing on this big picture of dietary health is that it simplifies eating! Nothing kills motivation like the feeling you have to follow complex rules, do math problems to make eating decisions, or track milligrams of this or that nutrient. Below are some red flags about nutrition advice and myths that you can put to rest. These tips should also help streamline your thought process and leave your attention free to focus on the exciting benefits of eating a plant-based diet:

Myth #1: If you don't eat animal foods, you need to practice protein-combining to get complete proteins. Protein is composed of amino acids, some of which are essential, meaning we have to get them from our diets. Foods have different profiles of amino acid composition, and most animal foods tend to have all of them. While most individual plant proteins have only some of the essential amino acids we need, as a group plant foods do contain all of them. Our bodies are designed to break down protein from the foods and recombine them with amino acids previously stored in tissue as needed. This process of protein breakdown and turnover is normal and happens continually, so specifically combining beans and rice at the same meal is not necessary. As long as you eat a variety of foods over the long term, your body will take it from there.

Myth #2: Counting calories and portion sizes are important to maintaining a healthy weight. The best way to prevent over-consuming energy is to eat foods that are nutrient-dense and calorie-dilute—and the best way to ensure this is to choose food with plenty of fiber. Fiber increases satiety with fewer calories by activating the stretch receptors in the stomach, so we can eat until we're full without thinking about it. Animal foods contain no fiber; it is exclusively found in plants. When you eat only plants, it's impossible not to meet the fiber recommendation of 14 grams per 1,000 calories per day.[45] In addition, it's difficult to actually measure portion sizes and calories with any degree of accuracy unless you are weighing your food and using computer software to calculate the embodied energy. How many of us are realistically going to do that on a daily basis? And who would want to? Remember that only a few hundred extra calories per day can put you over the edge of weight gain. By eating food that physically fills your stomach without sneaking in excess calories, your body can execute its beautiful and sophisticated regulatory signaling with much more precision than you can achieve by estimating cup measures of mixed dishes.

Myth #3: Any one nutrient (insert the latest nutrient in the news) is the key to everything from weight loss to world peace. Beware of individual nutrient fetishes. They're hard to avoid because research lends itself to studying one thing at a time and the mainstream media love to exaggerate and simplify research data. These results are best interpreted in the context of the overall diet. The most beneficial and safest practice is to get your nutrients from food. While nutrient studies make great headlines because it's easy to take a pill, supplements are not equivalent to eating food! The benefits ascribed to specific nutrients, like antioxidants, magnesium, or vitamin C, have launched the rise of the supplement industry, and individual nutrient supplements have produced not only disappointing but often dangerous results. Taking antioxidants like vitamin E or carotenoids (a variety of pigments that convert to vitamin A in the liver) in the form of a pill just hasn't produced the same effect that is thought to occur when people consume these same substances as part of the food matrix. The *food matrix* is the packaging of fat, protein, carbohydrate, fiber, and other micronutrients that come together in the proportion and combination determined by nature. In fact, taking individual nutrient supplements over many years has been associated with increased risk for heart disease and certain cancers.[46] So when you hear about the benefits of particular nutrients, use that as a reminder to consume a widely varied diet of whole, plant foods.

CONSTANT CONTACT
KEEPS MOTIVATION ALIVE

Despite your enthusiasm for dietary improvement, an initial burst of motivation isn't enough to maintain a healthy lifestyle. Long-term success occurs by forming new habits, which are behaviors that are thought to originate from an impulsive or nonrational part of people.[47] In this context, impulsive isn't a bad thing. It simply means you don't have to stop and think about what you're doing, or make a conscious choice to eat differently.[48] But while you are integrating these new patterns, and even afterwards, you need to stay plugged into your motivating force. There will be moments when your willpower, your energy, and your commitment may wilt. You'll need a pick-me-up, and staying in touch with your inner impulses in those moments can spark the flame to get back in the game and keep going. The more contact you have with your reasons for your new behaviors, the easier it will be to take the steps required to make them permanent.

How can you do this? There are some key strategies you can use to keep infusing the freshness of your initial motivation into daily life, almost all of which center on being able to see or visualize where you are headed. We all have an innate preference for food and objects that are closer rather than farther away.[49] This is consistent with our innate drive to conserve energy, as well as our preference for goals that seem attainable. So do your best to remind yourself with inspiring images, ongoing education, and celebrating how far you have come—it's only going to strengthen your belief in your capacity to get there. Try any or all of the following techniques.

Surround Yourself with Inspiring Images

Describe in as much detail as possible the goals that you want to move toward. What do you want your life to be? How do you want your body to feel? Is there a health condition you want to change? How do you want to spend your time?

Good fiction paints a picture in the mind of the reader so vividly you feel like you are in there. Become the author of your future. What do you see for yourself? What are you doing? What does it look like? To identify everything you want, it may help to articulate both what you want to move toward and what you find disturbing. What will happen when these conflicts have been resolved? What are you eating? What does your dinner table look like? How do you relate to your friends around food? Write these scenarios down and post them somewhere that you can review them daily, experience the feelings they give you, and visualize them again and again.

You might also consider saturating your environment with images of plant-based meals and delicious recipes you can't resist trying in your own kitchen. The easiest way to do this is to subscribe to social media feeds from plant-based chefs and educators. We all know how much people love photos of food on Facebook, Pintrest, and Instagram! This is one of the most efficient ways to keep up your excitement around cooking and trying new recipes. If you have time to look at the news feeds on social media, it can be a quick way to check in with the pulse of the movement, get ideas for dinner, and recharge your motivation and commitment to keep cooking. You can also invest in a few cookbooks as well for that visceral page-turning experience. There are so many lovely choices with mouth-watering images of food. Check out the Ongoing Support Resources section beginning on page 291 for suggestions of social media you may want to subscribe to and cookbooks you may want to acquire.

Yet another approach is to create a vision board with photos of beautiful food, nutrition facts you find particularly striking, and photos of people modeling the behaviors you want to embody. These might be images of people exercising, cooking, meditating, or anything you want more of in your own life. You could do this on the wall, in a paper format, or even add images into a screensaver file to be displayed on your computer.

Stay Engaged with Ongoing Education

This book will give you the tools you need to implement a sustainable healthy lifestyle, as well as to interpret health information critically. However, there's no reason to stop there! The more learning you do, the more informed you will become, the stronger your motivation will be, and the firmer your commitment will feel. This is especially true if you are currently facing a chronic disease. Ongoing learning through books, videos, live events, or programs will keep you engaged, both at the beginning of your journey to a plant-based diet and as you continue on this path. More suggested reading lists, residential programs, and other educational opportunities are listed in the Resources section, including information on disease-specific resources.

Celebrate the Changes in Your Body

In addition to all the great imagery and information you have at your disposal, pay attention to how your body feels. As you eat a more whole food, plant-based diet, it's likely that you will feel better quickly. How is your energy? Is your constipation going away? Are you starting to get signs that you might not need that Viagra anymore? Are you feeling some of the symptoms you've dealt with for so long fading away? Is your doctor decreas-

37

ing your medication? These are the kinds of outcomes that can't be matched by standard medical treatment, and celebrating these changes can really add to your momentum!

YOUR PATH GOING FORWARD

The transition has begun. You're on the road to a plant-based diet! Below are some suggested first steps in crystallizing your vision for your life, staying connected to your motivation, and taking best advantage of your support and accountability structure.

Remember that the most effective way to set goals for yourself will be to use the SMART goals format. You can review that in *How To Use This Book* for a refresher. Once you've created your goals, do you have a visible place to post them? That could be the refrigerator, above your desk, next to your bed, on the bathroom mirror, or anywhere that you know you'll look at them several times a day. If you are creating an inspiration or vision board, do you have a good place to hang it? If it's bulletin-board style, make sure you have push-pins, scissors, and whatever you need handy to make it really easy to grab or clip inspiring images from magazines or the Internet. If you're thinking of making a screensaver slideshow, do you know how to use your software? Remember, now's the time to share your plans with your support buddy, ask for feedback on the relevance and specificity of your goals, and ask for a follow-up, or schedule a check-in after your time limit has past.

The three paths described below are tailored to a gradual (Easing In), moderate (Rev It Up), or rapid (Total Transformation) pace of change. If you're not sure which one to take, revisit the self-assessment *How Much Change Am I Ready? For* on page 13. As we discussed in *How to Use This Book*, the path you take and the goals you set for yourself are your choice and, whatever they are, they will be most effective if they challenge you but do not overwhelm you. You want to be able to visualize yourself reaching them.

1. **Easing In:** Take the time to write down your goals. When you have some clearly defined targets, post them in a visible place. Choose two to three social media profiles to subscribe to and start checking in at least once a day. Browse the Resources section of this book, and make the time to watch at least one movie on the benefits of plant-based diets. Is there anyone you can invite to watch it with you? ▶ *Suggested time frame: two weeks.*

2. **Rev It Up:** Start with what you want from your life. Are there medical conditions you face? Excess weight you'd be happier to leave behind? Make it relevant and make it real by writing your goals down. When you have some clearly defined targets, post them in a visible place, and find a place in your house to create a vision or inspiration board, either paper or electronic. Choose three to five social media profiles to subscribe to and start checking in at least once a day. Browse the Resources section of this book, and make the time to watch at least one movie on the health benefits of plant-based diets. Think about whether there is anyone you can invite to watch it with you, or perhaps even a group of people. Are you particularly interested in one reason for, or one aspect of, plant-based eating? Select a book that focuses on that angle and either order it online or request it from your local library. ▶*Suggested time frame: one week.*

3. **Total Transformation:** This is the start of total immersion in your dietary transition! If you are going for a radical change or want to bump your commitment up to that ultimate goal of being totally plant-based, make sure you can see, taste, and feel where you're headed. Start with your big vision for your life and health, and then outline some intermediate goals to stay connected to that motivation. When you have the big picture and supporting goals identified, post them where you can see them every day. Find a place in your house to create a vision or inspiration board, either paper or electronic. Choose at least five new social media profiles to subscribe to and start checking in at least once a day. Browse the Resources section of this book for suggestions for more plant-based education. Make the time to watch at least one movie on the health benefits of plant-based diets. Consider whether there is anyone, or perhaps a group of people, who can watch it with you. It's critical to a Total Transformation that you stay connected to other people, so make sure you reach out to your support buddy for feedback and accountability. Are you particularly interested in certain reasons for plant-based eating, or certain types of plant-based lifestyles? Create a reading list for yourself, and start by either ordering one book online or requesting it from your local library. Finally, watch at least one lecture via YouTube, or listen to at least one podcast from the authors of the recommended reading list on page 297. There are many teachers with worthwhile input,

39

and the more varied the source of information, the more deeply it will sink in. Do everything you can to immerse yourself in this lifestyle! ▶*Suggested time frame: one week.*

Alright! This is an exciting beginning—you've launched a new chapter of your life and your diet.

ADD PLANT-BASED FOODS TO YOUR DIET
welcoming new friends

G IVEN THE RIGHT FUEL, materials, and rest, your body is capable of enormous healing. Now that we have discussed how to find your motivating force, we are going to focus on the tools and knowledge you need to effectively add whole, plant-based foods into your diet, naturally displacing what you currently eat. Rather than concentrate on what not to eat, we will ease you in to your new diet by adding more whole plant food than you've been eating. Many people call this approach *crowding out*. By making healthier choices first—without denying yourself anything—the proportion of unhealthy food in your diet is reduced and replaced.

This approach offers several advantages. First, it's a kinder and gentler way to get started. If you feel a tremor of alarm at the thought of giving up your favorite dinner or dessert, you're not alone. However, crowding out can be the perfect way to shift your diet without psyching yourself out with an untenable resolution. People who break self-imposed rules, such as vowing never to eat a specific food again for the rest of their lives, are more apt to feel stressed and guilty when they surrender to temptation. This can result in throwing their hands up and, in frustration, going on a binge eating spree.[1] The more this happens, the harder it can be to get back on track. Women are even more prone than men to binge eating behavior.[2] Try to let go of value judgments about yourself and what you eat. That kind of thinking gets in the way of being able to stick with your choices and enjoy your new diet.

The beauty of practicing crowding out is that it can remove the element of "I should." Let's be clear about something: You will find no "should" in this book, or at least not in the sense of expectations about your goals. There are a few things you *should* consider doing, though, *if* you want to be successful at establishing a plant-based diet, but that is based on the assumption that this lifestyle is your goal. Whether this book helps you to simply add more fruits and vegetables to your meals or to achieve a complete whole food, plant-based diet is up to you. The information presented here will just help you move ahead in your chosen direction more effectively.

In Step Two, we will clarify what plant-based eating consists of, and allow you to plan, purchase, and prepare as much plant-based food as you choose to incorporate for yourself and your family. There are also strategies for making the lifestyle affordable, more convenient, and a positive experience for kids—important elements in making plant-based eating habit-driven. You'll learn the basics of how to cook and eat totally plant-based, but again, how far you go along this path is up to you. Remember that delectable appetizers and snacks, hearty main courses, fresh salads, mouthwatering desserts, and many other dishes await you in the Recipes for Everyone section on page 147.

WHAT IS PLANT-BASED EATING?

Expect your plate to look different from that of an omnivore. Even people who eat vegetarian or vegan meat substitutes may make the mistake of keeping the same format of a starch, vegetable, and heavier "protein" food—which can contain a lot of fat and salt if it's a faux meat substitute. Including a food reminiscent of meat doesn't make your plate a real meal; getting enough volume and sufficient calories to satisfy you sets the standard. Remember from Step One that you will likely need to eat more food than before to achieve this. Many people mistakenly fear that plant-based eating will be restrictive, but it truly opens up a whole new world of tastes and ingredients. As you consider which goals to set for yourself, you may choose to incorporate certain foods or ingredients, eat plant-based for certain meals, or choose certain days of the week at first. You may also decide

42

to base your meals on the foods shown in Table 2 and then see what happens when you fill up on healthy food first.

So what is a plant-based diet composed of? For optimal nutrient intake, variety is key. However, of all the foods in the table below, the relative nutrient content of greens and vegetables cannot be beaten! For this reason, including plenty of greens and vegetables every day is ideal. Table 2 indicates the relative contributions and proportions of food groups making up a healthy plant-based diet, but the guidelines leave a lot of room for individual variation and preferences. The list is not exhaustive, but it paints a picture of the color and variety you have to work with.

Table 2: **THE BIG PICTURE OF PLANT-BASED EATING**

FOODS TO INCLUDE	
Whole Plant Foods *Include unlimited amounts of a variety of these foods on a daily basis*	**WHOLE GRAINS:** rolled and Irish oats, brown rice, wild rice, quinoa, barley, teff, millet, wheat or spelt berries, buckwheat groats, and amaranth
	LEGUMES (*dried or canned with minimal salt*): lentils, black beans, navy beans, black-eyed peas, chickpeas, kidney beans, soybeans, tempeh, green beans, peas, mung beans, fava beans, lima beans, adzuki beans, homemade veggie burgers, and more
	GREENS (*fresh or frozen*): kale, collards, spinach, chard, bok choy, lettuce, arugula, beet greens, dandelion greens, purslane, parsley, cilantro, and sprouts
	ROOTS: potatoes, onions, sweet potatoes, leeks, carrots, daikon, burdock, radishes, turnips, beets, parsnips, garlic, and ginger
	OTHER VEGETABLES: summer and winter squash, celery, cabbage, brussels sprouts, broccoli, cauliflower, mushrooms, corn, asparagus, scallions, peppers, and tomatoes
	FRUIT (*fresh or frozen*): apples, pears, peaches, nectarines, apricots, cherries, kiwis, grapes, plums, bananas, papayas, pineapple, mangoes, berries, and melons
Lightly Processed *Okay to include, but use less frequently*	**PLANT MILKS** (*unsweetened*): oat milk, almond milk, hazelnut milk, soy milk, and rice milk
	WHOLE-GRAIN: pasta, crackers, and unsweetened breakfast cereals
	WHOLE-GRAIN FLOUR: whole wheat, spelt, oat, buckwheat, or gluten-free mixes, or legume flours like chickpea and fava bean
	STORE BOUGHT (*read labels and try to minimize the added salt, sugar, and oil*): tomato sauces, hummus, salsa, guacamole, and other dressings
	Tofu

cont. on next page

43

| Richer Whole Plant Foods

Use as condiments or ingredients only and, for most, not necessarily every day, because of the high fat content | AVOCADO: straight avocado and guacamole

NUTS, SEEDS, AND SPREADS/BUTTERS: peanuts, almonds, cashews, pine nuts, Brazil nuts, pecans, walnuts, macadamia nuts, flaxseed, chia seed, sesame seeds/tahini, and sunflower seeds

COCONUT: fresh coconut flesh, canned coconut milk, and coconut cream |
|---|---|
| Use in Cooking

These make food flavorful but still healthy | ADDITIONS: Fresh and dried herbs; fresh and powdered spices; vinegars; limited amounts of salt and sweeteners such as rice syrup, maple syrup, honey, or dates; limited amounts of miso, tamari/soy sauce, and vegetable bouillon |
| Treats for Special Occasions

Remember that "special occasions" happen infrequently | DESSERT: recipes made with lots of nuts, coconut, or added sweeteners

DRINKING: plant milk by the glass—save the plant milk for use on cereal or in baking; if you are thirsty, just drink water |

If you follow the guidelines described in Table 2, you will consume about 10 percent protein, 10 to 20 percent fat, and 70 to 80 percent carbohydrate. Coincidentally, this is just about what our bodies need.

But wait, you may be thinking, "I thought eating carbs made you fat?" While avoiding sugar and sugar-sweetened food products does improve blood lipids and lowers risk for cardiovascular disease,[3] carb-counting is a misinformed interpretation of this data. Carbohydrate is an essential nutrient (meaning we must get it from our diet). It's the fuel of choice for our muscles and our brains.[4] The only thing wrong with carbs is that many of them are refined. The white bread, sugar, and processed snacks that so many people eat on a daily basis are the carbs to eliminate. Whole plant foods, on the other hand, are largely composed of carbohydrates—complex sugars that are digested slowly alongside the fiber and don't lead to a spike in blood sugar. Relax about carbs and remember that they are in all whole foods—which is a good thing because you need them.

Following these guidelines while consuming enough calories to feel satisfied allows you to get plenty of the nutrients you need, while also minimizing your risk for the chronic diseases we discussed in Step One.

Essential Vitamins

44

In addition to the macronutrients of carbohydrate, fat, protein, water, and fiber, we also need a variety of micronutrients—vitamins, minerals, and phytochemicals. Phytochemicals are other chemical substances in plants generally thought to be beneficial, though at this time they are not considered essential. Essential nutrients are those we have to consume through our diet or we run the risk of deficiency and the symptoms associated with those deficiencies. The essential vitamins and minerals do have recommended levels of consumption, and there are a few nutrients that require a little extra attention for optimal health when eating a totally plant-based diet.

VITAMIN B$_{12}$

Vitamin B$_{12}$ is a water-soluble essential nutrient that is important for nerve function, healthy blood cells, and creating DNA (the genetic blueprint of our cells).[5] It is produced by bacteria in the soil and, to a small extent, the bacteria in your gut, though the amount is generally not thought to be adequate compared to the dietary requirement.[6] When you eat animal foods, you also consume the vitamin because during their lifetime, the animals ate grass or other plants that contained small amounts of soil, and therefore bacteria and B$_{12}$. This is probably one way that humans got B$_{12}$ in the past, before the food was washed in the harvesting process and public water was treated and sanitized as it is now. Today, people eating a totally plant-based diet (as well as all older adults because of absorption issues) should take a B$_{12}$ supplement to ensure adequate levels,[7] even though fortified foods such as soy milk, cereal, and nutritional yeast often have B$_{12}$ added to them.[8]

VITAMIN D

Vitamin D is considered a conditionally essential nutrient—meaning that only under certain conditions (low sun exposure) do you need to ingest it. However, the vitamin has many important roles, including regulating calcium absorption in the gut and supporting bone health.[9] Vitamin D is actually a hormone produced by your skin upon exposure to ultraviolet B (UVB) radiation from the sun.[10] UVB radiation is released most often during the hours of 10 A.M. to 3 P.M., and you can also check the UV index on a weather website for your area, which most weather apps on smartphones display. A higher UV index (usually three or higher) means that UVB radiation is likely reaching your area at that moment, but it's also more likely you can burn if you stay in the sun too long. For a light-skinned person, five to ten minutes of exposure two to three times per week during the hours of 10 A.M. to 3 P.M. should be enough to produce the required level of vitamin D.[11] The more melanin you have in your skin, the longer

45

you need exposure to the sun to produce adequate vitamin D compared to a lighter-skinned person.[12]

The vitamin D recommendation from the Institute of Medicine assumes minimal sun exposure.[13] Depending on your lifestyle, the season, and the area of the country where you live, this assumption may hold true for you. Since vitamin D is not found in most foods, except for fatty fish and fortified cow's milk, it may be a good idea for you to take a vitamin D supplement under these conditions: if you have darker skin, if you tend to be inside during the aforementioned hours of 10 A.M. to 3 P.M. most days, if you live farther from the equator and the UVB index doesn't reach above three in the winter, or if your area tends to frequent clouds and rain.[14]

Your doctor can order tests to check the levels of vitamins B_{12} and D levels in your blood, and determine whether taking a vitamin D supplement is necessary.

OMEGA-3 FATS

Omega-3 and omega-6 fatty acids are the two essential fats that humans must consume for many reasons, including appropriate cell membrane flexibility, regulation of blood clotting and inflammation, and to help ensure that our blood vessels can relax and contract.[15] We can make other fats from other food substances in our diet, but the essential fatty acids (EFA) are fats we have to consume. The richest sources of omega-3 fats are vegetables and vegetable oils, soybeans, walnuts, flax seeds, chia seeds, and coldwater fish such as salmon or sardines.[16]

Some of the omega-3 fats you may have heard of, EPA and DHA for instance, are actually synthesized by our bodies from the omega-3 fats we get in plants. EPA and DHA get a lot of attention in the news, because higher blood levels of them are directly linked to lower risk of cardiovascular disease (CVD).[17] Fish synthesize EPA and DHA, too, which is why they are rich sources of both of these fats.[18] For this reason, as well as the fact that we're not sure how efficient that conversion from the omega-3s in plants to EPA and DHA is, the Dietary Guidelines for Americans do recommend eating fish as part of a healthy diet.[19] However, this recommendation doesn't take into account the fact that fish, too, will push your consumption of animal protein over the 10 percent threshold (check page 32 for a refresher on this), that only 10 percent of the ocean's predatory fish remain compared to 50 years ago, and in 40 years from now there may be no fish left in the oceans if we don't change our consumption patterns.[20]

We have seriously compromised marine health due to our overconsumption, and this isn't something that can be quickly repaired. If you eat a totally whole food, plant-based diet, you're ahead of the game, because your lower consumption of omega-6 fats, the other type of essential fats that are widely present in many foods, may help your conversion rates from omega-3 to EPA and DHA.[21] There is a popular belief that the ratio of omega-3 to omega-6 fats is very important (one omega-3 for every two, three, or four omega-6s, or so, is considered ideal), but this may vary according to what the rest of your diet is like, as well as the absolute levels of the fats in your diet.[22] You can try to include a tablespoon of ground flax seeds or chia seeds on a daily basis to increase your omega-3s. Some people eating a totally plant-based diet also choose to consume an omega-3 supplement made from algae (usually called *vegetarian omega-3 supplements,* or *algae omega-3*), which will provide more EPA and DHA directly.[23] At this point, it looks as though this may provide some increased benefit for CVD, but there isn't really enough data on whether people eating a low-fat, whole food, plant-based diet need this.[24]

As you begin the process of crowding out your old eating habits, worrying about any one nutrient, even the three above, isn't necessary. However, once you've moved into eating a totally plant-based diet for some time, or once you've eliminated all processed food (since much processed food, including breakfast cereals, is fortified with both B_{12} and D), for optimal health pay attention to your consumption of vitamin B_{12} and your vitamin D levels.

Occasional Treats Versus Everyday Fare

The concept of "moderation" holds a lot of traction for people in the United States, and in theory, moderation is a great concept. It adds a non-neurotic, reasonable quality to the discussion of diet and behavior, a feeling that is helpful in creating a sustainable lifestyle you can maintain without constantly feeling challenged. The problem is that our food culture has so shifted the dietary definition of normal that the idea of moderation has become equally distorted. Daily, we eat food that should be reserved for special occasions, and we have trained our palates to expect intense combinations of salt, sugar, and fat. We're so accustomed to this that we've forgotten what it's like to reserve these kinds of foods for a truly special treat, like holidays.

47

With this in mind, be forewarned that as you start adding in simpler food, it may taste a bit bland to you. That is normal—soon you'll start to taste flavors more intensely—but you have to stick with it long enough for the change to happen! That's where your commitment to stick with your dietary transition from Figure 1, Your Path to Change, comes into play. We'll get into why and how commitment matters more in Step Three, but for the time being, practice all the strategies from Step One for staying connected to your motivation. As you read on and learn the new cooking skills and simpler ways to conceptualize a meal, take advantage of all the recipes beginning on page 147 to get going. These recipes are mostly appropriate for everyday fare, but there are a few exceptions! Even whole, plant foods can be unhealthy if you overdo the nuts, avocado, and coconut daily. (The piecrust on page 271 and the coconut cream on page 274 should definitely be limited to special—and very occasional—occasions.)

Everyday foods are whole foods, meaning the nutrient composition of fat, protein, carbohydrates, and vitamins and minerals hasn't changed much since they were grown and picked. This includes whole grains, fresh and frozen greens and vegetables, legumes, and fruits. Nuts and seeds are nice garnishes, but it's not important to include them daily. The one exception is ground flax seeds or ground chia seeds, which you can include in small quantities (one or two tablespoons) daily to augment your consumption of omega-3 fats.

That being said, there is no need for everyday food to taste boring or bland! It's not difficult or expensive to prepare delicious, varied meals. Once you get into the rhythm of it, you don't need more time than for any other cuisine. To get started, take a look at the three-week meal plan in the Ongoing Support Resources section on page 291 and use that as a template for your own timeline for crowding out, or move on to follow it completely as you advance into replacing and letting go of unhealthy food in Step Three. Know that while recipes are terrific inspiration and can help you branch out into trying new dishes, eventually you may establish a pattern of regular meals that don't require recipes.

PLANNING PLANT-BASED MEALS

48

Cooking food requires having the ingredients in the kitchen, which necessitates having purchased them, which involves having a plan. To whatever degree you are transitioning to your plant-based diet, you will have an easier time of it if you plan your meals in advance for the first three weeks. After that, you will probably find that planning still helps, but for that initial 21-day period it is likely to be essential. Here is a sampling of some approaches to meal planning—from adding particular ingredients to arranging entire meals:

- To add a whole grain into your breakfast cereal for the coming week, you decide to mix your current cereal with an equal amount of rolled oats, 50/50.
- To incorporate more produce into your weekly meals, you include a green vegetable at three dinners, make a big salad as the main course of three lunches, and prepare a big bowl of fruit for one weekend breakfast.
- To plan ahead, you choose two or three new dinner recipes to try in the evening with your family and one lunch that can be based around the previous night's leftovers by perusing the new recipe sources you subscribed to via social media in Step One.
- To orchestrate some meals as a family, you make a trip to the library or bookstore to browse cookbooks. With your kids, you select certain dinner recipes for the coming week, discuss how you can make the meals together, and decide which nights each of the meals will happen.
- To prepare for being pressed for time on Wednesday with its late afternoon staff meeting that almost always runs long, you plan to make an extra large dinner on Tuesday, choosing a basic recipe that's not too complicated—perhaps a grain, green vegetables, and beans that you season with herbs and spices—and think ahead about how you can make a quick meal of the leftovers the next day by dressing it up a little differently.
- Consider creating a paper list you can post on the refrigerator, putting specific recipes for specific days into your electronic calendar, or making a colored schedule of meals with your kids. Once you know what you'll be making, you'll know what you need and you can make a shopping list. The meal planning doesn't take a lot of time, but remember, "You don't get what you value, you get what you schedule/plan." In addition to what you intend to make, schedule time for the shopping and preparation. At the very least, do a spot check of your calendar to make sure your cooking aspirations are realistic for that day; otherwise, you are failing to plan, which, as we know, means planning to fail.

49

SHOPPING MAKES COOKING POSSIBLE

We are lucky to have an increasing number of healthy options for eating on the go, such as fruit stands, salad bars in grocery stores, and even sandwich shops that will do their best to accommodate special requests. However, preparing food at home is the best way to ensure that you eat what you want and stay on budget. You know what ingredients are used, the food tastes better because it's freshly made without copious amounts of salt and preservatives, and you have the ability to cook extra for leftovers. Any strategies that facilitate more home cooking are worth considering.

Shopping well is also important because without a well-stocked pantry and kitchen you'll be left scratching your head and ordering takeout. Virtually every one of the long-term, successful plant-based eaters I spoke with as I was writing this book has an established habit for their food shopping. Their common strategies include:

- Planning what they'll prepare in the coming week, whether that consists of a general sense because of long-time experience cooking or actually making meal plans and selecting specific recipes ahead of time.
- Using a list for food shopping, whether it's a running list in their kitchen as they run out of food or apps on their smartphone.
- Knowing the geography of their usual stores to make efficient use of their time, or even organizing their lists according to where the foods are in the store.
- Shopping weekly at only one or two places for the majority of their groceries, though they might visit the store again for little things that come up during the week.

Using a list can give you authority while you're in a store. It can help you to avoid the hazardous environment (aisles full of temptations) and allow you to emerge unscathed because you can lean on your list for direction. As you get more accustomed to your new eating patterns and less entrenched in your old ways of doing things, all these little tricks will become less important because you will develop new habits. But in the beginning, or when you are starting with new intentions that brush up against old habits, anything you can do to make it easier on yourself is worth trying. Here's what successful plant-based eaters *don't* do:

50

- They don't go shopping when they're hungry, which can lead to overbuying and impulse buys, as well as indulging cravings while surrounded by food they are trying to avoid.[25]
- They don't go to the store without a list or at least an idea of what they need.
- They don't shop for just one meal or one day at a time.

Given the fast pace and busy schedule most of us have to navigate, the old-world vision of going to a local farmer's market or small grocery each day to get ultra-fresh ingredients for that day's dinner isn't usually feasible. In fact, the traditional 20 hours per week that housewives spent on food preparation in the 1920s isn't feasible either.[26] Nowadays, we have jobs, commutes, kids with school and extracurricular activities, and more, and it's an accomplishment just to have a family dinner. Only slightly more than half of American adults spend time cooking on a given day.[27] Even though family meals at home are associated with healthier weight in children, lower risk of alcohol and drug abuse, and better nutrient intake,[28] the majority of American families are now eating out regularly for family meals, often at fast-food restaurants,[29] where healthy options, much less plant-based options, are few. Less than half of adolescents report at least seven at-home family meals a week.[30] With limited time and a whole world of unhealthy food to avoid, it's more important than ever to use our time as efficiently as possible in order to be able to carve out enough of it to actually cook real food (and eat it together).

Even if you end up food shopping without knowing specifically what you need, it helps to have a simple fallback list you know will yield a meal you and your family will like.

Though someone in your household has to do the planning, shopping, and cooking, it doesn't necessarily have to be the same person. You have three options for each of these jobs:

1. Yourself
2. A family member
3. Someone you pay

Doing it yourself or negotiating with a family member are most common. Different families organize these activities in different ways. Camille said that for years her husband, Bill, would plan the menus and make the list, and she would take the list and do the grocery shopping. For a long time, this worked well, but eventually they began planning only some of their meals each week in order to take advantage of seasonal produce and fresher ingredients they found in the store or their local farmer's market. If you have adolescents, some of their weekly household responsibilities could include planning and preparing one or more meals. If you have teenagers (and you trust them to drive and use your credit card!), you can even make grocery shopping one of their weekly chores. While this requires a complete list in advance, this can free up more time each week that you can actually spend cooking.

Many people are pressed for money or time—or, unfortunately, both. Think about the resources at your disposal, your household budget, and how much you spend on incidentals that could be reallocated to get home help. Do you have the time to do the planning, shopping, and cooking? Do you have room in your budget to hire a personal chef to cook for a few hours on the weekend and set you up for an easier week? Could you hire a housecleaner for a few hours a week instead of ordering takeout for two nights? (A clean house often facilitates more home cooking.) If you don't have room in your budget for a professional, you can try hiring a local teen through a youth employment bureau to help you cook or to clean. Often, people with full-time jobs face a second full-time job at home, and doing the cleaning, shopping, and cooking can be overwhelming. Think about how you spend your time at home, and prioritize ways to relieve the burden of other chores so you can have more time to cook and eat with your family.

If you are the primary shopper in the house, you already have a big advantage for adding in new foods. You are the locus of control—the groceries must pass between your hands! If you are not the primary shopper, you may need to step up and get involved. Your family member, partner, or spouse may try his or her best to satisfy your new diet, but you'll probably get more of the food you want, and with less frustration, if you put it in the shopping cart yourself.

Where to Shop

Once you start eating a plant-based diet, you may find that some of your regular places to shop no longer offer what you need. Most larger grocery stores have good produce sections, as well as "natural food" sections. Be wary of the natural food aisles, because many of the products here aren't necessarily healthy. They include processed meat substitutes and prepared

52

foods that contain white flour, along with added sugars, salt, and oil. Those foods may be useful during your transition period, but they are not components of an optimally healthy diet. Many grocery stores do carry bulk products, which can be a good way to save money on certain foods. Grocery store options continue to improve as well as more people find their way to healthy eating and stores respond to consumer demands.

Chains like Whole Foods and Wegmans have great bulk sections with a variety of dried beans, grains, nuts and seeds, dried fruit, and trail mixes. Local health food stores or grocery co-ops also tend to offer extensive bulk sections. The purpose and structure of a small, local store varies—some co-ops have better prices for members while others are specialty stores with higher prices. In both cases, you may be more likely to find foods that regular supermarkets don't carry. Trader Joe's, another national chain, has medium-small sized stores that carry mostly the store brands and a limited inventory. In this way, they consistently keep costs low and have a great price point for frozen fruits and vegetables, potatoes, onions, carrots and other root vegetables, nuts and seeds, and many cooking supplies.

Another way to emphasize whole plant foods is by getting involved in your local farm community. Community Supported Agriculture (CSA) is a rapidly growing movement that connects farmers directly with consumers. Members buy a share of the farm's produce for the season and pick up shares on a weekly basis.

By getting a CSA share, you can buy fresh, locally produced food at affordable prices. You also create a relationship with the people growing your food. You know exactly where your food comes from, and you are supporting a local farmer as well as the local economy. Most people feel some amount of pressure not to waste food coming in, so they tend to eat more produce with the weekly influx of fresh vegetables from the farm. This automatically crowds out old food choices.

Becoming a CSA member can support your plant-based diet in a multitude of ways.

Over the course of several months, CSAs are usually the most affordable way to buy local, fresh (and often organic) vegetables. Many farms calculate a price comparison for their own produce versus locally purchased produce from a grocery store in the area. In all the comparisons I've seen, the farm has come out less expensive every time over the course of the season. In addition, many CSA farms offer scholarships or work-trade opportunities. They may also participate in programs with the local cooperative extension to offer free or reduced shares to income-eligible families.

53

This may or may not be an option in your area, but it's worth checking out.

Farmers usually prefer that members pay upfront, but some farms offer more flexible payment plans. Some CSA farms require members to work a certain number of hours during the season or to volunteer on the farm in return for a reduced membership fee. Most simply have a price for the season. In exchange, you receive a weekly box of produce all season long, often well into the fall, even in more northern climates. The length of a CSA season varies between farms, and also by climate, and there are now quite a few winter CSA shares even in cold winter climates. Often, these are heavy on root vegetables and kale, which do quite well in the cold. While the winter selections may require some creativity in the kitchen, they provide a great base of ingredients for your cooking.

Check the Ongoing Support Resources section for websites that can help you to locate CSA farms and food co-ops in your area.

Strategies to Make Plant-Based Diets Affordable

Many people mistakenly believe that plant-based eating is more expensive, but it doesn't have to be. What can get expensive quickly is buying lots of "faux" meats and cheeses (real meat and cheese is already costly), packaged and prepared food, and takeout. A diet composed of simple, wholesome ingredients can actually cost less than one that includes meat. Here are some strategies you can use to keep costs low:

- Join a CSA.
- Buy foods from the bulk section of a store.
- Place wholesale orders together with other people.
- Prioritize whole, plant-based food over organic.
- Shop at Walmart and big-box stores for staples (their inventory is expanding).
- Start a garden or container garden; you can get free seeds from your local Cooperative Extension.

Given all the sources of affordable plant-based foods, it really is possible not to spend more. Table 3 compares the cost of two plant-based dinners using groceries purchased at Walmart in Pennsylvania in 2015 to the epitome of cheap food—McDonald's—for a family of four. These meals assume you have a few spices and vinegars at home in the kitchen, but the cost of these is factored into the comparison.

54

Table 3: **DINNER FOR FOUR, FOUR DIFFERENT WAYS**

Meal	BIG BURGER MEAL	CHICKEN MCNUGGET MEAL	BEANS AND RICE MEAL	PORTOBELLO STEAKS, SWEET POTATOES WITH KALE, AND SALAD
Food Prices	2 Big Mac meals = $12.38 2 cheeseburger Happy Meals = 6.58 Tax = $1.14	2 Chicken McNugget meals = $12.78 2 Chicken McNugget Happy Meals = $7.18 Tax = $1.20	Spicy black beans = $6.77 Savory brown rice = $1.99 Steamed herb vegetables = $3.99 Salad with dressing = $5.08 No Tax	4 portabello mushrooms = $6.15 4 sweet potatoes = $2.50 1 bag kale = $4.68 Salad with dressing = $5.08 No Tax
Total Cost	$20.10	$21.16	$17.83	$18.41

While exact prices will vary from place to place and year to year, this comparison drives home the point that pricewise, nothing beats buying simple, whole food ingredients, even the food we typically think of as cheap. If you want to try the Portabello Steaks or the Sweet Potatoes and Kale yourself, see pages 253 and 265. For my own grocery shopping, I am fortunate to live near both Trader Joe's and Whole Foods. We usually buy most of our groceries at Trader Joe's, choosing organic whenever we can, receive a weekly box of vegetables from our farmshare, and then buy a few specialty items and certain other fresh produce at Whole Foods.

My friend Kathy describes herself as weak and sick as a child, with little energy and lots of stomachaches. As an adult, she always chased vitality because she'd never had any in her youth. Kathy got involved with yoga and the outdoors in college and it helped, but her typical, heavy American diet kept her feeling lethargic and sluggish. Finally, when she and her husband decided to start a family, she became determined to produce and raise the healthiest kids in her power, and she centered this goal on plant-based eating.

Reality hit Kathy as a young mom without cooking skills or a chef's intuition. Preparing meals was daunting; making a veggie-based dinner every night for a family of four was even more daunting. She knew she had to devise a survival plan. If she could just have a few easy recipes in her head, she believed, then perhaps she could successfully navigate through meal planning, cooking, raising a family, and working.

So Kathy started keeping track by jotting down every dinner she made for a few weeks straight, and to her surprise, patterns emerged. She had gathered enough reliable, healthy main dishes to get through a couple of weeks. What a relief! She was then able to plan out dinners for a week and make a grand shopping list on Sundays. Having this weekly plan gave her confidence and relieved the stress.

Kathy based her meals around fresh produce and "went local" before it became a thing. To save time and money, she planned meals around a weekly stop at the farmer's market and later joined a CSA. Having the seasonal produce in the kitchen encouraged her to make meals based on those ingredients, like local eggplant or asparagus, or leeks and potatoes. And having kids around motivated her to teach them cooking skills so that they could help her prepare!

Today, Kathy continues to be amazed at her health and energy, which improves as she travels through middle age. And as for her grown kids, well, they are a shining example of the beautiful health and vitality that she had always strived for, which has made her plant-based transition such a shining success.

PREPARING PLANT-BASED MEALS

After a long time eating plant-based foods, the need to use recipes lessens substantially. Most people who cook any type of cuisine on a regular basis don't always use recipes (some may *never* use them), but they also tend to rely on the same seven to ten dinner recipes, a few lunch options, and a few standard breakfasts.

When I had just graduated from college, I lived in Toulon, France, for the school year as a *fille au pair*, a live-in nanny who was treated as a member of the family. I took care of four children, ages two, three, five, and ten, and hoped to become fluent in French after taking so many years of language classes. Several highlights and challenges of that experience remain with me, but one of the somewhat unexpected benefits was picking up many cooking skills from watching and cooking with Monique, the mom.

The family never ate out. Monique cooked a fresh dinner every day, and when the children came home from school for lunch, I was expected to prepare them a fresh lunch with a nicely set table. When Monique went food shopping, she always chose different types of cheeses (no, I was not able to avoid eating cheese while I lived in France for a year), fish, and yogurts, as well as diverse brands of packaged foods. When she went to the local farmer's market, she chose vegetables and fruits depending on what looked good and fresh. The family didn't seem to have any particular loyalty to specific brands. Their dietary pattern practiced an intentional rotation of foods, expressing variety in a way I hadn't encountered before—not just a broad variety of food groups, but a purposeful choice to not eat the same thing every day, or even every week.

Monique also always refreshed leftovers; if something was left over from the previous day or meal, she wouldn't serve it as is but incorporate it into a new dish. None of this food preparation or shopping took an unreasonable amount of time. I was there to take care of the children because Monique had gone back to school for nursing and so was a full-time student. That steady pattern of fresh cooking was her habit, made possible because of her expectations about the proper way to eat. After my time watching and learning from the activity in their kitchen, I'm convinced that you don't need to be French to develop the skills and habits to incorporate freshly prepared meals into your lifestyle.

Consider the amount of time it takes to get takeout: 5 minutes deciding, 2 minutes calling, 10 to 20 minutes driving to the restaurant, 5 minutes parking and paying, 10 to 20 minutes driving home, 3 minutes parking and unpacking the food. All this adds up to between 35 minutes to just under an hour—plenty of time to prepare a fresh, plant-based meal, as long as it's not overly complex. Of course, if you pick up your takeout on the way home you might shave off 10 to 15 minutes, but not necessarily, if you have to sit in traffic or drive outside of your normal route.

Besides swimming in the turquoise Mediterranean Sea, one of my favorite parts of that year in France was learning to cook from Monique. I learned to make perfect crepes—buckwheat French crepes with just flour and water, dressed with chocolate inside, a dessert that's easily included in a plant-based lifestyle (see Buckwheat Crepes with Chocolate on page 284).

I learned to work with different kinds of dough, with vegetables, and with sauces, and to make full meals without using a recipe. To this day I rarely use recipes, but I do own many cookbooks and love browsing through them for inspiration. I often start with an idea from someone's recipe or from a restaurant dish I've heard of, and then use what I know about temperature, the ratio of liquid to dry ingredients, and cooking time to improvise. Improvising becomes easier the more experience you have with a cuisine, so if you feel intimidated at the thought of learning a whole new

57

cooking style, remember that the learning curve is temporary. Once you've gotten into a new rhythm, you won't need recipes either.

That being said, the recipes in this book are delicious and inspiring options from my friends, mentors, and heroes in plant-based eating. These recipes can completely satisfy you at all hours of the day. Ongoing Support Resources has three weeklong meal plans and shopping lists. This kind of instruction and structure can help you branch out from your usual cooking routine if you're experienced (other people's recipes can help you out of a rut), and provides structured guidance if you're just starting out and not sure what to do.

But rough sketches of ideas for dinners that don't require exact quantities or even the same ingredients are really useful to have in your back pocket as well. Here are some examples of quick and easy meals when you're not sure what to make and want to keep the prep time really minimal:

- Quinoa cooked with garlic and frozen vegetables like broccoli, sweet bell peppers, mushrooms, and fava or lima beans. Throw in chopped fresh tomato and basil at the end and it's an Italian delight. I'm not opposed to pre-chopped garlic from a jar, by the way.
- Brown rice with steamed vegetables and tofu. You can top with a quick peanut sauce or tamari-ginger sauce, if you prefer.
- A big salad meal that uses enough greens to fill a large serving bowl. Try chopping the greens into smaller pieces to make the salad more uniform, then add leftover rice, beans, and cut-up raw vegetables, and top with a citrusy fruit dressing (see Raspberry Vinaigrette or Peanut-Lime Dressings on pages 232 and 233) and a few pecans.

Once you have a few new favorites in your rotation, you can rely on them when you don't have the energy to try something completely different. You can also simplify your favorite recipes to make them easier to prepare, but don't stop browsing recipes! They help to keep your excitement up.

COOKED VERSUS RAW

Cooking food does cause certain nutrients to become more available as cell walls are broken down and softened by heat. Cooking also makes certain foods more palatable, which means they will be more sustainable for people to continue eating over the long-term. Of course, cooking doesn't change the proportion of fat, protein, and carbohydrate.

However, all-raw diets are gaining in popularity, and many people claim to feel much better, or to have reversed a disease condition, after starting one. There are a growing number of "raw chefs" teaching many raw food preparation techniques that yield delicious meals. Hopefully we will have research in the future that can shed some light on the nuanced differences between cooked and raw plant-based diets, but for now, it's reasonable to assume that your diet should include some raw food dishes as well as vegetables and fruit, but unless you have particular reason to go all-raw, don't worry about trying to consume an all-raw diet.

Many proponents of raw food diets claim that living enzymes in the food confer specific health benefits. We are far from understanding everything about how nutrition works, but this is something that is fairly unlikely because stomach acid kills or inactivates enzymes in food by the time the food gets to your stomach.

PLANT-BASED PANTRY AND KITCHEN

As you add more and more plant foods into your diet, you'll need to stock your kitchen to keep it ready for making delicious meals! Wondering what you should keep on hand? What you should expect to find in the kitchen? What should you buy on a weekly basis? As you set your goals in *Your Path Going Forward* at the end of this chapter, consider purchasing at least some of these foods to try new recipes, and make room for them in the cupboard. Check Table 2 for more specific ingredient recommendations.

- **Staples to keep on hand:** dried whole grains and beans, cans or jars of diced tomatoes, beans, tomato sauce, a selection of flavored vinegars, smaller amounts of nuts and seeds, nutritional yeast, vegetable bouillon or broth, dried seaweeds (such as nori and kombu), a wide selection of spices and dried herbs, aluminum-free baking powder and baking soda, frozen vegetables and fruits.
- **Foods used less frequently but still good to keep on hand:** jars of pickles, capers, olives, sauerkraut, and heart of palm, nut butters and jars of fruit spread (no-sugar jams), natural sweeteners (date sugar or maple syrup, for example), baked tortilla chips, popcorn.

- **Foods to buy on a weekly basis:** fresh vegetables and fruits, fresh herbs and greens, whole-grain or corn tortillas, tofu, whole-grain pasta or pizza crust, plant milk (soy, almond, rice, oat, or others).
- **Kitchen equipment that helps:** a cutting board, at least one sharp knife, mixing bowls, glass or ceramic bakeware, stainless steel pots, wooden and stainless steel cooking utensils, whisk, food processor, electric immersion blender, and a high powered blender. If you can swing it, the Vitamix and Blendtec high-powered blenders are excellent. If you need to stay more budget-conscious, many less expensive models will be just fine; you just may need to blend things like smoothies and sauces longer to get a smooth consistency.

Translating Recipes to Plant-Based

One purpose of this book is to empower you, the reader, the shopper, and, of course, the cook, to become comfortable enough with plant-based cuisine that you can create your own delicious and healthy recipes. The recipes in this book, as previously mentioned, are a starting point. They provide plant-based versions of some basic—and some more gourmet—dishes that you'll love and enjoy. However, the list could never be complete, and most people have particular family favorites they would love to continue eating if a healthier version existed. You may find the following substitutions helpful in modifying your favorite recipes into a whole food, plant-based version.

- Use whole-wheat flour, or other whole-grain flour, instead of white or even wheat flour. Flour is still a processed food, although minimally processed, so better choices for everyday eating are whole grains like rice, quinoa, oats, barley, and millet. When you do bake or need flour to thicken sauces or stews, choose whole-grain flour. It rises almost as easily as white flour, and it retains the fiber and nutrients found in the intact grain. Your palate will soon appreciate the rich, nutty taste of the whole grain. If you are sensitive to wheat or are avoiding it, try whole spelt, oat, barley, or millet flour, or a gluten-free flour mix (which often contains brown rice and potato).

60

- Use whole-grain pasta instead of white pasta. There are many varieties now on the market. You may have to look in your local health food store, or a larger grocery store with a natural food section, but you'll find spaghetti, fettuccini, lasagna, angel hair, and even macaroni in a variety of whole grains. They could be made from rice, spelt, wheat, quinoa, corn, or even beans. Make sure you choose brown rice pasta instead of just rice pasta, so you are getting the whole grain nutrients.
- Use fresh or frozen vegetables instead of canned. Commercial canning often uses copious amounts of salt and oil to pack food, and the closer you can get food to the state it was in when freshly picked, the better. Frozen produce is a better choice than canned, and can even be more nutrient-packed than fresh, at least for nutrients that degrade in the presence of light (like vitamin C).

Tofu, tempeh, and seitan (a denser substance made from vital wheat gluten flour) are often presented as a substitute for meat when people are switching over to a plant-based diet for the first time. It's not a good idea to overly rely on seitan because it does tend to be salty, and some people are sensitive to wheat gluten, but tofu and tempeh are excellent substitutes for meat ingredients.

Achieving the Texture and Flavor

What many people miss most when switching to a whole foods diet are the intense tastes created by sugar, salt, and fat. Some of this desire will pass with time. Often at least three weeks is needed for taste preferences to shift. But there is no need for meals to be bland or flavorless, and making food especially savory and flavorful is an important strategy in making this diet sustainable for you.

Many people crave specific foods, especially when hungry or in the grocery store. It can be helpful to think about the qualities of the food you crave. Is it savory or sweet? Is it crunchy, chewy, or fluffy? Is it served warm or cold? For instance, a craving for macaroni and cheese might be comfortably satisfied by eating mashed potatoes made with plant milk and seasonings. Avoiding cheese will keep from prolonging the withdrawal from dairy, but often a dish seasoned with nutritional yeast (a deactivated yeast that can be found in many supermarkets and most health food stores) can lend

61

enough of the savory, cheesy flavor to help you pass through the craving. A craving for sweets and desserts might be dealt with by eating a piece of fruit and making a deal with yourself to wait and see if you are still hungry after 10 minutes.

Sometimes people aren't in the habit of eating fruit as a snack, but if you can remember to choose fruit first for several weeks, it will soon come naturally to you. A great strategy during the transition for all foods, not just sweets, is to mentally "allow" yourself to eat whatever it is you crave, but to eat a healthier version *first*. Once you do that, you may find that you are satisfied and don't need anything else.

Your taste buds register five main flavors: salty, sweet, sour, bitter, and umami (Japanese word for delicious that refers to a rich, savory flavor). People are most familiar with salty and sweet in cooking. As your body and tastes adjust to a less processed diet, you will probably be comfortable with less salt—most processed snacks like potato chips have way too much salt—as well as foods that have a lower intensity of sweetness. The following strategies may help you achieve flavorful, delicious dishes, all plant-based!

For savory grain dishes:

- Add vegetarian bouillon cubes or flakes, or cook the grain with some liquid bouillon, or tomato juice instead of all water. This will make the grain extra delicious.
- Try adding a piece of kombu seaweed (just a one inch by one inch square) to your pot for a tiny bit of extra flavor and minerals.
- Cook the grain with minced carrot and celery, à la Julia Child's recommendation.

To make soups and stews satisfying:

- Take out a portion from the dish, blend it to be creamy, and then add it back. This infuses flavor and texture, and brings that thickness and extra body we associate with comfort food. When your body is used to the caloric density of fat, and you're trying to adjust to a lower-fat diet, the new foods might seem unsatisfying. This is true for all levels of fat consumption.
- Add white wine, miso, onions, potatoes, carrots, garlic, mushrooms, and kombu seaweed to accentuate the umami flavor of the dish, which many people find more satisfying.

62

To make salad dressings and sauces:

- Try using dates as the base for the sweet kind of salad dressing and try beans, silken tofu, or nuts as the base for the savory kind. This will add bulk—thickness and creaminess once you blend it—as well as flavor. Add other fruit in different combinations; it's almost like pouring a smoothie on your salad. Yummy, too. Most "fat-free" salad dressings you buy in the store are loaded with corn syrup, artificial thickeners, and preservatives. We have several delicious recipes in this book, but don't stop here—try making your own.
- Use silken tofu, chickpeas, or cauliflower as bases for creamy sauces for pasta or other dishes. Make sure to add ingredients with intense flavors to cover up the tofu taste, though silken is mild compared to regular tofu. Sundried tomatoes, herbs and spices, a little lemon juice, mustard, nutritional yeast, and cooked onion are all effective components of savory sauces. Adding different vinegars to your savory dressings and sauces will also change the flavor; take the time to experiment. You have apple cider, balsamic, umeboshi, rice, coconut, and both white and red wine vinegar, among others.

For general flavoring and seasoning:

- Add ketchup and soy sauce (or tamari or shoyu) together to lend a smoky/meaty flavor to bean dishes and homemade seitan.
- Combine a small amount of vegan Worcestershire sauce to peanut sauces to lend them a more robust flavor.
- Use herbs such as tarragon, sage, or thyme with white wine, lemon, salt, and garlic in tofu and bean dishes, though those same herbs do not mix well with tamari/soy sauce.
- Replicate coconut-based curries, a staple of Thai cuisine, by using the condensed curry paste and fresh lemongrass stalks for a fresher flavor.
- Incorporate nutritional yeast (though it doesn't taste like cheese) for a smoky, savory flavor and a satisfying, cheese-like experience. Nutritional yeast ground with toasted walnuts can make a dry Parmesan-like condiment to sprinkle on food, or creamy sauces with a substantial amount of nutritional yeast can make a version of mac 'n' cheese, or a liquid cheesy pizza topping, possible.

63

For marinating:

- Start the marinade, which offers baked dishes a much richer flavor than food with sauce simply poured on top, by preparing the dish the night before and letting it sit. Then bake it just before serving. It's a great way to incorporate a lot of flavor without using oil.
- If you didn't have the chance to start a marinade the night before, it's still worth doing even if you have only 30 minutes to let the food sit in it. If you are marinating tofu, make sure to press the water out of the tofu with a cloth as much as possible—this will allow more liquid to permeate the tofu.

VARIATIONS IN RECIPES

Think of this book as a jumping-off point for further exploration in the kitchen. Some variations are included with the recipes, but take the recipes and change them. Try different seasonings, vary your veggies. Whether you are a beginning cook or have lots of experience, you may find that eating a more plant-based diet means that you have a greater variety of food in your diet, not less.

Cooking is dynamic—the experience and results change depending on who is involved, their background, how they feel that day, which foods are available, and which foods they use. There are infinite possibilities, so don't be afraid of failure. Learning what doesn't work can be as valuable as finding what does. The more you test out variations, the less you will need written recipes to cook. You will develop a sense of which flavors work well together, how long things take to cook, and which dishes might complement each other in a meal.

REFRESHING LEFTOVERS

Sometimes, leftovers just sit in the refrigerator, waiting for you to do something about them. It's great to make enough food for leftovers, as few people have time to cook for every meal, so think about creating a new meal tomorrow with today's dinner, and consider freezing for future meals. As I learned from Monique, taking a few extra minutes to make the leftovers different is well worth it. A soup that tastes mouth-watering the first and second time will become increasingly boring if you eat it for days.

Additionally, eating straight out of the pots standing around the refrigerator is quite a bit less appealing than eating off a pretty place set at the table. Practice mindful eating. People are more prone to overeating when they're watching television or in the car than when they're sitting down at the table.[31] Taking the time to prepare a nice presentation will more than pay you back with the pleasure you experience in the meal.

Here are some techniques for rearranging different kinds of leftovers, making them more interesting, more appealing, or different tasting, all without cooking a full meal over again.

For leftover grains:

- Add them to your leftover soup and make a nice stew.
- Add them to cold salads.
- Add some plant milk, raisins, cinnamon, and apple, and simmer in a pot and you have a nice pudding for breakfast the next morning.

For leftover soups and stews:

- Try adding miso to soups to give a new twist to the flavor. Almost any soup will taste good with miso, except for soups with tomatoes, eggplant, peppers, or potatoes.
- Use leftover soups made of tomatoes, eggplant, peppers, or potatoes as a sauce poured over leftover grains or baked potatoes to flavor them.
- For soups that contained miso in the first place, you can add more tofu, seaweed, onion, or celery to bulk it up a bit.
- Put leftover stews of grains, beans, salads, and vegetables in wraps. If you love cilantro, add some.
- Turn leftover stew into a casserole by adding broth, pouring into a casserole dish, and topping with corn bread batter; then pop it in the oven.

For leftover cooked vegetables:

- Try adding them to a new soup or bean dish.
- Add them to a wrap for lunch, with hummus, salad dressing, or refried beans.

For leftover fruit salads:

- Who wants to eat leftover fruit salad? It was so delicious the first time, and now just seems sad and verging on brown. Instead of composting cut fruit that is still fine to eat, throw it in the blender and make a smoothie. Smoothies have a creamier, more substantial texture with banana, so add another one, and you may want to add in plant milk or greens to make a green smoothie. Peeled bananas kept in the freezer make a delicious addition.

For leftover raw salads:

- Try throwing this in the blender with the smoothie.
- Add some new vegetables to old salads, or leftover grains, nuts, or seeds, and use a different dressing.
- Add steamed potatoes or yams to otherwise raw salads, too, helping to bulk up the second-time-around experience.

For leftover bean dishes:

- Make bean burgers by opening another can of beans, cutting up an onion, and mixing everything with some spices, flour, ground flaxseed, and plant milk. In no time you'll have a nice mixture you can use to form patties and make bean burgers in the oven. Add some ground rolled oats if the mixture is too moist. Breading the outside with cornmeal adds a delicious texture.

For leftover pasta:

- If the pasta is unsauced, try going in a different direction. For example, if you used tomato sauce the first night, try the Mac and Cheeze sauce on page 252 the next day.
- Lightly steam some different vegetables to add in, or add them raw.
- Try using pre-flavored tofu for a quicker dish.
- If the sauce from the first day is already mixed with the pasta, throw it all into a pot of soup. Just adding new vegetables makes a big difference.

66

Of course, if you don't mind eating exactly the same thing more than once, you can save a little time! Yet, taking a bit of care to change things up makes your meals more interesting and satisfying, so give it a try.

INVOLVING YOUR CHILDREN IN COOKING HEALTHY FOODS

Cooking is an excellent way to get children on board with eating healthy food. The more involved they are, the more invested they feel, and the more likely they will be to swallow! Most kids are fascinated by cooking and love the idea of getting involved. By preparing food together, you can spend quality time with your children, teach them about nutrition, and create an empowering experience all at the same time. Research shows that one important contributor to children's well-being and success is when the adults in their lives have high expectations and hold them to high standards.[32] Expecting that your kids *do* understand the nutritional implications of what they eat, and that they will try new foods, even if they make different choices when they are around friends outside the home, will serve them better in the long run. So will expecting them to participate in creating the healthy food eaten at home. Plus, they'll have fun. Of course, parents or caretakers are responsible for making and initiating time for cooking together, for creating teachable moments, and for finishing the experience by cleaning up together.

Above all, be patient. Having little helpers in the kitchen usually means more work for you, not less. If you can have fun guiding them, it can set a foundation that will serve them for a lifetime. Imagine the difference between a child who associates cooking and eating whole, plant-based foods with fun and with feeling loved and respected and a child who is uninvolved in making dinner but is pressured to "eat your vegetables" in order to get dessert. When the experience of preparing and eating healthy food is a reward in itself, no link is created between sugary, fatty foods and being rewarded. At the same time, you avoid the implication that vegetables or "healthy foods" are unpleasant and something to be endured for the sake of the "pleasure" of dessert.

Particularly in the United States food is often used as a reward to bribe children to eat or do what we want, to celebrate successes, or as consolation. Going out for ice cream to celebrate good grades or a soccer win is

67

common. Why not instead get your child a book or some music he or she particularly wants? Or go for a walk or see a movie together? There is no need to make unhealthy foods a reward. Food is fuel, and preparing and eating delicious food lays the foundation for the highest quality of life. It will serve children better to keep food in its appropriate place in the larger context of living well. This means talking to them about nutrition, about what the different kinds of foods do when entering the body—animal foods versus plant foods, and processed foods versus whole foods—and how the body can be tricked into cravings by high-fat, salty, sugary foods.

As you cook together, you can point out how beautiful the colors of the vegetables and fruits are, teaching them to appreciate that beauty. Take the time to make sure you have healthy snacks on hand and that you earmark enough time to prepare healthful meals together. Teach children that food is nourishment for the body; that it's not a solution for boredom or loneliness; that it's not something to be mindlessly included in every other activity, such as driving, reading, or watching movies; that it's not reward for good behavior, good grades, or achievement. Teach them that food is something to be honored, appreciated, and enjoyed—and also something to be kept in its place.

The patterns set in infancy and early childhood truly have a lifetime of influence. Research shows that lifetime taste preferences are affected by the diet of the mother during pregnancy and nursing, and also by what the child consumes in the first 18 months of life.[33] It is absolutely critical to provide the best nutrition possible during this time—whole, plant-based foods with no added sugars or oils. It's important to point out, too, that during infancy and the toddler stage there is absolutely no need to share less-than-healthy food with your baby, even if you are making less-than-optimal choices yourself. Your toddler doesn't know the difference! If she is used to eating only whole, plant foods, she won't feel at all left out if you don't share your birthday cake with her. It will serve your child better over the course of his lifetime if you simply do not allow him to develop strong taste preferences for unhealthy foods. Of course, as children get older, it becomes less possible to control everything they eat, but those early years offer an important opportunity to influence what tastes good to them permanently.

At the same time, if your child is older and you are making a transition to healthier foods for the first time, do not be discouraged—it's definitely not too late. Remember that taste preferences are learned, and even adults can learn to like a healthy diet. Your children will take the lead from you, so the more open you can be about your struggles *and* your motivation to

68

maintain a healthy diet, the more respect they will have for the process, and the better equipped they will be to make their own decisions.

As children get older, the opportunities to cook and prepare food together become more numerous. Growing a garden is an easy and fun way to help children get invested in healthy food. Even if you live in a city, it's possible to grow greens like kale and collards—as well as tomatoes—in buckets. Although you can't expect to contribute significant bulk to your food supply with container gardening, for young children the purpose is more to create a positive association in their mind with growing food, nutrition, and taking care of their bodies.

Even fairly young children can use knives with supervision, and learning to cut vegetables for dinner is a great way for them to be involved. Kids can practice math by measuring for baking, and if they can read, they should be able to do some baking with minimal help from you, or perhaps with your supervision in the kitchen. Kids are proud to be able to say, "I made this all by myself!" There are many ways for them to be involved, and probably the only limit on what is possible will be your patience.

If you embark on this transition for the first time with older children, you'll have to decide what kind of food environment you want to create in your house and what you are comfortable allowing your children to do outside of the home. The older they are, the more self-agency they have, the less you'll be able to control their choices when you're not with them. Recognizing what you do control and being clear about your boundaries will require some persistence (know that your children are just as addicted to unhealthy food as you are).

Additionally, if you have a spouse or partner who isn't on board with the new diet, it can be harder to enforce your standards with kids. We'll talk about these challenges in more depth in Step Five, but even if parents are united, it can be hard when kids aren't ready to play along. Many parents facing this situation choose to navigate these dynamics with some of the following compromises:

- Only certain foods (where you draw the line is what you have to figure out) will be purchased with the family grocery budget.
- Older children (preteens and teens) who may have their own spending money are free to buy what they wish outside of the home, but if that includes foods that are no longer being kept in the kitchen, they can't bring them home and put them in the refrigerator.

69

- A policy for special occasions, like eating out in restaurants, can serve as a compromise for making exceptions—as long as nobody brings the leftovers home.

For practical reasons, it may make the most sense to have a frank conversation with children about your own goals and the new rules you set in the house, and to acknowledge that while you hope they will make healthy choices on their own, you know they make their own decisions the older they get. While you don't and can't monitor everything they do, if you focus on your own goals, you will model the satisfaction and happiness that comes from following through with what you want. That, on its own, can inspire your kids to join you in this healthier path.

EATING OUT AND TRAVELING

Restaurants can be hard, especially if they are not vegetarian-friendly. Nowadays, many restaurants will have plant-based options on the menu, but this depends on where you live and the kind of restaurant it is. Do some investigating. Which restaurants in your area offer plant-based dishes? This information will come in handy whenever you are involved in the decision about where to go. Most Asian restaurants—Thai, Chinese, Japanese, Korean, and Indian—offer many vegetable dishes, and you can usually choose tofu in place of meat.

As you plan to add in healthy foods, consider challenging yourself to a totally plant-based meal the next time you go out to a restaurant, or a totally whole foods meal if you are looking to move up to the next level of health.

Surprisingly, diners and steak houses are often some of the best choices for truly healthy, whole plant foods that are oil-free. You can order baked potatoes and large salads with vinegar or no dressing. Most restaurants are accommodating. You can tell your server you are on a special diet, or not, as you feel comfortable, but be specific. Don't be shy to ask for what you want, as your new way of eating is becoming more commonplace. Ask for modifications on meat dishes, for instance, requesting beans on the roasted chicken salad instead of the chicken, or requesting a certain dish without the cheese. At Chinese restaurants, you can ask for steamed rice and vegetables with the sauce on the side, instead of fried in oil. The more you ask, the more you create the demand for it.

But what about when your boss takes the office out for seafood? Almost every restaurant has a salad section as well as various side dishes. There may be rice, vegetable, or bean dishes that together would make a nice meal. I often order several side dishes in situations like this and feel very satisfied.

Eating a plant-based diet while on the road is frequently challenging. Try to prepare road snacks ahead of time so you aren't starving in the car or the airport. Some good choices are fresh and dried fruits, cut vegetables in a bag, no-oil crackers and hummus—try Oasis brand for no-oil dips—and mixed nuts. Most grocery stores and airports carry fruit smoothies and juices with no added sugar that are helpful in a pinch. If you have the time and inclination to carry food with you, there's nothing better than a home-cooked dinner in an airtight container.

Many hotels have coffee makers in each room, allowing you to make hot water for instant, healthy soups that you can pack. You may want to consider investing in a travel blender to make your own smoothies with fresh fruit from local stores.

YOUR PATH GOING FORWARD

Step Two has been packed with information about how to incorporate more plant foods into your diet; how to plan, purchase, and prepare plant-based meals; how to work the routine into your family dynamic; and even how you can handle eating while traveling and for special events. This is your time to start changing what you eat. Remember, at this point we are approaching the change from the perspective of crowding out unhealthy foods. Life doesn't come with a set of rules for eating. You will always be "allowed" to eat whatever you want, but the more whole, plant-based food you can add in now, the faster your path to optimal health. Remember to make your goals SMART and to share your goals with your support buddy. You can reexamine both in *How to Use This Book*. Above all, remember to review your motivation(s) and add to your vision board. Stay plugged into the social media you subscribed to in Step One. These contacts will introduce you to recipes and new foods as well as keep up your resolve.

The three paths described below are tailored to a gradual (Easing In), moderate (Rev It Up), or rapid (Total Transformation) pace of change. If you're not sure which one to take, look again at the self-assessment *How Much Change Am I Ready For?* on page 13. As we discussed in *How to Use This Book*, the path you take and the goals you set for yourself are your choice, and they will be most effective if they challenge you but do not overwhelm you. You want to be able to visualize yourself reaching them.

1. **Easing In:** Think about how you want to start the crowding out process. Take your time, and sketch out a plan for the next three weeks. Post your plan in a visible place—the refrigerator is a good bet. Do you want to focus on adding certain foods or dishes, making a plan to eat healthy food first whenever you feel a craving, or switching from refined products to whole grains, for instance? Consider planning to replace sweet snacks with fruit, choosing certain days of the week or certain meals to be completely plant-based, or making a point to include bean dishes at several dinners per week. Start with an overall plan to increase the amount of plant-based foods each week: the first week you might start with two days out of seven, or six out of twenty meals, and then gradually increase that for weeks two and three. Stick to what feels like a manageable amount of change for you. Check the recipes and meal plans in the Three Weeks of Meal Plans (page 291) for ideas, and make sure to shop with a list so you have the ingredients to fulfill your plan. Make a point to let your immediate family members know you are embarking on a new path with food and could use their support. ▶*Suggested time frame: three weeks.*

2. **Rev It Up:** You're ready for more significant change, and crowding out is a terrific first step. What do you want to happen over the next few weeks? You might want to start by planning half your meals, or make three of the seven days of the week completely plant-based (or whole food and oil-free if you already eat plant-based). With each successive week, plan to increase the amount of whole plant-based foods you are cooking and eating until you are close to targeting mostly plant-based foods all the time. Remember that this step focuses on adding in healthy food, not worrying about avoiding unhealthy food, so don't fret if you still eat things you eventually want to cut out. Your diet will shift significantly simply by adding in new food. Think about the time you spend on household chores and revisit the suggestions for saving time and getting help. Can you implement any of these strategies to carve out more time to cook? Make time to have an open and authentic conversation with your immediate family members; you are starting a new dietary path and their help and support will be essential

for your success. If you are frustrated with your health, your weight, or emerging new values around compassion towards animals, share with family members how you really feel without trying to control their responses or trying to convert them to your new way of thinking. Consider whether you'd like to set some boundaries about what foods you'll allow your kids to bring into the house, and try to come to an agreement about the new rules with your spouse or partner. Remember to use the meal plans and shopping lists in the Resources section for support in planning and shopping. ▶*Suggested time frame: three weeks.*

3. **Total Transformation:** Time to take your diet to the top! This is a great move for people who are open to radical shifts. While you don't need to worry if you still include animal foods or processed foods, take the meal plan and shopping lists in the Resources section to map out the next two weeks of completely plant-based meals. Make sure you think about your schedule on a daily basis— when you can shop, and how you'll work enough time to cook into your routine. Writing down the time you've scheduled for these steps makes the plan realistic. If you already make plant-based meals that you prefer, switch out some of the recipes in the meal plan for your own, and adjust your shopping list accordingly. Make sure the plan looks appealing and manageable, and post it somewhere visible (again, the refrigerator is a great choice.) Is it possible for you to reallocate some household chores, hire professional help, or hire a teenager to assist you? Set your goals for contacting these people and starting the appropriate conversations with your spouse/partner or kids. If you are taking your diet to a new level of healthy, it's possible you'll be adding in a lot of new food that your immediate family may at first not know what to think of. The power of an open and authentic conversation is that your family can get inside whatever pain or frustration you are feeling and empathize with that. This helps them get on board with your change for yourself and support you even if they want to eat differently. Now is also the time to think about what kind of boundaries you and your partner/spouse will set for the food that kids can bring home, or exceptions for special occasions. If you eat plant-based already, it's likely that processed food still creeps into your kitchen, and these are some refinements you can target as SMART goals. ▶*Suggested time frame: two weeks.*

73

CHOOSE HEALTH OVER HABIT
letting go of the foods that no longer serve you

A T THIS POINT IN the book, you owe yourself a thank you and an encouraging pat on the back. You've set out on a powerful path of dietary change. In following this path, you've taken some steps toward actually shifting your diet by incorporating more whole, plant-based foods. You've also likely been reading about nutrition, watching some documentaries on diet and disease, and following some new chefs and recipe blogs on social media.

You may be feeling both energized and challenged by these new routines. At the same time, you may be dealing with your own emotions of elation, satisfaction, or worry, as well as reactions of happiness, or maybe consternation, from family members.

In Step Three, we will take you further forward along the path of good health by not only choosing to *add in* healthy foods, but by developing habits that will enable you to choose healthy foods *in place of* what you used to eat as well. Our purpose here is to create lifetime habits, so we'll discuss how to accurately interpret the messages from your body, how certain types of foods can distort these messages, how to recognize and replace unhealthy food, and how to sail gracefully through food withdrawal and create new habits more effectively while also leading a balanced life.

WHAT YOUR BODY IS TELLING YOU . . . AND HOW YOU CAN CHOOSE TO RESPOND

You started the process of changing your diet based on your own needs and wants, and with your own goals in mind. Those goals may or may not have initially included eliminating foods or food groups. So take this chapter as an invitation, rather than a requirement. Whether you choose to shift your diet in small steps or break free of certain food groups entirely, you'll benefit from the information presented here. However, if you want to have the most energy possible, the lowest risk for chronic disease, and the easiest time maintaining a healthy weight, then moving to a totally whole food, plant-based diet is your best opportunity for doing so.

You may, perhaps, be feeling a little fearful or alarmed, even if you have strong reasons for wanting to change your diet further. Nutrition can be an emotional topic. Diet and food practices are with us from birth. They form part of our culture and—in some ways—part of our identity. As you move forward, be attentive to how you feel and how your body reacts to the change—not solely after you eat, but how any anxiety, fear, regret, or other emotions express themselves in your body. The body doesn't lie when it comes to your feelings, and it's important to acknowledge them with kindness, wherever you are with your eating goals.

My friend Samantha struggled for years to change her eating patterns, but every time she made a little progress, her longtime love of fried food and sugar derailed her. In spite of her good intentions, the fried chicken drumsticks, peanut butter and bacon sandwiches, and unbaked cake batter she ate with a spoon became irresistible in moments of craving. Her resolve would last for half a day, sometimes until the evening, and occasionally even for a few weeks. But, inevitably, she felt hungry, she felt tired, or she craved dessert and gave in, after which she would eat the foods she knew kept her feeling sluggish, congested, and overweight. In addition, even on the days and weeks when she controlled her eating fairly well, she didn't really see the results she hoped for—a pound or two would temporarily disappear, but the weight never stayed off and she continued to always feel tired. Plus, she struggled continually throughout the day to function with the distraction of hunger. She was stuck—as many of us were or are—until she learned that instead of eating less of the same foods, she needed a deeper transformation of the *kinds* of food she consumed.

76

My own experience with dietary change was deeply influenced by my childhood eating habits and my tendency to go for a high-fat diet. As I learned more about what a truly whole food diet means, I was reluctant at various points to change my diet any further—even after I already had stopped eating all animal products. I didn't want to take out the remaining added fats and oils because, well . . . I thought I liked them, and my physical addiction to fat colored my beliefs about what would make me happiest. It took time to be ready to let go of that, not to mention actually preparing foods differently and beginning to enjoy my new cooking style.

Living a whole, full life supported by healthy food is an empowered existence. Food is fuel to support our activities and allow us to express our unique gifts in the world. Fuel makes the car go, but it isn't the purpose of the journey. On the contrary, the less we have to think about the fuel in our cars, the more fun it is to drive!

The three biggest culprits that cause unnecessary food distraction are added fat, sugar, and salt. The more you eat foods with these ingredients, the more your taste preferences shift to expect even more of them in everything. We'll discuss this further later in the chapter. What this state of food addiction means, though, is that the old maxim "trust your body" isn't necessarily a good principle to follow. Your body, if it's addicted to calorie-dense foods, will send you unreliable signals that are not based on your actual need for energy. This is the definition of cravings.[1]

Without sufficient information and perspective on your diet, it's easy to interpret cravings as "messages" from your body that should be accommodated. Here are a couple of examples: We say we just need a little something to get us through the afternoon, so we eat some cheese and crackers, or perhaps a brownie or a cookie, or we tell ourselves that we really need some protein, so we prepare a dinner of a hamburger on a white bread roll with potato salad. In both situations, we are hungry and need enough calories to be satisfied in that moment. Now, the fifth taste receptor—the umami receptor, which picks up the taste of glutamate, an amino acid in protein—appreciates the savory flavor of glutamate-containing amino acids.[2] But that's not really what is going on here. These "just-a-little-something" foods contain a lot of fat and/or sugar, which we crave when we are hungry if we're accustomed to high-fat and high-sugar food. Because our culture bestows a special reverence on protein, in certain moments our genuine hunger combines with our cravings and we interpret these signals as real messages from our bodies, when, in fact, they are the product of our misinformation applied to a cycle of addiction. If we don't have a context of nutrition knowledge in which to interpret our cravings, it's easy to get confused and interpret cravings as our inner voice speaking to us about what our bodies need.

THE ADDICTIVE ALLURE OF HYPERPALATABLE FOODS

Most people are familiar with some of the more obvious forms of addiction—cocaine, heroin, morphine, alcohol, and, of course, even more people experience the addictive effects of nicotine and caffeine. A little at first produces a noticeable effect, a little more does almost as much, and then tolerance builds and eventually you need quite a bit more to produce the same experience that originally hooked you. You start to feel like you need the substance just to feel normal.

Many of us feel that we may struggle with being "addicted" to certain foods, and science backs us up on this one.[3] Paralleling the growing concern with obesity, researchers have coined the term *hyperpalatable foods* (listed as "Foods to Avoid" in Table 6, on page 90) to describe the intensely refined and artificial snacks and treats we face in supermarkets, gas stations, parties, and even in stores where food was not even sold in the past. These foods are created with *food fragments*, extracted, concentrated, individual nutrients (the fat, sugar, protein, or vitamins and minerals) that are added to foods in quantities and proportions impossible to achieve naturally. These hyperpalatable foods made of food fragments inspire behavior that easily falls within the definition of addiction—a strong desire to consume a substance in spite of negative consequences.[4] At this point, we have more research on the addictive potential of hyperpalatable foods than there was on alcohol and other drugs when they were declared officially to be drugs of abuse.[5] Drs. Doug Lisle and Alan Goldhamer, who see patients at TrueNorth Health Center, a residential medical facility in Santa Rosa, California, use a whole food, plant-based diet as the foundation of their program and have coined the term "the pleasure trap" to describe the lure of hyperpalatable and calorie-dense foods.

When these addictive substances are consumed on a regular basis, they lead not only to overeating, but also to increased risk for a host of chronic diseases. And these foods are everywhere. For many people, they make up the majority of their diet.[6] Table 4 describes the methods by which macronutrients (carbohydrate, protein, and fat) are altered, and the consequences of adding them to foods.

78

PROCESSING TECHNIQUE	LEADS TO...	EXAMPLES (A FEW!)	RISK FOR:
Concentrating carbohydrates	Isolated sugar lacks fiber; more calories fit into less space; sweet taste trains the palate to expect sweeter food.	White sugar, turbinado sugar, corn syrup, agave syrup, dextrose, fructose, and even maple syrup and honey	Overweight and other chronic diseases[7]
Concentrating fat	Isolated fat lacks fiber so more calories fit into less space; rich taste trains the palate to expect richer food.	Butter; lard; coconut oil; and bottled oils such as olive oil, safflower oil, sesame oil, and canola oil	Overweight, type 2 diabetes, heart disease, and other chronic diseases[8]
Concentrating protein	Overall protein consumption is much higher than requirements.	Protein powder supplements used in "protein shakes"	Cancer and other chronic diseases, especially with whey or other dairy protein supplements[9]
Removing fiber	More calories fit into less space; people can eat more calories without realizing it.	White flour products or any processed food or juices	Overweight due to overeating leads to many other health risks[10]
Adding sugar	Proportion of simple sugar calories out of total calories increases; total calories increases.	Soda and punch, cookies, crackers, chips, canned soup, dips, yogurt, and most commercial breads	Overweight, elevated blood triglycerides, heart disease, type 2 diabetes, and other chronic diseases[11]
Adding fat	Proportion of fat calories out of total calories increases; total calories increases.	Soup, sauces, fake meats and cheeses, cookies, crackers, dressings, pastries, almost all commercial foods	Overweight, type 2 diabetes, heart disease, and other chronic diseases[12]
Adding salt	Flavor is intensified and the added salt trains the palate to expect saltier food.	Virtually all processed food, even food that says "low-sodium"; most restaurant food contains more salt than home-cooked food	Hypertension and heart disease[13]

79

When you think more deeply about the practice of isolating and concentrating fat, carbohydrate, and protein, it may seem a bit strange to go to so much trouble to create foods that contain these elements when the whole foods you started with contain all of them anyway. The other strange thing is that it's extremely common to do this! There are even food products on the market whose major ingredients are isolates of all three of the macronutrients, such as sports nutrition bars and meal replacement shakes.

The end result is what food writer Michael Pollan likes to call "edible, food-like substances." You can chew them. You can swallow them. But they are not actually food. When you take food fragments out of the context of whole food and concentrate them, the balance of macro- and micronutrients is disturbed, leaving us with only some of the nutrients our bodies need, and a huge excess of calories that we don't need at all.

The characteristics of hyperpalatable foods parallel those of drugs of abuse in several important ways:

- **Brain chemistry:** Both drugs of abuse and high levels of fat, sugar, and salt activate the hedonic, or pleasure centers, in the brain via the dopamine and opioid neural pathways. These are the same pathways activated by cocaine, heroin, morphine, and alcohol. Compared to unadulterated, whole plant food, both drugs of abuse and hyperpalatable foods stimulate unnaturally high levels of reward.[14]

- **Absorption:** Both drugs of abuse and hyperpalatable foods are processed in such a way as to concentrate the potency of the substance of interest, and cause rapid absorption into the bloodstream, increasing their addictive potential.[15] Think of cocaine versus coca leaves or high-fructose corn syrup versus corn.

- **Tolerance and triggers:** Both drugs of abuse and hyperpalatable foods trigger various addictive responses, such as the body becoming biologically ready to deal with the impending substance when particular environmental cues are encountered. For instance, the pancreas might secrete insulin when you see food you want to eat, so your body prepares for the impending overconsumption of sugar and the subsequent need for insulin. This can increase your craving or ability to eat more even without needing it. All of these dynamics play a role in wanting food—the motivation to seek the food in question, without a commensurate increase in the satisfaction derived from actually consuming it. This is how tolerance develops.[16]

When our mechanisms for pleasure developed, our ancestors lived in an environment in which eating as much as possible whenever possible benefited them.[17] The food environment required a lot more work for a lot less payoff, and no one needed to stop themselves from eating too much. On the contrary, the more you could eat, the better. Period. We've evolved to seek the most calories possible with the least amount of effort, yet now that our food environment is completely unnatural, we're starting to self-destruct. We have an excess of artificial, calorically dense options (the processed food we discussed) and an artificially increased frequency of the naturally calorically dense options (meat and cheese). It's like handing over the keys of a racecar with unlimited acceleration to a speed addict and making him navigate an impossibly difficult race course with large rocks strewn all over the track. What else can he do but speed ahead? It's only a matter of time before he crashes.

> Curious about the dark side of food processing? Read *The End of Overeating* by David Kessler, physician and former commissioner of the Food and Drug Administration. He takes a hard look at the struggles with overeating caused by the precise and powerful manufacturing decisions made by food industry scientists and executives to concoct the perfect combinations of fat, sugar, and salt that will uncontrollably hook consumers and keep them coming back for more, even when they want to stop. It's a page-turner of a book.

The struggle caused by hyperpalatable food is intense. An acquaintance of mine recounted her horror at discovering a bag of Cheetos her teenage son's friend had left in the kitchen and facing the possibility that she might actually eat them if she didn't take immediate action. With the Cheetos menacing her through the bag, her solution was to shake them out into the trash and cover them in detergent. Personally, I admire her singularity of purpose. Not everyone would go so far, and there's no question the detergent chaperoned her irreversibly past the threshold where she might break down and eat the snack. But who wants to have to navigate food choices by taking such extreme measures? Fortunately, when you eat a whole food, plant-based diet, instead of simply eating less of the hyperpalatable foods, your taste preferences do change and eventually you no longer want a lot of the things you previously had to resist. This happens across the spec-

81

trum. Even vegans who are ready to let go of oils have to go through the same adjustment. It takes a bit of time.

Once you've become habituated to hyperpalatable foods, healthy foods seem bland and tasteless, so you crave those salty, rich, sweet flavors in order to feel satisfied. What you perceive to be your preferences are really just learned responses. Your experience eating is most determined by what you've been used to eating recently—yesterday, last week, and last month. And, fortunately, multiple intervention trials have demonstrated that tastes can change in as little as a few weeks or months with the introduction of lower-fat foods.[18] At the same time, your own expectations about what you like also shape your expectations and experience of liking something again.[19] The very good news is that you can train your palate and your brain to prefer something different!

READING LABELS TO AVOID ADDED FAT, SUGAR, AND SALT

Training your palate to enjoy healthier tastes can be a lot of fun as you eat your way through the change, but of course you have to be eating the right foods for this taste preference transition to work. The tried and true method for eating truly healthy meals, as we discussed in Step Two, is preparing them yourself with ingredients you purchased. When you do purchase prepared foods, a key change is to read the labels. Be prepared for grocery shopping to initially take a little longer as you start scrutinizing what is actually contained in the foods you're used to eating. You might also want to budget some time in the store for a moment of shock after reading these labels.

As far as shopping goes, most of the ingredients you'll really need to create delicious, homemade, meat- and dairy-free foods are listed in "Foods to Include," in Table 2 on pages 43–44. However, if you're like most people, you'll experiment with and search for packaged foods of various kinds. Healthy packaged and prepared foods are one element that makes the diet sustainable and doable for many people, so don't feel that you have to give them up entirely. You do have to read labels carefully, though. Certain packaged products you'll probably want to continue using at least some of the time, including flour and corn tortillas, pasta, crackers, cans of beans or tomatoes, hummus or bean dip, plant milk, and dried fruit. Healthier versions of all of these may not be sold in a typical supermarket, so it's worth searching out new stores for grocery shopping—online options, food co-ops, larger stores with "natural food" sections, or stores like Whole Foods or Trader Joe's. Use the following tips to recognize added fat, sugar, and excess salt on food labels and choose differently, but also take time to do some quick Google searches for all the names for fat and sugar that you may not recognize.

Added Fat

Oils and fats come in many varieties. Some of the most common are canola, safflower, sunflower, olive, vegetable, and grapeseed—and of course, butter, margarine, and lard. If your only choices for prepared foods all contain added oil or fat, chose one with a lower percentage of fat calories out of total calories, preferably 15 percent or less. Multiply the grams of fat by nine to calculate the fat calories, and then divide that number by the total calories. For instance, if the total calories in a serving is 300, and there are 15 grams of fat, multiply 15×9 to get 135, and divide by 300. That's about 45 percent fat—not something you want to eat if at all possible. Watch the label for added sugar on products labeled "low-fat" or "lower-fat", though—many food products can appear to be low-fat because they've added so much extra sugar—and as you know, any sugar you don't burn gets stored as fat.

The percentage of fat in most foods on the store shelves is much higher than 15 percent, and you will have to say no to many products to find something that satisfies the guideline. And remember, fat also creeps into products you wouldn't necessarily anticipate, including dried fruit, plant milk, and bread.

Added Sugar

Besides well-known characters like cane sugar, turbinado sugar, honey, and other syrups, many highly refined foods contain more esoteric varieties of sugar you may not be familiar with. Avoiding anything with ingredients you can't pronounce is a good rule of thumb, but any time you see something that ends in -ose, it's likely a sugar. Based on their biochemical structures, simple sugars (or *monosaccharides*) are carbon-containing rings, and every carbohydrate ring can be classified as either an *aldose* or a *ketose*. Glucose, fructose, and galactose are some of the more common ones, and sucrose (table sugar) is made of two single rings of glucose and fructose joined together. Ingredients are listed in order of descending volume, which means that if you see sugar as one of the first few ingredients, a significant portion of the product is sugar. Quite a few manufacturers get around this by using several kinds of sugar, which allows them to be listed separately.

Intuitively, you wouldn't expect savory food to need substantial sweetening, but the addition of sugar to almost everything has become commonplace, at least in the United States (Europeans often comment on how sweet American food is). Double-check salad dressings, hummus and dips, pasta sauce, and soup, as well as the more obvious items like bread and crackers.

Added Salt

Currently, the Dietary Guidelines for Americans state that most people should consume no more than 2,300 milligrams of sodium per day, and people who have high blood pressure or who are at higher risk for high blood pressure (African Americans and those over age 40) should consume no more than 1,500 milligrams.[20] You don't really need more than 1,500 milligrams—this is considered the "Adequate Intake" for the general population.[21] However, most of us get about 1,000 milligrams more than the 2,300 limit suggested (as much as 3,200+) per day.[22] Jeff Novick, RD, uses a handy trick for screening foods for unreasonable sodium content: Just make sure that the milligrams of sodium per serving is roughly the same as or less than the number of calories in a serving. Since most people eat around 2,000 calories per day, this works out rather perfectly. Unrefined plant foods, like fruits, vegetables, beans, and grains have low sodium content anyway. Except for canned versions, you can trust that these unrefined foods follow this rule without further checking.

You've probably heard that most Americans get the majority of their sodium from restaurant and processed food and not from home cooking or salt added at the table, but you may be surprised to learn just how enormous those quantities of sodium can be.[23] Be sure to check the labels on sauces, pickles, sauerkraut, ketchup, canned soup, cereal, and any snack you can find in a gas station. Don't be surprised to find that the milligrams of sodium are four, five, nine, or more times the calories in a serving, even for some foods you had planned to keep eating. Don't worry—lower sodium versions do exist for most of these. Just be patient and shop carefully until you've nailed down your new brands and remember to check the Recipes section for homemade versions.

Though chips, candy, soda, pastry, and other refined products are the obvious culprits in triggering food addiction, not all processing is a problem. We have evidence that as far back as 30,000 years, humans ground their starch grains,[25] indicating our long history with food processing. As we discussed in Step Two, frozen produce still contains most micronutrients and is often more affordable than fresh. It's our industrial version of processing that substantially changes the nutrient composition of an ingredient that is the issue.

Not only do the modern versions of processed foods with added fat, sugar, and salt grab us, but the naturally calorie-dense animal foods also disrupt our eating mechanisms. The food environment we have to navigate doesn't just present intense combinations of extreme ingredients, it also offers most people the opportunity to consume meat and dairy products far more frequently, and in much greater quantity, than we ever did as hunters and gatherers.[26]

Earlier hominids in the Plio-Pleistocene era, *Ardipethicus* and *Australopithecus*, were most likely generalist eaters, meaning they could eat and process a wide range of possible foods, including animal foods. They had to, as food availability constantly changed. Their choices are best predicted using foraging theory, a method of modeling eating behavior that takes into account the larger environment and the availability of competing foods.[27] The evidence supporting the theory of generalist foraging offers little support for "Man the Hunter," an image initiated by Darwin's famous sketch of human evolution and then expanded upon by Aldous Huxley and a stream of other artists and writers. The diet of the real Paleolithic human ancestors was likely highly varied and flexible, shifting as food sources and availability shifted, and it was largely plant-based. Meat and sweet foods like berries were available in small quantities or infrequently.

We can certainly take a lesson from our ancestors, who made choices that supported their primary goal of survival in the face of an unavoidable challenge—possible starvation. The dietary challenge we face today is similar in that it is unavoidable, but the actual danger is chronic disease due to dietary excess. Most members of developed countries have been relieved of the need to worry about getting enough energy (calories). Instead, we have the opportunity to focus on making choices that will give us the best chance for good health, not simply survival. And as we discussed in Step One, that

85

means avoiding animal foods, whose protein and fat content increases the risk for chronic disease and whose calorie density plays right into our propensity for fat addiction.

The sensations of pleasure you experience when you eat are intensified whenever the food is more calorically dense than usual. Your palate is innately so sensitive that you can tell the difference between a ripe and unripe banana—a difference of only a few calories of additional sugar. (There aren't actually more calories in a ripe banana, but the greater proportion of sugar as opposed to starch is perceived by your palate as sweetness, which is a clue that a food contains energy and is easier to digest. Starch is converted to sugar as fruit ripens.) The more calorie-dense food you eat, the less obvious these more subtle differences become to your palate; if you're used to eating calorie-dense foods like meat or cheese, or food that's had sugar and fat added to it, the calorie density gradations become less noticeable and you experience your food as less satisfying. Table 5 shows the energy content of various foods, as well as their fiber content. Keep in mind that fiber contributes to bulk, which triggers the stretch receptors in your stomach to signal you to stop eating.

Table 5: **THE CALORIC DENSITY OF VARIOUS FOODS**[28]

FOOD	FIBER	CALORIES IN ONE CUP (CHOPPED OR SLICED)	CALORIES IN ONE LITER (ROUGHLY THE VOLUME OF THE STOMACH)
Lettuce	0.3	4	17
Apple	3	65	275
Banana	3.9	134	567
Brown rice	3.5	218	922
Black beans	15	227	960
Mixed nuts, dry roasted	12.3	814	3443
Chicken	0	231	977
Scrambled eggs	0	328	1387
Bacon	0	484	2047
Ground beef	0	530	2242
Cheddar cheese	0	536	2267
Sugar	0	774	3274
Candy bar	8.3	1084	4585
Potato chips	6.6	1236	5228
Vegetable oil	0	1980	8375

As you can see, it's pretty easy to eat a lot of calories without your stomach realizing you've had enough when you make energy-dense choices. In the days of the hunter-gatherers, none of these calorie-dense foods were encountered in great quantity or frequency. That's why we've evolved without brakes to slow our appetite for them.

You may be wondering why we aren't all overweight, if the fault lies in the food that almost all of us are eating. How are some of us able to eat less, when most of the food cleverly tricks our satiety mechanisms? Why are some of us able to eat exactly the same type of diet as others and yet not gain weight? It doesn't seem fair.

Well, you're right, it *is* unfair, colossally unfair. But it's not random. Being able to regulate your calorie intake is a natural, innate ability, but the extent to which that ability remains functional as you continue eating highly processed and calorie-dense food over time varies from person to person, possibly affected by genetics. In studies with siblings raised in the same family environment, the extent to which normal-weight siblings were able to compensate for already being full when presented with food was far greater than the ability of their overweight siblings.[29] However, this doesn't necessarily mean your genes determine whether or not you'll be overweight. On the contrary, remember that the majority of adults in the United States *are* overweight, regardless of whatever personal genetic advantage they started off with.

Our bodies are incredible regulators of energy intake, but when we pound them with meat, cheese, and processed snacks, they slowly lose their ability to send our brains a signal of "Enough! I'm full." Children do have more success when they are young in regulating their intake based on caloric density, but the ability is lost over time as they grow accustomed to the high-fat, high-sugar diets of artificially and naturally energy-dense foods. By the time they reach adulthood, most of us are prone to eating just a little bit too much. The large portions and often enormous plates, the stimulating advertising and packaging, and the ubitquitousness of eating opportunities doesn't help either—it all contributes to what Cornell researcher Brian Wansink called "mindless overeating."[30]

When you eat nutrient-dense but less calorie-dense foods, it becomes physically impossible to overeat because your stomach is so filled with fiber that your stretch receptors send loud and clear signals to your brain to stop eating. In this way, even those of us with "mischievous genes," as Dr. T. Colin Campbell likes to call them, can maintain a healthy weight.

Thus, eating naturally means an overall eating pattern that will not overwhelm the system—your body—and that facilitates appropriate signaling for satiety. This means eating whole food, reducing or better yet eliminating animal food, and including calorie-dense food sparingly.

FOODS TO INCLUDE, AVOID, OR ELIMINATE IN YOUR DIET

With all the pitfalls of processed and naturally calorie-dense food, it's a big improvement to shift the majority of what you eat. However, even if you are eating a mostly whole food, plant-based diet, a dedicated period of abstinence from all processed and animal-based foods is what will most effectively allow you to withdraw from food addictions, so that you can trust the messages you get from your body. This is where the *commitment* component of the conceptual model for what it takes to change your diet comes into play (see Figure 1 on page 7). Physical withdrawal from any addiction is an uncomfortable process, but it eventually passes. Along the way, you may face craving, longing, and distraction. Although it can be tough while it lasts, the good thing is that the health benefits you receive far surpass any initial discomfort you might feel!

As we discussed in Step Two, the variety in eating plant-based can be surprising. Many people find that they eat more varied foods than ever before. And this continues even as you eliminate animal and processed foods. What does eating a totally whole food, plant-based diet look like? Table 6 expands on what can be included in your diet from Step Two, with the remaining guidelines on what you should avoid or eliminate.

In place of all of the items listed in "Foods to Avoid" and "Foods to Eliminate," choose more of what is listed in the following sections as general guidelines to make replacements:

■ **Instead of processed and prepared foods:** Some minimally processed foods are okay, such as what is mentioned in the "Lightly Processed" section of "Foods to Include" in Table 6. These products may even be essential in helping you stick with the diet in a comfortable way. Become a label reader and shop carefully for brands that are whole grain, have minimal added sugar, have reasonable amounts of salt, and do not have added oil (or very little). Many people do go for faux meats and cheeses when they initially transition. If these foods make you feel more confident, they may be worth including initially, but plan to eventually let go of them as well.

88

TABLE 6: PLANT-BASED EATING:
FOODS TO INCLUDE, AVOID, AND ELIMINATE

FOODS TO INCLUDE	
Whole Plant Foods *Include unlimited amounts of a variety of these foods on a daily basis*	**WHOLE GRAINS:** rolled and Irish oats, brown rice, wild rice, quinoa, barley, teff, millet, wheat or spelt berries, buckwheat groats, and amaranth
	LEGUMES (*dried or canned with minimal salt*): lentils, black beans, navy beans, black-eyed peas, chickpeas, kidney beans, soybeans, tempeh, green beans, peas, mung beans, fava beans, lima beans, adzuki beans, homemade veggie burgers, and more
	GREENS (*fresh or frozen*): kale, collards, spinach, chard, bok choy, lettuce, arugula, beet greens, dandelion greens, purslane, parsley, cilantro, and sprouts
	ROOTS: potatoes, onions, sweet potatoes, leeks, carrots, daikon, burdock, radishes, turnips, beets, parsnips, garlic, and ginger
	OTHER VEGETABLES: summer and winter squash, celery, cabbage, brussels sprouts, broccoli, cauliflower, mushrooms, corn, asparagus, scallions, peppers, and tomatoes
	FRUIT (*fresh or frozen*): apples, pears, peaches, nectarines, apricots, cherries, kiwis, grapes, plums, bananas, papayas, pineapple, mangoes, berries, and melons
Lightly Processed *Okay to include, but use less frequently*	**PLANT MILKS** (*unsweetened*): oat milk, almond milk, hazelnut milk, soy milk, and rice milk
	WHOLE-GRAIN: pasta, crackers, and unsweetened breakfast cereals
	WHOLE-GRAIN FLOUR: whole wheat, spelt, oat, buckwheat, or gluten-free mixes, or legume flours like chickpea and fava bean
	STORE BOUGHT (*read labels and try to minimize the added salt, sugar, and oil*): tomato sauces, hummus, salsa, guacamole, and other dressings
	Tofu
Richer Whole Plant Foods *Use as condiments or ingredients only and, for most, not necessarily every day, because of the high fat content*	**AVOCADO:** straight avocado and guacamole
	NUTS, SEEDS, AND SPREADS/BUTTERS: peanuts, almonds, cashews, pine nuts, Brazil nuts, pecans, walnuts, macadamia nuts, flaxseed, chia seed, sesame seeds/tahini, and sunflower seeds
	COCONUT: fresh coconut flesh, canned coconut milk, and coconut cream
Use in Cooking *These make food flavorful but still healthy*	**ADDITIONS:** Fresh and dried herbs; fresh and powdered spices; vinegars; limited amounts of salt and sweeteners such as rice syrup, maple syrup, honey, or dates; limited amounts of miso, tamari/soy sauce, and vegetable bouillon

cont. on next page

FOODS TO INCLUDE (continued)	
Treats for Special Occasions *Remember that "special occasions" happen infrequently*	**DESSERT:** recipes made with lots of nuts, coconut, or added sweeteners
	DRINKING: plant milk by the glass—save the plant milk for use on cereal or in baking; if you are thirsty, just drink water

FOODS TO AVOID	
Processed and prepared foods *Based on refined flour or isolated plant fragments and loaded with added fat, salt, and sugar*	**REFINED CARBOHYDRATES:** anything made with white flour or white rice, including bread, pasta, chips, cookies, candy, pastries, and crackers
	ADDED SUGAR (*sweeteners are extracted and concentrated carbohydrates that add calories but may not make you full***):** white table sugar, brown sugar, fructose, dextrose, syrups, and others
	ADDED FATS AND OILS (*concentrated fat is a processed food just like sugar***):** Butter, lard, shortening, and olive, canola, safflower, sunflower, and grapeseed oils
	FAUX MEATS, CHEESES, AND ICE CREAM: *(fake animal foods are packed with fat and salt, and often contain isolated proteins that are not a whole food)*: vegan lunchmeat, veggie burgers and veggie dogs that contain protein isolates, vegan cheese or cream cheese, and vegan ice cream

FOODS TO ELIMINATE	
Red and processed meat, poultry, and fish *Any animal flesh contains more protein than we need and often a lot of fat and saturated fat*	Steak, hamburger, ground beef, pork, bacon, chicken, turkey, hot dogs, lunchmeat, and fish
Eggs and dairy products *These have a similar nutrient composition to meat*	Eggs any style, hard and soft cheese, yogurt, butter, ice cream, and milk
Liquid calories *Get most of your calories by eating solid food*	Soda, fruit punch, fruit juice, energy drinks, and milk

Meals can be any combination of whole grains, legumes, fruits, and vegetables, as long as you eat sufficient calories. To be filling, as we've discussed, your meal may need to be bigger than you're used to! And if you can't eat a large meal all at once, you may need to eat more often to keep yourself fueled. A meal doesn't need to center on meat or faux meat—and if you are a vegetarian or vegan making your move to a totally plant-based pattern, this may be where your nutritional edge lies.

- **Instead of meat:** Again, remember that a meal can be any combination of whole plant foods as long as you consume enough quantity to be satisfied. Many people are accustomed to meat being the main focus of a dish, but if you want to choose a filling substitute to build the plate around, try beans for ground meat and/or the meat in soups and salads and try tempeh or tofu for a more traditional presentation.

- **Instead of eggs:** Eggs are actually not necessary in baking. When they are used, they serve the functions of binding and leavening, but these functions are easily performed by a variety of plant-based substitutes, which you can find with a quick Google search. Chickpeas make an excellent substitute in salads, wraps, and sauces where you're looking for a little bit of that eggy-flavor (this is because of the sulfur content of chickpeas), and chickpea flour can make a great omelet batter. When I first stopped eating eggs, I did miss them scrambled and deviled for a few years, but after so many years of not eating them, I no longer miss them, and the smell of cooking eggs is a bit off-putting to me. I do enjoy a delicious tofu scramble and mock-deviled creations using potato skins and chickpea dip. So investigate the alternatives. There's a lot to choose from!

- **Instead of milk and yogurt:** There are a wide variety of plant-based milks on the market, as listed in Table 6, but if you are in the habit of drinking glasses of milk with meals or as a snack, try to replace that choice with fruit, crackers and hummus, or other solid food. Otherwise, plant-based milks work well in baking and batters—soy milk works best because it has higher protein content, and oat milk would work second best for this same reason—and almond and hazelnut are just fine for most purposes. I do put oat milk in my bowl when I eat raw oats and fruit, but that's probably the only time I use plant milk to eat. If you are a yogurt fan, there are certainly some choices in the supermarket made with plant food bases (make sure you choose unsweetened), but it's also not too hard and much less expensive to make your own.

- **Instead of cheese:** A lot of what people love about cheese is the high fat content. As you get used to an overall lower-fat diet, it will become easier to forget about cheese. However, the savory, sometimes pungent flavor is something you can replace with nutritional yeast used in a variety of ways: dried flakes as a topping, ground with walnuts for a parmesan condiment, mixed as a sauce for a melted cheese effect, and more. There are now a number of producers of actual cultured plant-based cheeses that use nut pâtés as the base and are successful in developing complex, pungent flavors, so for those occasional treats and wine and cheese parties, it may be worth placing an order online.

- **Instead of soda or other liquid calories:** You may have noticed that humans are the only animal who gets calories from liquid (except, or course, for the young of mammals, who nurse from their mothers). Liquid calories do not stimulate satiety (feeling full) the same way solid food does, which can lead you to eat more than you need.[31] You can include smoothies in an overall healthy diet, but some people who are trying to lose weight find that a breakfast salad keeps them feeling full longer. Many scientists now regard fruit juice as more similar to soda than fruit. The next time you are hungry, eat solid food, and the next time you are thirsty, drink water.

UN-TRAINING YOUR PALATE

Though babies naturally prefer sweet foods and avoid bitter tastes (an adaptive mechanism to help them get enough energy to fuel growth and to avoid being poisoned), their acceptance of the salty taste is learned.[32] You may have certain predispositions toward flavor, influenced by what your parents fed you when you were very young, as foods consumed in the early years of life do have some influence over our lifetime taste preferences.[33] However, this is only one element in a variety of influences leading you to your current taste preferences. Even as adults, our tastes are learned behaviors, and that means we can train ourselves to genuinely enjoy healthy food, even after we've developed a liking for burgers and fries.

This learned preference has also been measured in a research context, using a low-salt versus high-salt soup. How much people liked the soup they ate was influenced by the salt content of the soup they had eaten previously![34] In fact, as most people switch away from a high-fat, high-sugar, high-salt diet, they find a similar change happens for the richness and sweetness of food as well as the salt. This is a critical point to get across—it's more

92

your mental attachment to the idea of eating certain things that is blocking you from actually changing your palate than it is the actual taste of the food. Once you're used to not eating certain things for a long enough time, you don't actually miss them. Facing the possibility of no longer missing a food you love now can even trigger a little bit of grief; you begin to mourn the future loss. That's why it's good to take it one day at a time, and commit to just a few weeks of avoiding the food, rather than thinking about eliminating it from your diet for the rest of your life. Remember to revisit the suggestions for dealing with cravings on page 77, for when they come up.

Plant-based diets are effective in helping you break out of the pull of addictive food because, when you eat a plant-based diet, you're already avoiding the things that therapists who treat clinical food addiction have been telling people to avoid for years—fat, sugar, and salt. Though most people aren't at the point of needing to check into a residential facility for treatment, we can all stand to take a lesson from the methods considered most effective in clinical contexts. These are:[35]

1. **Use principles of clinical food addiction treatment:**
   - Eliminate the "offending" food to eradicate the physical addiction (a totally whole food, plant-based diet makes this really easy). Be prepared to wait out the withdrawal period—initially you may find yourself craving the "forbidden" foods more intensely.
   - Ask for help and be honest about how much control you currently have over what you choose to eat. Are you still eating little bits of oil or sugar on a daily basis even though you've been trying to cut back? Keeping a food diary is an objective way to evaluate what you are actually consuming on a weekly basis.
   - Get the right amount of support to help you stick with your goals. If talking to your support buddy once a week was enough to add more plant-based foods in, you might need to talk to her or text her once per day while you're cutting out the cheese or the oil.

2. **Try behavioral therapy:** Use a cognitive behavioral approach to analyze the cues that lead up to the behavior you are trying to change, continually revisit your goals, and figure out how you can interrupt that cycle of decisions so you choose a different behavior

93

in the end. You can do this yourself, or seek out a therapist. For example, if you know that your most vulnerable time occurs mid-afternoon and you're likely to grab a slice of pizza from the cafeteria, make sure you bring a second lunch to work. Thirty minutes before you typically get hungry for pizza, eat your second lunch, and then schedule a meeting for your typical pizza time so you're busy. Figure out how you can interrupt your routines to steer yourself into making different choices. If you can maintain this for a few weeks, you'll have gotten over the hump and it will start to feel a lot easier to maintain.

Exiting from these food addictions is a real withdrawal process. This is one of the most important things to acknowledge. While you are still withdrawing from food addictions, you are going to have a much easier time of it if you think of the transition as your hobby for at least a few weeks and keep your life relatively free of additional stress. If you are a tax accountant who loves steak and French fries, don't pick March and the first half of April to substantially change your diet. You get the idea.

CREATING HABITS OF HEALTH

Not only do you want to interrupt your patterns to break free of food addictions, you also want to develop lasting new habits that will support you permanently. Habits are strengthened just through repetition, so the more you can do to help yourself repeat your new behaviors, the more likely you are to continue. While this doesn't always serve us, you can turn it to your advantage the more times you've made a healthy choice.

- **Change the environment that triggers the behavior:** Environmental cues can trigger certain behavior as well as hinder you from making the choices you want. We'll discuss this more in Step Four, but in addition to getting rid of the food in your kitchen that you no longer want to eat, making changes to your environment that are seemingly not related to food can support you in interrupting the patterns you typically follow.[36] Shop in a new grocery store? Rearrange the furniture in your house? Take a different route to work? If you are orchestrating a change for the whole family, maybe a family vacation is the perfect opportunity to start serving

94

fruit instead of chips as the go-to snack? You want to mentally shift your feeling about what is normal, and changing your normal environment can help make other changes seem normal too.

■ **Plan yourself out of your habitual response:** The dilemma you face is that addictive foods are reinforcing in the immediate moment. However, people who create *implementation intentions* tend to be more successful at creating new habits than those who don't.[37] This means making a plan with yourself before you get to the decision-making point. Going out to eat with friends on Friday? Look at the restaurant's menu online and figure out what you're going to order in advance. When you get there, enjoy the company and don't spend your energy debating how to navigate the menu. Just carry out your plan without thinking about it further.

■ **Create new reinforcements for your behavior:** What can you do to reward yourself for your new choices? Subtle reinforcements (complimenting your children on their willingness to try a bite of broccoli instead of paying them to eat vegetables) can play an important role in creating new habits. For yourself, the more you can appreciate and savor the taste of healthy food, touch base with your motivation for making a change, and appreciate the benefits you know you will receive (feeling great), the more your new way of eating will be self-reinforcing. We'll discuss this more in Step Five, but you want to try to elicit positive responses from other people about the food you're eating or preparing as much as you can, too—it's community that turns our individual habits into a shared culture. This is where posting pictures of your food on social media can save the day. All those comments like "Wow, I'm hungry!" and "Hey, want to be my personal chef?" are very encouraging.

Adopting Comfort Rituals Without Food

Another aspect of developing new habits is to change your lifestyle in the way that you make use of food. Many of us come from households where sugary or fatty foods were used as comfort or reassurance. Part of interrupting that cycle and changing your environment is to change the behaviors you engage in at that time of day. Consider any of the following food-free options:

95

- **Making tea:** Many cultures throughout the world practice a tea ritual. It can be a way of calming your system, slowing down, and nurturing yourself. Perhaps you could make a cup of herbal tea before going to bed or brew a pot of tea with loose leaves in the midafternoon. With all the herbal varieties of tea available, there's no need to use caffeine if you don't want to.
- **Implementing relaxing routines to replace late-night snacking:** Many people are stuck in the rut of late-night snacking, and it can easily derail you from healthy eating habits. It's best not to eat for a couple of hours before going to sleep to give your body the chance to digest the food (surprisingly, digestion itself uses a fair amount of energy). One thing to try is going to bed earlier. You don't need to fall asleep right away, but getting into your bed can provide a transition and keep you away from your old habits. You can read in bed before nodding off. Evening showers or baths are another comfort ritual that many people find very satisfying. Taking a shower right before you go to bed is relaxing and an activity you can look forward to. I love evening showers to relieve muscle tension, mentally wash off the day, and take a bit of personal transition time between being active and resting.
- **Taking afternoon walks instead of having afternoon snacks:** When the urge for a brownie hits in the midafternoon, try moving around first and see if you still feel sluggish. If you're experiencing true hunger, bring some fruit and water on your walk with you; by the time you get back you probably won't want that brownie anymore. If you can't leave the office, try at least carving out a stretch break in front of the computer.

Leading a Balanced Life

While changing your physical taste preferences is primarily a biological transformation, it can be helpful to think about shifting your mental attachments and patterns.

- Where is the sweetness in your life?
- Where is the salt in your life?
- Where is the richness in your life?

Being able to easily point to parts of your life and identify where you get these elements is a sign that they are in balance. If you can't really think of anything, it might be time to seriously consider how you *are* satisfying those desires. This may not be necessary for you at all. Your transition may just revolve around food, but if you feel like these questions could help you, they are here for you to use. Consider the following suggestions:

- Sweetness can be play, lightheartedness, laughter, joy, or delight. It can mean seeing a friend, giving yourself the time to enjoy a hobby, making time to have fun, or feeling appreciation and gratitude for what you have.
- The salt of your life can be the savory stimulation—perhaps intellectual or business stimulation. Excitement, interest, or discovery. It could mean taking on the challenge of putting on an event, navigating a difficult conversation with your child, or training for a race. It could mean the books or articles you are reading, academic dialogue, business planning, your learning, or your own curiosity.
- The richness you can consider your abundance, your access to plenty, your more-than-enoughness. It could mean feeling loved and connected to friends and family or keeping a wide variety of groceries in the house (recommended anyway) so you always have a choice about what to eat. It could mean managing your money well so you can take care of your needs and goals without feeling pinched.

Whatever your particular mix of sweetness, savoriness, and abundance, the more replete your life feels, the less you'll feel the need to "treat" yourself with food, and you can let food stay in its proper place—as energy to help you express yourself in the world.

DECIDING WHAT TO DO WITH THE FOOD YOU NO LONGER WANT TO EAT

So you've decided to make some changes. You're ready to let go of the foods currently in your home that are standing in the way of you changing your diet. If you are the sole eater of these foods, your job is easy. You can:

- Compost them (if they compost).
- Throw them out.
- Give them to friends.
- Donate them to a food pantry or food drive.
- Feed them to a pet.

If not all the food is yours: First, speak with the people who brought this food into the house. Be honest and vulnerable. You started this conversation in Step Two when you started adding in healthy food, and you may have begun some new house rules for your kids. Now is the time to go more deeply into the conversation and share how much you need the support and help from your loved ones. Explain you are really trying to do what is best for your body, but remind them you are not trying to control their choices. You can say that to be successful, it's important that you eat a specific diet, and it's extremely challenging for you to have other food in the house. These can be sensitive conversations to engage in, so much so that often some of us don't even know how to approach the topic. It can also be tricky when some of the food you want to let go is food that you've been sharing with a partner or a spouse. If you're feeling particularly challenged by how to discuss your new diet with immediate family members and close friends, Step Five contains a variety of suggested scripts for dialoging with them, as well as for less personal situations.

If you're not the type of person who wants to throw everything out all at once, you can take it slow. But continue to analyze the effect this is having on you. We'll discuss the importance of this more in Step Four, but the longer the food remains in your house, the harder it will be to stay away from it in all situations, including outside of your house.

THE BOTTOM LINE

Today, Samantha is successfully eating a totally plant-based diet and feeling great. She eats when she's hungry and stops when she's full. She maintains a healthy weight, her energy is up, her skin is clear. She's happily married and she can stick to her diet even though her husband eats meat. She sticks with her plan even though her work requires regular lunches and dinners out with clients. The guilt, tension, and sluggishness generated by her old eating habits are gone.

Samantha achieved this only by cutting out the foods she used to try to "eat moderately." With her childhood training in tow, there wasn't any other way for her to stick with a healthy diet without feeling challenged and continually slipping. Samantha ate her way through a childhood generously padded with every kind of sugary drink and processed treat. For parents not much inclined toward cooking, fast food was convenient and affordable. Dinner for their busy family with three kids was graciously provided by Carl's Jr. Father-daughter bonding developed over Krispy Kreme donuts and Tommy Burgers. Snacks were potato chips, cookies, and even unbaked cake batter. Drinks were soda. By the time she became an adult, she struggled with food and literally couldn't resist when a craving hit. At last, by letting go of all the foods that stimulated the addictive reactions, she was able to break free and get on with her life. She never thought it was possible, but going totally plant-based turned out to be better than anything she had tried.

YOUR PATH GOING FORWARD

Step Three has taken you on a grand tour of the research and implementation around food addiction, what it looks like, how to break the cycle, and how to use that information to support yourself in making healthy choices and replacing your habits of convenience with habits of health. While Step Two got you started adding healthy food into your diet, at this point you're armed with the knowledge of what calorie-dense and processed food is doing to you and why your health is best served by taking these foods out. This is the point at which you start, at your own pace, to remove the meat, dairy, and processed snack foods from your diet and replace them with healthier choices. As you consider where to begin, think of the foods to reduce, avoid, or eliminate as belonging to one of three major categories— meat, dairy and eggs, and processed food. Depending on what will be most effective in your lifestyle, you may be ready to focus on one in particular— or you may already have given up two of them.

With the three paths below, set SMART goals for your next steps and make sure to share your goals with your support buddy. As we discussed in *How to Use This Book*, the path you take and the goals you set for yourself are your choice, and they will be most effective if they challenge you but do not overwhelm you. At this point, you've gone through Steps One and Two, and you might be feeling a need to slow down, or you might be ready to turn it up a notch! Now is the perfect time to fine-tune your pace.

Remember to tell your support buddy your plan and ask for his or her assistance with holding you accountable.

1. **Easing In:** Looking at the goals you set for crowding out in Step Two, consider where you can go next. If you are ready for a more gentle transition, consider the three big categories of food to replace and try starting with just one: meat / fish, dairy / eggs, and processed food / snacks. Which one feels like the right place to begin? If you generally feel tired or tend to have allergies and/or respiratory problems, you may want to consider starting with dairy or processed food rather than meat. Choosing a category of food to eliminate, rather than preparing whole food, plant-based breakfasts, say, or dinners, is a more straightforward way to begin and will probably be easier because there is less room to make decisions on a meal-by-meal basis. Sketch out the next few weeks and post your goals in a visible place. What are your most common instances of eating your chosen candidate for elimination? What kinds of dishes do you cook that use that ingredient? Make sure to plan some replacements for your meals and adjust your shopping lists accordingly. Consider whether you need to discuss this with any friends or family, or if it's better to say nothing and simply adjust your cooking without mentioning it. Remember to be kind to yourself. If you backtrack and eat something you were planning to give up, just start over and let go of the judgment. Practice makes better. ▶*Suggested time frame: three weeks.*

2. **Rev It Up:** Ready for the next level? This choice is well suited for someone who's ready for a substantial change, or for vegetarians who are ready to cut out either the dairy products or the processed food. Take stock of what you used to eat and make a plan for replacing what you've decided to let go of. That means planning meals, snacks, grocery shopping, and your routines. Do you want to make any environmental changes to shake things up mentally? Choosing a new grocery store is a great option here. Aside from the fact that you might have to anyway, telling yourself "I don't buy X, Y, and Z in this store" is a great use of implementation intentions. Think about whether you need to have any additional conversations with friends and family, revisit any new boundaries for

household food with your family, or clear out other aspects of your life to eliminate stress and distraction. Remember, it's best if you can temporarily think about changing your diet as a significant hobby or a new part-time job. ▶*Suggested time frame: two weeks.*

3. **Total Transformation:** Great decision! You're headed for a massive overhaul of your diet. This is the big moment, as Steps Four and Five are geared toward helping you sustain this change. If you are feeling up for a radical shift in your energy, your habits, and cooking, this is for you! A total transformation for Step Three is also well-suited to someone who eats a vegan diet already but is ready to make that final shift to totally whole food, plant-based and cut out the oil and sugar. Because there's a lot of animal-free processed food on the market now, this change will require additional commitment to cooking at home, bringing food with you, and planning your grocery shopping to support a completely whole foods path. This total transformation may require deeper conversations with the people you are closest to, but reminding them that you are embarking on this change for yourself without trying to control them can alleviate a lot of their discomfort. Take advantage of the three-week meal plans in the Resources section and make sure to clear stress, extra activities, and distractions away from the very important work of changing your diet. For at least three weeks, try to not plan other significant trips or extra work. Just consider your diet and yourself to be your only priority besides the necessities. You are doing awesome. Truly. ▶*Suggested time,frame: one week to ramp up, and then continue.*

101

MAKE YOUR FOOD ENVIRONMENT MATCH YOUR BIOLOGY:
creating the context that guarantees success

Y OU'VE DONE GREAT WORK so far. Finding your motivating force, adding in plant-based foods, and letting go of the rest are huge steps in cultivating a healthy eating habit. You're now ready to take the next step, which happens to be one of the most fun parts of this process because it lays the foundation for a life of dietary ease. Personal choice can go only so far. Your most effective strategy for easy and permanent success is to reshape your environment so that it is rarely necessary for you to rely on willpower. When the easiest, most obvious choice is the healthiest one, you are set.

In Step Four, we'll explore more deeply the challenges to eating a healthy diet in the modern world, identify the context of your eating decisions, and reshape your food environment to make healthy eating a no-brainer.

MORE CHALLENGES TO EATING A HEALTHY DIET

Not only do the physically addictive properties of food take their toll on many people's success in maintaining a healthy diet, but the food environment itself makes it difficult, and this can cause people to internalize a negative view of their own ability to eat well. You may be one of the many people who feel resignation and sadness around their eating habits. No matter how strong your intentions, and how clear your vision for the kind of diet you *want* to be eating, you just can't maintain the discipline to stick with it in the long term. "If only I had the willpower," you might think, with a litany of failures readily parading through your mind. When it comes to eating, willpower is tested at every turn—relentlessly.

Roy F. Baumeister, a social psychologist whose research has popularized the concept of willpower, has done extensive work tracking the challenges to it that come up in the course of everyday life as well as how people respond to them. In one of his studies, his team tracked 200 adults' desires for a week by asking at randomly selected moments and intervals whether or not they were experiencing a desire. The participants, notified via beepers they had agreed to wear, shared whatever desires they were feeling, if any. The researchers also asked the participants if they gave in to their desires. As it turns out, people have a lot of desires. And what was the most frequently resisted desire? The urge to eat.[1]

Willpower

Now, this may come as no surprise to anyone with even a mild orientation toward nutrition. In Western cultures particularly, it's no secret that we constantly fight pressure from advertising, the aroma of donuts wafting through the office, the late-night snack for those late-night owls, or the golden arches calling our name, catching us in moments of transit—hungry (or bored, or stressed) and, therefore, vulnerable. This is "common sense," you may think, and as we've discussed in Step Three, the physical addictive quality of calorie-dense food is powerful. Resisting the urge to eat is a battle for almost all of us, and it's fought on an almost continual basis.

What is significant about Dr. Baumeister's research is that he has found extensive evidence that people's willpower and decision-making ability is a finite resource that can be depleted through physical or mental fatigue. What does that mean? The more times you say no, the more times you have to think through a variety of choices and make a decision, the more tired you become, and the more likely you are to go with the default, or give in to temptation.

104

With eating, we commonly talk about willpower, but when you consider the challenges most people face, what they're really exercising is "won't power" in order to stick with their intentions. Willpower, or self-control, is essentially the ability to resist immediate temptation in favor of longer-term goals, to choose behavior without being buffeted off-course by external influences. And what most people don't stop to consider is that won't power, or willpower in the form of restraint around food, is 100 percent unnatural. Self-control most likely evolved to protect social order. How else are we able to get through the day without reacting to the typical rudeness, annoying habits, or stupidity we may encounter in our families? In people we work with? In our children? Our bosses? How could we even function without a highly developed ability to let these things roll off our backs? At various points in history, these same people who tried our patience so intensely have also been community members and individuals on whom we depended in a real sense for our survival.

> **Intrigued? Read *Willpower, Rediscovering the Greatest Human Strength* by Roy F. Baumeister and John Tierney. Dr. Baumeister leads readers through the evolution of his lifetime of work to some very surprising conclusions about success and human nature. Any student of the human condition will love this book.**

What were self-control and willpower *not* used for? Stopping ourselves from eating too much. Before we practiced agriculture, such a behavior would be very, very counterproductive. When there was food, it was in our best interest to eat until we were very full, no matter what kind of food was in front of us. The natural availability of edible substances for humans was in balance with our caloric needs, so we never evolved the capacity to regulate our eating to the degree that we now must do.

What else does this mean? It means that almost constantly throughout the day, you are being challenged to engage in a behavior (actively not eating, or refraining from eating more) that runs 100 percent contrary to your biology and therefore might be accumulating a much bigger toll on your willpower than some of the social needs for self-control that you've evolved to be able to handle. As mentioned in Step Three, we've evolved to eat as much as possible, every time food is available. And what happens when you are faced with challenges to your self-control? You get tired. And what is then more likely to happen? Your self-control, willpower, won't power, or whatever you want to call it, will be temporarily diminished. And then you have almost no resources left to deal with temptation, making it much more likely you'll go for the fast food, the pizza, the pastries, or even the vegan cheese instead of a healthier sandwich or salad.

Ego Depletion

Dr. Baumeister, in a nod to Freud, has coined the term *ego depletion* to describe the state you're in when you're fatigued by having exerted yourself to maintain self-control, or after having made many or difficult decisions.

What's interesting is that practicing self-control, and the capacity for it, are both also correlated with stored glucose levels in the brain.[2] So not only are you getting tired facing temptation after temptation, you're also getting hungrier.[3] Can you see where this is going?

As if all that weren't enough, being in a state of ego depletion removes some of the boundaries that keep your feelings in check. If you already feel fatigued from practicing self-control, you might feel more irritable than normal after an annoying encounter, more sad than normal after seeing a movie about animals being hurt, and more euphoric than normal after receiving good news. Even cravings can be intensified, as researchers have long noted in the context of studying withdrawal.[4] Someone exerting self-control during the withdrawal phase will actually experience intensified cravings because of being in a state of ego depletion . . . just when their willpower is compromised. And, as Drs. Doug Lisle and Alan Goldhamer, as well as others, point out, sugary, fatty, salty foods constitute a low-grade food addiction.[5] And, as we learned in Step Three, exiting the addiction to these foods *is* a real withdrawal process; there is no shortcut around that.

The one-two punch of an environment that requires constant saying no combined with the physical addiction of calorie-dense foods like cheese, potato chips, and cake leaves only a very narrow window for success if you're depending on self-control. That type of success is usually only temporary, because it's not sustainable—it means exercising sheer force of your will to surmount biological tendencies in a completely unnatural way, and you can't live like that for the rest of your life. That is why diets don't work.

Consider Lily's history with diet programs. Growing up in North Carolina, she was born into the heart of Southern cooking. Lily reminisced, "Mother used four flavors in her cooking—salt, pepper, sugar, and bacon grease. She fried everything in bacon grease." Waffles with bacon grease, vegetables cooked all day in bacon grease, and homemade biscuits of white flour and Crisco every evening. Chicken, pork barbeque, and slaw with a lot of mayonnaise. Fried squash and onions, and black-eyed peas, all cooked in bacon grease. Dessert was usually the same biscuits, additionally enriched with butter and sweetened with molasses. Bacon and eggs for breakfast every day (that bacon grease had to come from somewhere). Sometimes they also had hush puppies—deep fried dollops of corn batter.

"Thank goodness for not having a lot of money and not eating between meals," she mused, recollecting. All the children in the family participated in sports and walked to school. These were Lily's saving graces until she got a summer job as a college student behind an ice cream counter and spent an entire summer eating ice cream, a summer from which her body never recovered.

So began a yo-yo of diet plans, weight loss, and weight regain. Lily tried Weight Watchers (it worked the first time), protein shakes, and a weigh-in diet center program, and each time she would lose and regain. The weight got worse during each of her pregnancies, and she remains convinced that the pregnancy vitamins she took made her terribly nauseated, a nausea alleviated by vanilla ice cream and roast beef sandwiches slathered with mayo.

With a mentally and physically demanding job, as well as being disinclined toward cooking, she was not the best candidate to be the family chef. However, her husband's cooking skills were limited to making toast, and people have to eat. Even during times of (temporary) success with the different weight-loss programs she kept trying, cooking for the family was the hardest part of her life. Her husband could not eat any fiber because of a colon condition, and both her daughters had singular and unwavering likes and dislikes. Instead of cooking for one family she was running a restaurant for four different diners. Ordering take-out food provided a welcome relief, and they frequently made use of it. Eventually, she would cave and go back to eating the fatty foods that everybody else enjoyed.

Why did she fail? Let's look at her food environment and lifestyle—busy, surrounded with demands, and cooking three meals in her own home that included foods she was trying to not eat herself. She had to exercise self-control all the time, and face temptation almost continually. How often did she have to make a personal decision using willpower or won't power? Virtually every time she ate. This is a pretty common problem for many women who are the primary food preparers in the home, but it doesn't stop there. A lot of men and women have to navigate a minefield of unhealthy choices in the work setting—at the office cafeteria, at business dinners, and even while entertaining. This is in addition to what's going on at home or in social contexts. Let's look into this issue of personal versus impersonal decisions a little more.

107

Personal Versus Impersonal Food Choices

According to researchers Wansink and Sobal, the average person makes more than 200 food decisions daily, most of which the person isn't even aware of.[6] Think about your own decisions. How do you typically make eating decisions in your everyday life? How are these decisions made? I'm explicitly saying "decisions *made*" because there are some decisions that you make, and then there are also some decisions that are made for you.

There is always *personal* choice—your decisions—and at the same time there is *impersonal* choice—the default path organized for you by the environment. Think of all your personal choices and the impersonal (default) choices presented by the environment (see Figure 3). Each decision you make in a day is included in one side of the pie or the other, including when to get up, what to wear, whom to call on the phone, how to best do your job, what to eat for breakfast and lunch, and what to cook for dinner. Your food decisions, like all your decisions, fall in one category or the other. Together, they comprise all the choices that happen in your life—and the ratio between them, especially when it comes to sticking with your intended eating path, is very, very significant.

Personal choice comes about because of an intention and then an action on your part—a desire backed up by your willpower to do something about your desire. This happens in the context of food, but it also happens more broadly in almost every context of your life. For example, you might have always wanted to live in a white house with a red door, and so your first action as a new homeowner is to paint the door of your house red. You might have committed to eating whole-grain instead of white bread, or making quinoa and a vegetable dish for dinner instead of steak, and so you start shopping at a different store to get a whole-grain bread that you like.

Figure 3: **PERSONAL AND IMPERSONAL CHOICES**

■ **Personal Choice, courtesy of your willpower**

■ **Impersonal Choice, courtesy of your environment**

Impersonal choice is what happens automatically, without you thinking about it or making any particular effort. Impersonal choice doesn't deplete your willpower—it's going with the flow, letting the world happen to you, such as living in whatever color house you ended up buying because you don't feel strongly about changing it, or taking either the stairs or the elevator depending on how close they are to the door of a building, or being satisfied with an apple as a snack because it's what your friend hands to you. Impersonal choice isn't necessarily a bad thing. As you have learned, you have room for only so many decisions during a day, and if you exert your personal choice at every step, you might end up exhausted or stymied. Impersonal choice doesn't take any extra energy.

Now, let's consider these two types of choices and the driving forces behind them. Your impersonal choice is steered by your environment—the larger environment. This can include your immediate physical surroundings, social influence from friends and family, marketing messages you absorb, and convenience. The environment guides much of your life—it's what will happen anyway, whether you do anything or not.

To what extent does your food environment support the intention of eating a whole food, plant-based diet and maintaining a healthy weight? Researchers have reviewed a variety of dynamics at play in the modern food environment and identified a group of possible culprits that are associated with the rise in obesity and may be working in concert.[7] The foods that are readily available, like soda, chips, meat, and cheese, are energy-dense, cheap, and often packaged in large portions. Americans eat more frequently, in more settings, and more often away from home. We snack more and we face constant marketing messages from those same food products that are so ubiquitous.[8] The way I visualize these dynamics is something along the lines of Figure 4.

Figure 4: **HOW MUCH HELP DOES TODAY'S FOOD ENVIRONMENT GIVE ME?**

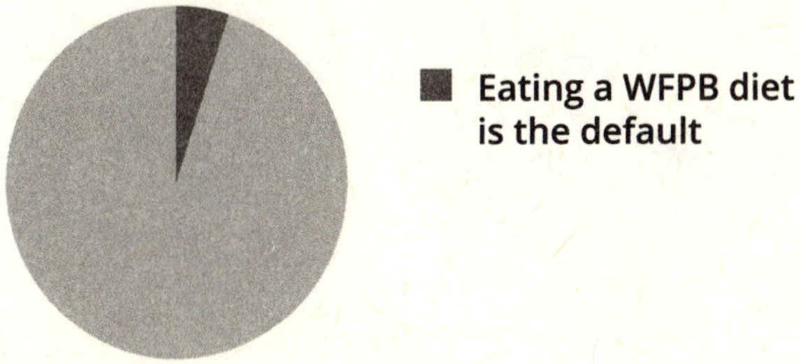

■ **Eating a WFPB diet is the default**

Depending on where you live, this could even be a generous representation. For people who live in areas with very poor access to grocery stores, often described as *food deserts*, it can be difficult to find anything other than what you might find in a gas station or convenience store.[9] This represents an even more extreme problem of social justice that won't be solved until it is addressed by public policy. Right now, if it's financially feasible for people, ordering food over the Internet is one of the only solutions in this situation to get healthier ingredients.

In contrast to the influences from the environment, personal choice is driven by willpower—*your* willpower. As we saw, willpower is something we all need to use when our choices go against the grain, when they come into conflict with what would otherwise be the default, or when we just make a specific decision from an array of choices.

Think of your personal choices as being fueled by a particular source of energy—your willpower, while the impersonal choices are generally facilitated by the circumstances around you—your environment. What happens if most of the decisions you want to be making are not supported by your environment but, by sheer force of will, you are succeeding anyway? What is your decision chart going to look like? Possibly something like Figure 5.

And, what do we know about willpower? Dr. Baumeister and others have shown us that willpower is a finite resource that can get used up. Make a lot of conscious decisions—use your willpower over and over throughout the day—and you're going to be that much more fatigued and likely to go with the default when it comes time to make more decisions—even if they really count and the outcome is important to you.[10] What would a decision chart look like for someone whose environment is supportive of their desire to follow a whole food, plant-based diet, that

Figure 5: **WHAT POWERS MY DECISION MADE IN A NONSUPPORTIVE FOOD ENVIRONMENT?**

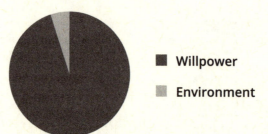

- ■ Willpower
- ■ Environment

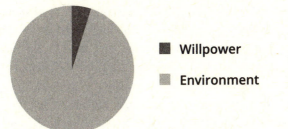

Figure 6: **WHAT POWERS MY DECISION MADE IN A SUPPORTIVE FOOD ENVIRONMENT?**

- **Willpower**
- **Environment**

is, someone who is more likely to succeed at their goals? Something along the lines of Figure 6.

The secret is that the environment is always going to have the advantage; it's always going to be lurking around the corner, ready to tempt you, but also ready to help you if it matches what you want to happen. Until you've kicked your food addictions, and even once you do, relying solely on willpower is like trying to outrun a cheetah on foot. You may have a fighting chance, but more likely you're going to be overpowered in the end. Willpower can take you part of the way, but you're going to be very tired, and then all your progress could get derailed.

Fortunately (and this is certainly not the case with diet programs that include addictive foods in "portion controlled" quantities), the longer you eat a whole food, plant-based diet, the less you need to rely on willpower, because certain foods will no longer call your name. In fact, they may even cease to look like food. And as we discussed in Step Three, the longer you eat a diet that doesn't trigger and support addictions, the more your tastes will change.[11] It will be easier and easier to be confronted by unhealthy food without it taking a toll on your energy or putting you into the state of ego depletion. Especially in the beginning, though, maximizing the support from your environment is crucial.

IDENTIFYING YOUR DIET AND EATING CHOICES

What can you do to take advantage of this information? Your dietary and other decisions are complex events, and shifting the outcome requires a broad-based look at what is happening. Self-awareness is the first step in understanding your decisions in context.

To successfully make personal choices that support your intention to eat a healthful diet and live a healthy life, you need to minimize the use of your willpower *as much as possible*, so that when you need to pull it out, it's there for you. Some of the unhealthy personal choices you make are not truly convenient—but you act out of addiction, and so your addictions can, in some moments, override willpower (for example, going out of your way to procure foods you crave).

If you primarily live and function in an environment that is not supportive of your goals, your willpower will be so worn down, so frequently, that you will have almost no chance in the long term. Since environment heavily shapes most decisions, your best chance for success will come when you can live in an environment where as many as possible of your most convenient choices are healthy.

Then, when you need to make personal choices not supported by the environment, you haven't been compromised to be in a state of ego depletion—you have willpower you can use. In moments of temptation that come to everyone—for instance, driving home from work, you think about driving the long way home to pick up your favorite unhealthy comfort food (pizza, donut, fill in the blank) as you often have in the past—you'll be better able to resist. In that moment, if your willpower is strong enough to keep you to your principles, you'll be able to override that urge.

The best strategy, though, is to focus on not getting to that point in the first place. Those moments will happen to everyone from time to time, but the less frequent they are, the easier it becomes to make your willpower count so you may live the life you truly want.

No matter what your path, taking action here starts with awareness. You may want to get out a journal or paper to write your answers to the questions in the decision awareness exercise presented in the chart that follows. These questions will help you describe your diet and eating choices in context, and allow you to figure out what truly empowers your decisions. Context is key. While you consider these questions, notice that "how much?" or "what quantity?" you eat is not included here. If you are eating the right *types* of foods, the beauty and simplicity of a whole food, plant-based diet is that "how much?" is not a major question you need to worry about.

This is an extremely useful exercise when switching to a whole food, plant-based diet. Think of it as akin to taking an inventory of your finances the first time you meet with a financial planner. Before you can develop a strategy to support your goals, you must identify what, exactly, is going on.

This exercise is also useful if you already eat a somewhat healthy diet but are experiencing leaks in your commitment or have hit a plateau and aren't sure why. Taking the time to identify and describe your "food life" in context helps you get to the bottom of which dynamics are at play and affecting your decisions.

In Chart 1, which you can also download from our website at HabitsofHealth.support, you can connect the answers of each question across the row. This allows you to see the context surrounding each food or type of food you eat.

Chart 1: **IDENTIFYING THE CONTEXT OF YOUR EATING DECISIONS**

FOOD	WHY	HOW	WHEN	WHERE	YOUR BEHAVIOR
					1. Habit 2. Environmental default/easy choice 3. Required willpower 4. Gave in to craving

113

What Foods Are You Typically Eating?

We start with the question of "what." What are the foods I am typically eating? This could include:

- Grains
- Vegetables, including:
  - Green leafy vegetables
  - Root vegetables
  - Fruits considered vegetables (peppers, squash, tomatoes, etc.)
- Fruits
- Beans
- Nuts, seeds, avocado, olives
- Meats
- Dairy—cheese, milk, yogurt
- Eggs
- Processed foods, including:
  - Pastries
  - Chips or salty snacks
  - Candy
  - White bread or white rice
  - Processed meats with added salt
  - Fake meats or fake cheeses
  - Added sugars
  - Added fats
  - Added salt
  - Specific brands
  - Specific dishes from specific restaurants
  - Specific meals or dishes in your house

Knowing what you are eating is the critical first step. You need to identify what you actually put in your body if you want to move toward any type of goal around health. What does your diet look like? It may help to think about this over the course of a week since there will always be day-to-day variation. It might be a good idea to carry this chart with you and use it as a food journal to help you track what you're eating.

Why Are You Eating?

The next question is "why." Why am I eating? What are all the reasons I might put food in my mouth during the day? This could include:

- I'm hungry.
- It tastes good and I'm full but I want more.
- I don't really want it but I can't stop myself.
- I'm bored.
- I'm stressed.
- I feel lonely or sad.
- Other people around me are eating and I feel pressure to fit in.
- I just kept eating and I didn't notice how much I ate.
- I deserve to treat myself.
- I don't notice that I'm even eating.

Let's unpack this for a moment. The reason to eat that is truly aligned with your natural biology and health is to eat when hungry. But there is so much more happening than that.

How have we gotten to a place where our behavior is shaped by so many other motivations? It often relates to being addicted to foods. The foods that foster addiction and stimulate overeating—such as potato chips, soda, cheese, chocolate, sweetened cereals, pastries, and other common processed foods—are low in fiber and contain added sugar, oil, or salt. This translates to extra calories in the same amount of space in the stomach. As Dr. Doug Lisle said in *The Pleasure Trap*, when you eat these foods, you *have* to overeat just to feel full. Your natural senses for satiation are fooled or distorted, and your natural tendency to stop eating when full isn't triggered. This is even more pronounced under stress.[12]

> **Your reasons for eating may change in different situations, and they will certainly change depending on *what* you eat. A key characteristic of addictive food is that your natural instincts can be distorted by what you eat. To learn more about some of the four biggest culprits—chocolate, sugar, cheese, and meat— check out *Breaking the Food Seduction* by Dr. Neal Barnard.**

Stress causes a reduced sensation of sweetness, which may naturally lead us to seek sweeter food,[13] but if you eat a healthy diet, that would mean a piece of fruit, not a candy bar. Everyone seeks comfort food from time to time, but if your comfort food is grapes or an apple or clementine, you won't be able to overeat much because of the fiber, and you're not going to get thrown back into addiction. If your comfort food is a Snickers bar or an

115

oily, hot, Reuben sandwich with melted cheese, the combination of emotional eating and foods that on their own promote addiction becomes difficult to resist.

How Are You Eating?

Now we move on to the question of "how." How am I eating? What are all the ways I get myself to eat this food? This could include:

- I cook this at home.
- My spouse/partner/boyfriend/girlfriend cooks for us.
- I stop at my favorite deli for lunch.
- I eat whatever is served in the office cafeteria.
- I always go out with my friends on Thursday nights.
- I hate cooking; I usually microwave frozen food.
- I stop at the grocery store for snacks and meals.
- My personal chef prepares some food for our family each week.
- My personal shopper does my grocery shopping and my daughter and I do the cooking.
- I live with my adult children and they do the cooking.

The "how" is an important question to consider because there may be ways to shift how you eat or how you seek food that better support your goals. And, of course, there can be both advantages and disadvantages when someone else does the cooking. Examining "how" can help you:

- Identify particular challenges about your situation that relate to other people's preferences, as well as your relationship.
- Notice if you eat out for more meals than you realized.
- Keep track of what you find convenient and which circumstances surround your typical habits.

When Are You Eating?

Next, let's think about the "when." When am I eating? When are all the times of day when eating happens? This could include:

- Breakfast
- Morning snack

- Lunch
- Afternoon snack
- Dinner
- After-dinner snack
- Other snacks
- When there's a special occasion
- 7:30 A.M.
- 11:30 P.M.
- After I get out of the gym
- After my class gets out on Tuesdays
- 1:30 even though I start getting hungry for lunch at 11:30 or 12:00

Where Are You Eating?

And, we finish with the question of "where." Where am I eating? Where are all the places or locations where I eat? This may include:

- The kitchen
- At home
- In my bed
- On the couch
- In my car
- At my desk
- In the break room
- At friends' houses
- Restaurants—maybe specific restaurants
- Specific delis
- Etc.

It's worthwhile to think about whether any of these locations may trigger you to eat certain foods, and how these factors of what, why, how, when, and where all relate to each other to influence your decisions.

Maybe you love watching your favorite movie while eating cake on the couch as a treat after a hard week, and it's easy to do since you buy your teenager's favorite Entenmann's cake for him or her and it's always in the freezer.

Maybe you feel motivated and energized after going running in your neighborhood, and it feels easy to come into the house and make a salad for lunch on the weekend.

117

Maybe you make a point to bring a small baggie of trail mix with you to work so you have some food that helps you resist the brownies your co-worker consistently dumps in the coffee room, and you use your willpower to successfully resist the brownies.

Maybe on some days you eat the brownies, even though you don't want to, and it happens to be those days when you've forgotten your trail mix.

Keep going until you've completed these questions for each of the first five columns in Chart 1.

THE DOMINANT MOTIVATIONS IN YOUR EATING DECISIONS

Finally, let's take an overall look at the context surrounding each food you have listed in the chart. Given what you know about those foods and the factors implicated in your decision, you now want to try to identify the dominant motivation in each decision in the final column. There may be more than one motivation at play, but choose the one that makes the biggest impact. This could be:

- Habit
- Environmental default/easy choice
- Required willpower
- Gave in to craving

Decisions that might be labeled "habit" could include:

- Eating cereal, banana, and milk for breakfast every day because you don't even think to eat anything else.
- Stopping at your favorite coffee shop on the way to work and adding sugar to your coffee because it's what you've always done.
- Making rice and beans for dinner because it's your go-to meal when you can't think of anything specific to cook.

Decisions that would be labeled "environmental default/easy choice" could include:

- You're hungry on your way out the door to your kids' soccer game, and you grab the leftover dinner from the fridge so you don't starve.

118

- You go out to dinner with friends at a restaurant that only serves cheesy or oily food, and though you're not really in the mood for cheese or oil, there isn't anything else on the menu except bread and lettuce so you order linguini in cream sauce.
- You swing by your favorite health food store that is on the way to your long-time client's office to get some fruit and healthy deli food for lunch.

Decisions that might be labeled "required willpower" could include:

- Making sure you first eat whole, plant-based foods before other foods when you're hungry.
- Avoiding the perpetual sugary banana bread residing in your office break room.
- Cooking oatmeal for yourself for breakfast though you're not really in the mood to cook.
- Walking across the street at work to get real food though there is a vending machine with candy on your floor.

Decisions that would be labeled "gave in to craving" could include:

- Your neighbor brings you Christmas cookies and, though you successfully resist eating them and intend to pass them on to your own hapless office colleagues, a late-afternoon urge for sugar hits and you eat three of them.
- You put on a movie and make popcorn, intending to eat it plain, but three bites into the bowl you put salt and butter on it because it just doesn't taste as good without them.
- You drive 15 minutes out of your way after work to get your favorite pizza because you can't stop thinking about it, though you know you have healthy food waiting for you at home.

This may seem like a good deal of work. It's time-consuming to map out all your decisions in this way, but the expanded awareness of your own patterns will pay dividends in allowing you to take advantage of what's known about the power of the environment. You will feel a real sense of accomplishment in completing the chart, and it will dramatically empower you in sticking with your healthy diet—for life. What you want eventually is for the majority of your food decisions to be either

119

habits or the environmental default. Let's look at how to shift those choices further.

RESHAPING YOUR FOOD ENVIRONMENT

Once you know what, why, how, when, and where, it's time to make a plan for reshaping your food environment, transforming your points of decision to make it work *for* you rather than against you. The following list of renovations covers your physical environment, shopping, routines and timing, travel routes, restaurants, and social situations. The more of these you can shift, the more you practice a habit or can take the easy path, the less energy it will take you to eat the way you want. Think of these changes as lifestyle renovations. Once they're done, they stay this way. You can use the strategies below to consider which specific areas you want to tackle, and then chose your path at the end of this section to make sure the changes are manageable.

Home

Remove and replace processed snacks and animal-based foods from your kitchen and your entire house. Remember to refer to Table 6 in Step Three for foods to include and to avoid. And then make sure you're stocked with enough options for when you do get hungry. We'll cover negotiations with family members in Step Five, but the more unhealthy foods you can remove the better.

Grocery Shopping

To get whole, plant-based foods into your home you've got to buy them somewhere—somewhere that sells them! Not every store offers what you need, and many emphasize processed and animal foods to such a degree that it can be hard to find kale, beans, or brown rice. Consider where you shop and ask yourself if it's easy to find what you need there. Access to healthy food is often a bigger challenge in urban areas with few grocery stores and more convenience stores than anything else. If you lack adequate grocery stores in your neighborhood, remember that the significant inconvenience you face—especially if you don't drive and don't live within walking distance of a bigger grocery store––is more than worth the trouble. This is one of the moments you must act with great initiative and take personal responsibility for making it work. (By the way, know that everyone who is aware of this problem is troubled by it, and researchers are working all the time to promote policy solutions.)

If you can drive to the stores you need, then do it. If you aren't sure what else is available, try Googling grocery stores in your neighborhood and look on a map. Find the closest large grocery stores. Are any them on your regular travel routes? How can you make time to get to them? If you don't drive and aren't near a store, does the bus or train run nearby? (Yes, you may have to take a bus or subway. Or even a taxi for a major shop. But again, it really *is* more than worth the effort.) Or perhaps you can carpool with a friend, a neighbor, or a coworker. And don't forget the grocery delivery services or CSA shares that we discussed in Step Two.

Office

Get those sugary treats out of your desk drawers and replace them with healthy alternatives. In general you want some fruit, some low-fat savory snack, tea, water, and maybe even dehydrated soups for emergency situations. Don't be caught without something to eat. If you have the luxury of a small refrigerator, it can make bringing your lunch to work easier and storing salad and veggies a pleasure.

Also, if your office colleagues tend to bring donuts and pastries to the common room regularly, try speaking with your supervisor about toning down the frequency, or suggest that colleagues share healthier snacks as well. You can choose to bring fruit or healthy treats from time to time to model what is possible on a plant-based diet. You can also request moving your work area farther away from wherever the junk food hangs out. Even turning your desk around so you face away from it may help you. As you eat plant-based food longer, you may continue to use some amount of willpower, but the need will diminish over time.

Commute

What kinds of snacks can you keep with you in the car or on your train or bus ride for emergencies? Healthy snack bars, crackers, or fruit may be essential traveling companions. They will especially be handy if there are delays in your commute or you take a long road trip.

121

Consider, too, taking the time to sit down with a map and study your commute. Plan out what you will do if you end up out of the house and hungry. Where will you buy food? How many minutes out of the way can you go? What will you buy? You can do this for both your work commute and any other trips you commonly take. It will help if you plan this ahead of time. Write these plans down on a card you can carry in your wallet. When the time comes and you feel hungry, you will have already made your decision and don't need to think about it. Just pull out the card and let yourself go on autopilot.

Schedule

Looking at your decision-making chart, think about when you normally eat. Are there adjustments you can make to your schedule? Make your lunch for the next day the night before? Cook several large dishes on the weekend for lunches the coming week? Make and freeze soup for hurried weekday dinners? Look for changes that will make your time spent cooking and preparing more efficient, and will save you the need to buy food when you're out.

Restaurant and Travel Preferences

Restaurants can be tough. Advance planning can assure that when you actually arrive, you know what you can eat. Nowadays, many restaurants offer vegetarian, or even vegan, options on their menu, but this depends on location and type of restaurant. Do some investigating. Which restaurants in your area offer plant-based dishes? This information will come in handy whenever you are involved in the decision about where to go. Most Asian food restaurants—Indian, Thai, Chinese, Japanese, and Korean—offer many vegetable dishes, and you can usually choose tofu in place of meat. Surprisingly, steak houses are often one of the best choices for truly healthy, whole plant foods that are oil-free. You can order baked potatoes and large salads with vinegar or no dressing.

Restaurants are usually accommodating. You can tell your server you are on a special diet, or not, as you feel comfortable, but be specific. Don't be shy about asking for what you want; your new way of eating is becoming more and more commonplace. You can ask for modifications on meat dishes, for instance, as well as requesting beans on the roasted chicken salad instead of the chicken, a salad without cheese, or steamed vegetables instead of fried. The more you ask, the more you create the demand for it. Just call ahead, look up menus online, and make a strategy so that when you get there you know what you'd like to order.

Eating a plant-based diet while flying is usually challenging. Try to prepare road snacks ahead of time so you don't starve in the airport. Most grocery stores and airports carry fruit smoothies and juices with no added sugar, and these are helpful in a pinch. If you're able to carry food with you, bringing no-sugar fruit and nut bars (Larabars are great when you're stranded) can save the day, as can bringing a simple wrap or leftover dinner in a sealed container.. Many hotels have a coffee maker in each room; the hot water allows you to make an instant, healthy soup or some instant oatmeal when you have no other options.

Social Gatherings

We're going to go into depth on this issue in Step Five, but for now, take this as an opportunity to think about frequent social situations and consider your strategies for avoiding pressure or inadvertent eating that you won't feel good about. You can also consider eating before you go or bringing a dish to events to make sure there's enough of something you want to eat.

If some people in your circles are very committed to meat-based eating, think about other activities you can share with them besides meals. Write down your possibilities for these situations and explore your desires. Are these activities important to you? Do you want to keep participating? What do you want to let go of and what do you want to shift? Plan your first step to be ready for the next gathering.

YOUR PATH GOING FORWARD

It's time to make it happen. Suggested renovations to your total environment are described below, and you're now ready to continue on your path. Remember to balance what you believe you can accomplish with something that feels like a challenge. Once you've selected your action steps, write them down and post them somewhere visible. This could be your bedroom, your desk, your car dashboard, or the refrigerator. If you have an accountability partner, call or email this person with your goals and ask

123

him to check in on you and your progress. If your friend is nearby, he might like to hang out with you while you throw out the mayonnaise! As we'll discuss more in Step Five, it's crucial to stay connected throughout this transition.

1. **Easing In:** Begin by completing the decision awareness exercise on page 113. It may take you several days, so take your time and think about everything carefully. Based on your results, work with your home environment, and get everything out of your house that you don't feel good about eating every day. If you're not ready to make a total change, remember that there will always be plenty of opportunities to eat anything you want out in the world. Let your home environment be a dietary refuge that supports your daily health habits. Take stock of where you shop. Are you able to find what you need? If not, find a new store and make a plan to get there. Check Chart 1 and see what kind of support you need. You're on a wonderful trajectory. ▶*Suggested time frame: two weeks.*

2. **Rev It Up:** Begin by completing the decision awareness exercise on page 113. It may take you several days, so take your time and think about everything carefully. Work with your home and grocery shopping environments as described in "Easing In" and also take stock of your schedule and travel routes. Once your home is a supportive zone, the most likely times to cave in to cravings are when you find yourself in transit or stuck away from home. A look at Chart 1 can help you see the priorities. Try to address the major points of breakdown. You're doing awesome. ▶*Suggested time frame: two weeks.*

3. **Total Transformation:** This is the big overhaul—no holding back. Begin with the decision awareness exercise on page 113. Take stock, using your results, and reshape your home, grocery shopping, your office, your commute, and your plan for restaurants and social gatherings. No worries, Step Five is all about making sure this diet doesn't isolate you. Do seriously consider every aspect of your life and take action to do a major reshaping, or make a plan for the next time you'll be in the situation. You're on a very exciting path. ▶*Suggested time frame: one week. Days one and two: your home. Day three: the office. Day four: rework your routes, commutes,*

and schedule. Day five: plan your restaurant meals. Day six: strategize about workarounds for common social situations.

🌶

Congratulations! No matter which path you are on, you have just taken some major steps in making a whole food, plant-based diet sustainable for a lifetime.

CULTIVATE CONNECTION FOR THE LONG HAUL
making your diet socially sustainable

ℐ

WELL DONE! YOU'VE MADE it through some significant changes and are probably by this time actively eating a more plant-based diet. Now that you've educated yourself about nutrition and found your motivating force, added new foods to your diet, let go of eating processed and animal foods, and altered your food environment to make it automatically supportive of healthy habits, you're ready for the final component to make plant-based eating a lasting and comfortable lifestyle.

In Step Four, we examined the method many people use to change in spite of an unsupportive environment—reliance on willpower—and explained how poorly that works in the long term. Willpower provides a short-term solution at best. Your physical environment can present challenges to it. So, too, can other people, whose challenges take a variety of forms, ranging from well-meaning concern or skepticism to unthinking offers of food you now find undesirable to subtle pressure to follow convention. For many of us, healthy relationships with people who respect and support our choices can make the critical difference between abandoning our diet and realizing lasting change. Lifestyle habits have staying power when you integrate them into your normal life. The more we cultivate relationships that celebrate our individual eating habits and the more we connect with other people around our plant-based lifestyle, the closer we get to a shared culture of health.

In Step Five, we'll begin by discussing the value of social support for your dietary choices. We'll then focus on the importance of both maintaining your connection with old friends as well as cultivating a new social network of people who are already excited about this way of eating. We'll also propose approaches to initiate difficult conversations with friends and family, discuss where and how to find new community, and suggest strategies to help you build a virtual community. These strategies will serve to enable you to stick with a whole food, plant-based diet permanently.

THE BENEFITS OF SOCIAL SUPPORT FOR YOUR DIETARY CHOICES

As with so many other behaviors, part of our struggle with eating a healthy diet is attributable to evolutionary tendencies for social approval that were at one time adaptive but no longer function properly because our environment has changed so drastically. As we discussed in Step Three, we've evolved to seek energy-dense food in quantities as large as possible. In the same way, we've also developed a basic drive to try to fit in, which extends to eating as well as other social behavior. Humans are sensitive to perceived standards for what is acceptable, and this sensitivity shapes our behavior so that we prefer doing what other people model and also what we perceive them to endorse. In the context of eating, researchers believe there may be overlapping benefits to this.

First, eating what other community members endorse makes it more likely you will select safe foods to consume. The learning process can be time-consuming and potentially dangerous if you were to test every food yourself, but learning through modeling shortcuts the trial-and-error involved in tasting every potentially nutritious but also potentially poisonous plant.[1]

Second, a basic instinct to eat the same things as fellow community members promotes food sharing and cooperation—essential traits to survive in the face of possible starvation. Social norms come into play more strongly when people are uncertain about the best behavior to engage in. And interestingly, the same neural pathways we discussed in Step Three—those activated by food reward—are also activated by norm following.[2] In other words, we are biochemically rewarded for going along with the group. At the same, we also experience negative consequences in the form of judgment or disapproval when we make non-normative choices, one example being our societal prejudice against overeating and obesity.

128

The jury remains out on the specific factors that affect whether or not social norms are followed in eating, but there is evidence for a few that likely play a role. These factors include being uncertain about the consequences of choosing a particular food (you're more likely to follow the norm when you lack other information), strong feedback from the group about one choice or another, and whether the group that sets a norm is a group you want to emulate and gain the approval of or distance yourself from.[3] While research in this area is still young, it's clear that social approval or disapproval really does make an impact on food choices. This holds true not only for adults but also for adolescents as they begin making independence choices. Adolescents' consumption of nutrient-poor and energy-dense foods outside of their home environment is most closely associated with what their friends are eating, not their own knowledge of food and nutrition.[4] So it's no wonder that in our meat-loving food culture, it can be hard to feel totally comfortable eating differently from our friends, family, or even strangers. When these people have direct questions, concerns, or even criticisms to air about what you eat, eating healthfully can become harder.

The influence of social norms actually can extend further than the people in your immediate sphere of contact. Social contagion is a theory that describes behaviors and social movements that catch on, moving across social networks with broad influence.[5] Traits and behaviors like obesity and smoking are found to cluster within three degrees of influence, which means that that you are likely to share certain traits, such as being obese or being a smoker, with your friends, your friends' friends, and even your friends' friends' friends.[6] You're also more likely to adopt new behaviors, shift your values, or make comparisons between yourself and others based on the influence of your social connections.[7]

Intrigued by the complexity of social influence? Read *Connected: The Surprising Power of Our Social Networks and How They Shape Our Lives* **by researchers Nicholas A. Christakis and James H. Fowler. The book examines the evidence for the profound influence we each have across social networks on one another's tastes, health, wealth, happiness, beliefs, and body weight. In our ultra-connected world, eating habits are a product of not just our own beliefs and values, but the multitude of influences coming to us from all our indirect connections.**

Social Influence Can Expand Incrementally

The story of Dr. T Colin Campbell and his wife, Karen Campbell, beautifully illustrates how influence can germinate from one or two people and spread throughout a network. As Dr. Campbell was conducting his early laboratory experiments on diet and cancer, he began to see patterns emerge in the results. The consistent theme was the ability of animal protein to promote cancer development, whereas plant protein inhibited it. These results were so startling and provocative that they led to a lot of discussion at home with his wife. Karen, taking very seriously the implications of these data, didn't waste any time and began to cut out red meat, then chicken, and eventually dairy products and all animal foods from their family meals. Their dietary transition happened over years as the research data gradually came in, but Dr. Campbell credits Karen with his success in "eating his own words," and this dietary success was transmitted to their children, grandchildren, and the public who have been touched by the information the Campbells share and the example they set.

Through Karen's translation of research into practice, Dr. Campbell's results took life as a simple, wholesome lifestyle that anybody could practice, with the single instruction to "eat whole, plant foods," subsequently inspiring a growing number of people to do exactly that. The Campbells mutually supported their own commitments to the diet and passed on those values to their children, grandchildren, friends, and the countless members of the public who've joined the plant-based community by reading *The China Study* (a project initially suggested by Karen), seeing Dr. Campbell lecture, and trying the diet out for themselves with incredible, positive results.

Today, the momentum of the larger community has taken off with more research being conducted, more recipes being shared, more restaurants opening, more businesses being started, more professional gatherings being held, and more people than ever eating whole, plant-based foods. With such a large group now connected through shared habits and values, plant-based eating has a life of its own, and it is easier than ever before for a newcomer to feel that the lifestyle is doable and enjoyable. Tracing the path of the Campbells' spark and influence shows us how we all have the potential to shape the course of events if we have unwavering integrity to our truth.

Interpersonal Social Support Predicts Success

Social norms and societal modeling and expectations contribute an overall context that promotes certain eating behaviors. However, when making specific dietary and lifestyle choices, like exercise, reactions from close friends and family—positive or negative—also exert a profound influence.[8] We are social creatures who live naturally in community. Making healthy lifestyle choices flows naturally out of feeling connected to the people around you. The degree of social connection or isolation you feel may even influence something as basic as the variety in your diet. In a large, observational study of 20,000+ adults over age 50, being single, widowed, or having less frequent contact with friends was associated with less variety of fruit and vegetable intake,[9] and it got worse for people who lived alone and *also* had less frequent contact with friends—they had even less variety than in those who were just single.

Social support from friends and family in the form of offering encouragement, establishing connection, providing accountability, and modeling or sharing a target behavior has been shown to help improve adherence for a wide variety of health behaviors, including taking medication,[10] eating less fat, and exercising more.[11] Doctors and the media also play an important role in facilitating healthy behaviors,[12] and women seem to be naturally inclined toward dietary support, because both women and men whose friends are women report more active verbal encouragement for healthy behaviors.[13] Spouses tend to have the biggest influence on each other,[14] and among couples, it's been shown that an individual who starts a new healthy behavior, such as quitting smoking, is much more likely to succeed if his or her partner already has the healthy new behavior (doesn't smoke).[15] It's a great reason to try to hang out with the people who are already doing and eating what you want to be doing and eating yourself!

Many of these results emerge in the context of a research intervention, which means someone else was providing the encouragement, feedback, and connection, but we can take a lesson from experiments like this and apply this information to inform how we can ourselves create a structure to support us through a dietary transition and beyond. The more role models, friends, and acquaintances we have who eat plant-based, the more we can share camaraderie over eating and celebrate our connection with food.

If you're not sure what kind of support you could be looking for, it may help to paint a picture of what supportive relationships look like. Social support from friends and family for your diet spans a spectrum of passive acceptance to active participation, and might take such forms as:

- Respecting your choices, giving you the space to make your own decisions
- Exhibiting open-minded curiosity about your diet
- Encouraging your eating intentions and celebrating your successes
- Accommodating your food choices by offering food that is compatible with your diet
- Offering to go to restaurants where you will be likely to find something to eat
- Checking in with you about whether you will be able to find food in a particular location or situation
- Eating a similar diet and sharing food with you over meals, potlucks, or other social gatherings
- Teaching, leading, or otherwise inspiring you to make even healthier choices through their own modeling

At the same time, if you don't live in a particularly supportive place or social context, you may be accustomed to a certain level of social disharmony or even criticism around your diet. It's a good idea to critically evaluate what kind of influences and messages you receive from the people around you and identify whether the interactions seem like any of the following:

- Displaying a lack of knowledge of and interest in plant-based diets in your community
- Expressing skepticism that you could be eating a healthy diet or that what you are doing is good for you
- Voicing energetic criticism of your food choices
- Discussing your choices with other people in a critical or unkind way
- Making little to no effort to accommodate your food choices, either at home or in the choosing of restaurants
- Offering you food you don't want to eat or pressuring you to "just have a little bit" even though you've explained you're not eating certain foods anymore
- Exhibiting tension, hostility, or derision when the topic of your diet comes up

If any of these non-supportive kinds of feedback rings a bell, it may be a sign you need to take a step back and evaluate how close to these people you want to be and how much of an effort you want to make to preserve the relationship, and in what context.

If your new way of eating causes you to feel alienated from the people you've known and loved for a long time, you may be tempted to discontinue your healthier diet, which, of course, isn't what we want to happen. You certainly want to maintain the majority of your relationships. However, you may need to figure out who can tolerate and respect your choices, even if they don't eat that way themselves, and who can't. For the people who can't, you'll need to make a bigger effort to redirect your energy in connecting with them so that you can connect in circumstances that do not involve food.

CREATING A NEW NORMAL

Our opportunity as we individually and collectively embark on a healthier eating pattern is to create a new shared culture, with new social norms that create a world where we don't eat animals or manufacture processed foods with added fat, sugar, and salt, and do encourage each other toward healthier lifestyles. Your best chance for making a significant difference in this shift is to set up your life so that your dietary transition is failproof, which means cultivating a sustainable, supportive social network.

The first component involves maintaining the majority of your relationships with existing family and friends, even if they do not share your interest in or enthusiasm for a whole food, plant-based diet. Finding ways to stay connected to them is critical for your stability and security, because losing these people who are important to you can be a barrier to sticking with your new diet long-term. This will necessitate gauging how interested these people are in plant-based diets and focusing on other ways of connecting with them if they do not share your values around food. It also means learning how to discuss your dietary choices in situations where your diet may trigger some unease or awkwardness between you and others.

The second component involves moving beyond your existing network of friends and family and cultivating new social networks for yourself. This may include both a live community and virtual communities.

133

Maintaining Your Relationships
Even When Food Preferences Differ

Not everyone is going to be excited about the idea of you eating a whole food, plant-based diet, and your new-found dietary differences can bring up unexpected areas of unease. It would be great if all of your friends and family suddenly wanted to hop on board with your new lifestyle, but that won't necessarily happen. This means that you'll have to make the effort to preserve those relationships. Try to stay sensitive to what others may or may not be interested in or find comfortable, and what kind of shifts they might be receptive to. Avoid expecting or demanding that others change their own diets to meet your needs, because it will place an uncomfortable burden on your relationship that may drive you further apart rather than closer together.

As you develop new connections, your shared values around food will nurture and sustain your commitment to the diet and carry you through the moments when your existing friends and family show a lack of interest. This is why forging new friendships with people who already eat plant-based is critical. They will allow you to circumvent asking those who may be closest to you for something they're unable to willingly give, and you won't risk taxing those relationships as a result.

Del Sroufe, plant-based chef extraordinaire at the Wellness Forum education center in Ohio, and former 475-pound vegan baker, created such a complete social support network that it would be virtually impossible for him to return to his old ways of 15-hour workdays ending with potato chips and beer. Thanks to his dedication to his health, his decision to place himself in a fully plant-based work environment, and his friendship and partnership with the center's executive director, Dr. Pam Popper, and other coworkers, Del crafted a situation of high social support and constant contact with like-minded people. Together, his new lifestyle and his supportive community of friends and colleagues enabled him to lose 200 pounds—something that would have never been possible without the encouragement of his mentors and friends. Del can even maintain his diet over family holidays in the midst of people who still eat candied yams and turkey. Through honest and loving conversation with his family, he's been able to make it clear that for him, a whole food, plant-based diet saved his life and isn't something he can take a break from. They understand that, so although he doesn't eat their food, they love each other and their dietary differences don't get in the way of what's most important.

134

There are a variety of situations that you may face after your transition to a plant-based diet that will benefit from some affirmation, smoothing over, or honesty on your part. When questions and comments arise, you will need to know how to handle them.

First of all, you will be happiest, and so will those with the questions or comments, if you do not try not to change others' views or expect that they will "come around" eventually. In each moment, you can either feel connected to them or not, and while it's much more enjoyable to share food with friends and family than not, if they don't want to eat what you eat, don't waste your time trying to manipulate them into changing. This may make it harder for you to stick to your target eating habits, but you have to do the best you can, given the circumstances you have. As you maintain your diet and the people around you become more used to it, it may cease to be a point of discussion or concern. As you stick to your principles with your children, they too will cease trying to negotiate or resist your house rules.

Here are some suggestions for how to navigate these potentially tense conversations without alienating those you care about:

- If your significant other, family member, or housemate just isn't into your plant-based diet, try to come to an agreement to keep food that does not fit your diet out of the house.

  FRIEND/FAMILY MEMBER: *I support you, but I'm totally not ready for this. I could never give up meat; it's my favorite food.*

  YOU: *I understand. I don't want to make you give up anything either. I just want the house to be an environment where I'm comfortable. I'm really trying to eat healthier because I feel better, and it's just so hard for me not to eat certain foods if they're around. I don't want to make you give up things you don't want to give up. Do you think you could use lunch out to eat what you want, and let the house stay plant-based?*

- If your significant other or housemate really refuses to get on board with the "only certain foods at home" idea and insists on maintaining a kitchen that includes things you don't want to eat, you may need to offer to step up the cooking.

  SPOUSE/HOUSEMATE: *I don't care what you do with your diet, I just don't want to feel like I can't eat what I want in my own house, and I don't think I can give up meat and dairy.*

You: *I totally get it. That's how I'm feeling too. I'm happy to cook dinner. Would you be up for me doing that and then you can add meat and cheese where you want to at the table? I feel like I should stay away from it so I'm not tempted to eat it, and that way we could each have the meal we want.*

- If your children or adolescents protest, you'll have to decide where you'll set boundaries and then stick to them, but expect some resistance initially. Remember, they may be exiting food addictions themselves:

    Child: *This totally isn't fair. There isn't anything good to eat anymore. Why do we have to do this?*

    You: *As you get older, you'll be making more and more of your own decisions. Right now, I/we make the decisions about the food we have in the house. No matter what you eat when you're outside the house, you have to stick to our rules in the house. I'm eating this for my own health, and it's because I love you that I want you to eat this way too. I'm learning to like it too, so we can learn to like it together—not to mention, I'm hoping we can do a lot more cooking together! I know you have talent waiting to come out.*

    Adolescent: *I can't believe you're doing this to me; it feels like the kitchen is a prison. Can't I just bring my own food home?*

    You: *I don't have a problem with whatever you choose to eat when you're not here—that's up to you, though, of course, I always hope you make healthy choices. But I really can't realistically stick to what I want to be eating if we have other food in the house. So I need to ask you for your support for me on this. Besides, I love you, and I want to make sure you're eating more than pizza, so these are the rules till you're on your own.*

- If you have friends who are disappointed in your new way of eating because it means they won't be able to share your former favorite foods with you, try to make light of the situation and affirm the connection you have with them without involving food. Also make a point to plan activities with them that don't involve eating.

FRIEND: *Can't you just cheat a little bit? I can't believe you're not going to have any (fill in the blank).... You used to love that.*

YOU: *I know, I can't believe it either! Seriously it's because I love you more.*

An alternative response might be:

YOU: *Why I don't meet you after dinner for a drink, I'll be coming from work anyway.*

■ If you encounter questions and concerns from friends, family, or coworkers, don't feel as if you have to justify your new dietary choices or otherwise explain yourself.

SOMEONE ELSE: *Where do you get your protein if you don't eat meat?*

YOU: *Well, I'm feeling good, so I don't feel worried about it. I've been doing a lot of reading and I found out it's actually not a problem to get enough protein from plant food as long as I eat enough calories.* [shrug]

SOMEONE ELSE: *Aren't you worried about a vitamin deficiency?*

YOU: *Well, I was at first, but I did some reading by some doctors, and it sounds like it's not a big cause for concern, so, I'm feeling okay for now.*

Of course, it's always possible you'll receive genuine interest and curiosity too. If someone in your life does want to know more, keep trying to stick to your personal experience in what you discuss directly, but steer them toward movies or books that you think might resonate with them. When they are ready to process what they are learning, be ready and listen with an open mind and heart. Everyone needs the chance to grapple with new information in their own way and at their own pace.

Cultivating New Social Networks

In addition to maintaining relationships despite dietary differences, creating a new normal entails making new friends as well. As previously mentioned, it's important to make friends who are already committed to the type of diet you want to be eating, because we all need that kind of shared experience and support. You can cultivate new friendships and community from two sources—real, live people and virtual connections. Each of these has unique benefits, but ideally you will find both as they complement one another and provide support for a plant-based lifestyle from different directions.

THE IMPORTANCE OF LIVE COMMUNITY

For inspiration and getting charged up for action, nothing substitutes for live interaction with others. Close conversation, the immediacy of the energy in a room full of like-minded people, and the personal feedback and sharing offer reassurance and normalcy. Find and create those opportunities to share food and conversation with those who already eat or are interested in trying a plant-based diet with you. Physically being in the same space as others naturally nudges you to absorb the social norms of the group, so the more plant-based group experiences you have, the more automatic the lifestyle becomes and the more natural it feels. Below are some suggestions to help you make your new social connections. (For a list of specific organizations,events, and their URLs, check the Resources section of the book.)

To locate like-minded people near you:

- Use the Internet and social media to make new, plant-based connections in your own locale. Vegan and vegetarian Meetup groups are popular and growing, so this may be the fastest path to live connections where you live. Thanks to the film *PlantPure Nation*, there are now local groups springing up around the world focused on promoting healthy, whole food, plant-based eating and activism.
- Identify local plant-friendly restaurants and grocery stores that offer ingredients or meals that meet your requirements. Check bulletin boards for announcements of groups, potluck dinners, or other interesting events that might yield a plant-based community to surround yourself with.
- Take an inventory of your friends and consider which, if any, may be friendly to or curious about plant-based diets. Reach out to them and invite them to try a new recipe with you or join you for an event. Would any of them attend a potluck or lecture with you? Nurture these relationships with extra attention while you create new habits.

138

Make it a priority to attend local events:

- Go to a local potluck dinner or gathering. Even if you don't feel like fast friends with the others you meet for the first time, you'll experience a deep pleasure in sharing food with a group that values and prioritizes plant-based eating, not to mention getting to taste some delicious new dishes!
- Bring a plant-friendly friend to this newfound event if you can, but don't let being solo keep you from trying. Plant-based groups are typically welcoming to newcomers; the new faces the first time may look familiar the next time around.
- Extend yourself to meet new people while you're there. Make the most of the experience, talk with others, and give them the chance to get to know you, which will help you to judge how you enjoy it and if it would be worth repeating.

Host a potluck or dinner party:

- Throw your own potluck or party, and invite your new plant-based acquaintances. Everybody is ready to have a potluck!
- Invite old friends to your party. Explain that you are hosting a themed get-together (the theme being all plant-based food, please) to try out some exciting new dishes and impress them, as well as to help everyone experiment with new cooking.
- Serve a fabulous dessert that everyone, including omnivores, can enjoy. While taste and enjoyment are important to plant-based eaters too, the more skeptical or curious folks find delicious desserts to be reassuring, which builds goodwill toward plant-based diets in general and your dinner parties in particular.

Consider attending conferences, programs, or special events:

- Find a lecture being given by one of the experts or authors you find appealing. You can check their calendars through their websites or social media sites, and make plans to attend. If possible, bring a friend so you can discuss the event together, as well as travel there with company.
- Immerse yourself in plant-based eating and learning at a confer-

139

ence or overnight program. A totally plant-based experience can be a powerful impetus to notch up your commitment, and the friendships and networking that develop in these contexts will introduce you to motivated, high-quality people—exactly the kind of people you want in your community.

- Attend an immersion vacation or residential medical program if you have the time and money to do so. Such programs are a goldmine of like-minded eaters, and no matter where you are in your journey to health, it's always valuable to get some professional guidance and supervision.
- Get involved and volunteer to help with plant-based activities or groups. Is there a vegetarian society in your area? A hiking group? A parents' group at school working to improve school food?

Your efforts to reach out to others will enrich your life with immeasurable value that personal connection brings us all.

THE BENEFITS OF VIRTUAL COMMUNITIES

Whether you live in an area with a substantial number of similarly minded eaters or not, virtual connection provides a feeling of immediacy that normalizes plant-based diets across distances, cultures, ages, and interests. Social media allows us all to plug in to the emerging shared culture with minimal expense, no matter who or where we are. The opportunites for connecting with like-minded people, sharing recipes, and participating in national dialogues through comments and discussion boards are all over. For people who live in more meat-centric locales, the connection through social media may be the most sustaining and important part of their social support network; really, if you can't think of a single person in your city who you talk to who eats plant-based, social media will be the backbone of your social support network, so make sure you invest the time needed to learn. If you're not already a social media user, don't worry, it's not hard. However, for the potential return, it's worth getting a tutor (perhaps a friend, child, or grandchild) if you have any hesitation. Consider using any of the following platforms for virtual plant-based connection:

- **Facebook:** Great for following educators of all kinds and recipe authors, and for joining public discussions and commentaries.

Check your favorite book authors to see if they have a Facebook page and "like" them to stay updated with their posts. Cooking dinner? Post a photo on Facebook of what you're making. All the positive comments will reward your efforts as well as point out who in your existing social network is friendly to plant-based food.

- **Twitter:** Limited to 140 characters or fewer, Twitter is the most efficient way to browse the news. In just a few moments, you can scroll through updates from thought leaders, teachers, and friends and decide if you want to click on the links to learn more. Policy updates, science press releases, articles, and events, as well as nutrition news and recipes can be posted on Twitter.

- **Instagram:** The focus on Instagram is photos, photos, photos. This is the perfect forum for staying energized with images of beautiful food and lovely people. Text takes a backseat to the images, so watch the newsfeed bring you one visual statement after another.

- **Pinterest:** Pinterest allows you to create online pinboards of images you like and want to keep track of—you can even create different categories and multiple boards, which makes it easy to peruse past sources of inspiration and review articles and recipes you like.

- **Email lists:** Many experts and groups have regular newsletters with valuable free content that also announce upcoming live events. Consider joining an email list from your favorite organizations to stay updated on opportunities for learning and in-person connection.

- **Online forums:** For more in-depth conversation, try discussion forums such as the McDougall Discussion Board

Remember, the more you learn, the more you do, the more you connect, the more successful you will be. Dive in and enjoy the ride.

YOUR PATH GOING FORWARD

Step Five has brought you full circle in the path of plant-based transitions to arrive at the final component of sustaining a dietary change—connection and relation to other people. It has to be more than just you in your kitchen to make the lifestyle last. Just as Step Four brought your attention to your physical environment, it's equally important to attend to your social environment, since a supportive social environment makes it that much easier to eat whole, plant foods as your default. A picture of what this can look like is all part of our collective vision for a new culture of eating, where whole, plant-based foods are normal. No matter how much or how little you want to change your diet, the more you can make your social environment compatible with those goals, the more likely you are to succeed and be internally satisfied and a positive influence on everyone, whatever they eat.

Part of your movement toward healthy social connections has been happening all along if you've been in touch with a support buddy. This person is your critical first step in reaching out, so take the opportunity to have another conversation with him or her and brainstorm about how you can incorporate more plant-based social connections into your life on a long-term basis. He or she may be a central part of that plan. Remember to commit to your support buddy with your goals and ask for assistance with holding you accountable.

1. **Easing In:** Check over the social media sites you subscribed to in Step One. Are you enjoying them? Are there any more you want to add? Try posting at least a few meals a week on Facebook and soak up the positive comments. Take stock of your friends and family. Are there any people who pop out as potential plant-based friends? Make a date to go out to dinner, or cook dinner together, and talk about what you'd like to try and see if they're interested in joining you. If the most obvious person is your support buddy, brainstorm with that person about what you can do online and in your community. Make a plan to attend at least one plant-based event in your area, or host a themed potluck if there are not events. ▶*Suggested time frame: ongoing, but make a concerted effort in the first two weeks.*

2. **Rev It Up:** Great choice to amp up your efforts—it will more than repay you. How are you feeling about the social media you belong to? Want to add anything else, or join any newsletters? You might make a daily ritual out of checking certain sites, or posting and commenting on your own food pictures. Don't forget to comment on pictures of food from your friends on Facebook to offer mutual support. How do you feel about your friends and family? Who do you want closer relationships with, or is there anyone you'd like

more distance from? Who do you consider a role model? Are there any people who pop out as potential mentors? Reach out to those people and let them know you're changing your diet further and you'd love their advice, support, or recipe suggestions. Make a plan for doing non-food activities with the people who don't feel as supportive. Reach out to your supportive buddies and brainstorm what you can do to fill in your social network with plant-based friends. Make a plan to attend at least one new plant-based event in your area, like a local lecture, and host a themed potluck. Look at your calendar and sketch out a rhythm for the contact you like to have on an ongoing basis. ▶*Suggested time frame: ongoing, but make a concerted effort in the first two weeks with an eye toward growing your social connections long-term.*

3. **Total Transformation:** It's time to totally renovate your social world! Check over the social media sites you subscribed to in Step One. Are you enjoying them? Are you subscribed to all the newsletters you want? Tried discussion forums online? Make a point to look at pictures of food from your friends on Facebook and post comments to their photos—support is a two-way street. Take stock of your friends and family—some are probably eating more plant-based already. Who do you consider a role model? Who would you like to be closer to? Are there any people who pop out as potential mentors? Reach out to those people and let them know you're changing your diet further and you'd love their advice, support, or recipe suggestions. Are there any people you want to distance yourself from because of their views of your diet? Plan some more potlucks or to attend dinners and events in your community. Do you volunteer? Have you been to a residential program or a conference? Map out your schedule in the next year and see if it's possible to plan for one trip or program where you will have full immersion. The more you seek, the more you will find support and success. Look at your calendar and sketch out a rhythm for the contact you like to have on an ongoing basis in terms of events, friends, social media, lectures, and anything else. ▶*Suggested time frame: ongoing, but you can make significant planning progress in a week and then continue to develop your social network long-term.*

2

ONGOING SUCCESS

keeping up
the momentum

RECIPES FOR EVERYONE

T'S MY PLEASURE AND honor to introduce the 100 plant-based recipes in the pages that follow. The authors of these recipes are my heroes, mentors, and friends, and they inspire me by the unique and beautiful way each of them expresses a plant-based lifestyle. Just as there are many ways to live your life, there are many paths to healthy, plant-based eating, and the people included here represent just a few. You can read more about the contributors on page 301.

Whether you are drawn to raw food, sea vegetables and slow-cooked grains, or traditional seasoning with garlic and herbs, you will find something here to love and make again and again. The recipes are categorized loosely as Breakfast/Brunch; Snacks; Appetizers; Soups; Salads and Sides; Sauces, Spreads, and Dressings; Quick Bites; Main Meals; and Treats. The beauty of plant-based eating, however, is that there are no rules about what you can eat at any particular time of day. So if you're like me and enjoy leftover dinner or salad first thing in the morning, go for it.

Most of the dishes are relatively simple with straightforward ingredients, though the more involved recipes are definitely worth taking the time to make as well! Remember to keep experimenting. You will end up with delicious food if you follow these recipes exactly, but the biggest gift we could give you is the confidence to try your own variations. Please visit michaelakarlsen.com/book for a slideshow of recipes.

Bon appétit!

BREAKFAST /
BRUNCH

everyday oats

MICAELA KARLSEN

For many years my standard breakfast was cooked oatmeal, but in the summertime the appeal of warm oatmeal dwindles. At some point I tried soaking the oats overnight and eating them cold, which creates an interesting raw oats experience, but thanks to my husband's preference for quick preparation in the morning and his childhood love of muesli, we've gradually transitioned to straight-up oats as our major breakfast cereal. The beauty of raw oats, beside super-fast preparation, is that you can eat a lot of them, which means you'll easily feel full well into lunchtime.

1 to 1½ cups thick rolled oats (optionally soaked overnight)
Blueberries, raspberries, or sliced strawberries (optional)
Raisins or dried cranberries (optional)
Dried dates or figs, chopped (optional)
Walnuts, almonds, or pecans, chopped (optional)
1 tablespoon chia seeds or ground flaxseeds (optional)
½ to 1 cup plant milk, such as oat, soy, almond, hemp, hazelnut, or rice milk

1. Pour raw oats in a bowl.

2. Add various toppings, as desired.

3. Top with plant milk, and enjoy!

SERVES 1

151

morning glorious

KRIS CARR

It's our motto and our morning beverage. Green juice is the rock-solid foundation of my crazy sexy life. Almost all of my juice recipes start with one or two cukes. Cucumber is the perfect base since it yields lots of mild and refreshing juice and minerals, and it's a fountain of alkalinity. Vive la révolution!

1 large cucumber
1 fistful kale (about ½ cup)
1 fistful romaine (about ½ cup)
2 to 3 celery ribs
1 big broccoli stem
1 green apple, quartered and cored
½ lemon, peeled and quartered

1. Wash and prep all ingredients.
2. Juice all ingredients.

SERVES 2

breakfast-and-beyond smoothie

KATHY POLLARD

This treat can be habit-forming. It can also be a healthy alternative to breakfast—sometimes one with unexpected benefits. When my husband switched from cereal to smoothies he experienced less eczema and fewer colds in the winter, and had more energy. However, because we humans are designed to chew our food, I make sure to accompany a smoothie with solid breakfast foods and snack options. Feel free to experiment with other vegetables.

1 tablespoon whole flaxseeds

1 carrot, beet, or tomato

3 to 6 kale leaves, stripped from stem, or other dark greens

1 to 2 cups frozen fruit (such as berries, cherries, pineapple, mangoes, or peaches)

1 banana (frozen works best)

⅓ cup thick rolled oats

2 to 3 ice cubes (optional)

2 to 4 dates (optional)

1. Place first six ingredients plus 1 cup water in a blender.

2. Add ice cubes if you prefer a slightly colder smoothie and dates if you want to make it sweeter.

3. Whiz until you reach desired level of smoothness. (Blending less creates some crunchy parts to chew on.) Add more water for thinner consistency, if desired.

If you don't have a high-powered blender, like a Vitamix, you may need to grind the flaxseeds separately. Some good flavor variations include: cherry, cocoa, vanilla, banana, and date; peach and dried apricot; strawberry, banana, and vanilla; and blueberry, orange, and vanilla.

SERVES 2

153

apple-lemon breakfast

MICAELA KARLSEN AND REBECCA MICHAELIDES

Rebecca Michaelides, former course instructor and instructor team leader for the T. Colin Campbell Center for Nutrition Studies, is my go-to source for healthy raw cuisine. When I was first getting to know Rebecca, exactly what she did eat was a little mysterious to me. I knew she didn't rely on loads of nuts in her everyday diet, but that was the only kind of raw food diet I was familiar with. She's always been kind enough to satisfy my curiosity, and I'm very grateful to her for expanding my ideas about what raw cuisine can look like and showing me how fresh, light, and delicious something as simple as apples can become. This my version of an everyday raw breakfast based on Rebecca's tutoring.

> 4 to 5 medium apples, any variety
> 5 to 6 dates, pitted
> 2 tablespoons walnuts (about 6 walnut halves)
> Juice of 1 lemon
> ¼ teaspoon cinnamon

1. Core the apples and cut into large pieces.

2. Place dates, walnuts, half of the lemon juice, cinnamon, and three quarters of an apple in a food processor. Puree until finely ground. You may need to scrape down the sides of the bowl a few times and restart.

3. Add the remainder of the apples and lemon juice and pulse until the apples are shredded and the date mixture is evenly distributed.

SERVES 1
(or 2 if you're eating something else for breakfast as well!)

almond-cinnamon granola

MICAELA KARLSEN

I love granola—not only for breakfast (although it's a classic choice), but also as a snack in the mid-afternoon (just dry out of a bag or mixed with homemade soy- or almond-based yogurt). Most store-bought granola, however, is akin to food crime: Oats are whole, healthy, and cheap, but once oil, sugar, and other stuff are added, the commercial product is high in fat, way too sweet, and really expensive. The first time I made granola myself I was amazed at how I didn't even notice oil and sugar weren't there. It was just delicious, and so satisfying!

1 12-ounce jar unsweetened applesauce
10 dates, pitted
1 tablespoon vanilla extract
1 teaspoon cinnamon
6 cups plus 2 tablespoons thick rolled oats
Suggested Toppings:
⅓ cup maple syrup
1 cup sliced raw almonds
1 cup raisins

1. Blend the applesauce, dates, vanilla, cinnamon, and 2 tablespoons of oats in the blender until smooth. For a sweeter granola, include the maple syrup.
2. In a large bowl, combine the applesauce mixture with the remaining oats.
3. Spread mixture evenly onto dehydrator racks or baking sheets. Cook in a dehydrator set on high (160°F) for 7 to 8 hours or in an oven set at 225°F for 1½ hours until slightly brown and crunchy. If you are using the oven, make sure to break up the granola and turn it every 15 minutes to ensure even cooking.
4. Once cooked, add almonds and raisins, if desired.

 Investing in a dehydrator is worth the money—especially for making granola because it means you don't have to tend to it or turn it while it's cooking (and mentally, that makes the recipe that much easier to execute).

MAKES APPROXIMATELY 7 CUPS
(before almonds or raisins are added)

green colada

KRIS CARR

This Crazy Sexy–fied piña colada will have your cells thanking you rather than cursing you in the morning. The half cup of raw spinach in this smoothie provides 100 percent of your daily vitamin K needs. Did you know that vitamin K helps keep your bones healthy and strong? Spinach is also high in calcium and magnesium—no wonder Popeye kicked ass!

- 2 cups cashew milk (or nondairy milk of choice)
- ½ cup pineapple chunks
- 1 orange, peeled
- 1 banana, peeled
- ½ cup loosely packed spinach

1. Place all five ingredients in a high-speed blender.
2. Blend until smooth.

SERVES 2

savory tofu scramble

MICAELA KARLSEN

My favorite way to spend Sunday morning is leisurely cooking an abundance of brunch dishes, especially when we have guests like our friend Craig, who has an unbeatable excitement for good food. Tofu scramble can be made in many ways—most of which are way more flavorful than similar recipes for scrambled eggs or omelettes. So be brave and experiment with other seasonings. If you start with onion and garlic, you can't go wrong!

1 large onion, chopped

2 garlic cloves, finely chopped

Salt (optional)

2 teaspoons vegetable base paste

6 cremini mushrooms, stems trimmed and caps and stems finely chopped

1 16-ounce package firm tofu, drained

1 teaspoon turmeric

½ teaspoon paprika

1 medium tomato, chopped

1 tablespoon nutritional yeast

Pepper (optional)

½ bunch parsley, chopped

1. Water-sauté the onion and garlic (with a pinch of salt, if desired) on medium-high heat starting with a few tablespoons of water in a covered pan until the onions start to become translucent, about 7 minutes. The lid should keep enough water in the pan so the onions cook (and don't burn), but check every few minutes to make sure the bottom of the pan is still wet and add small amounts of water as needed. Meanwhile, dissolve the vegetable base paste in ¼ cup hot water.
2. Once the onions have become translucent, add the mushrooms and dissolved vegetable base paste. Stir, re-cover, and cook until the mushrooms have softened, about 7 more minutes. Uncover halfway through, stir, and add more water to prevent sticking as needed.
3. Crumble the tofu with your hands, breaking it into small bits, and add it to the pan. Sprinkle the turmeric and paprika evenly across the tofu and stir the mixture until the tofu turns yellow.

recipe continues

4. Add the tomato and nutritional yeast, sprinkle with salt and pepper (if desired), stir, and cook uncovered until softened, about 5 more minutes. The water from the tomato should prevent further sticking.

5. Add the chopped parsley, stir, and turn off the heat. Don't overcook the parsley or it will turn brown. Serve with either soft corn taco shells or Sweet Potato Hash (page 159) and Jacked-Up Fruity Appetizers (page 183).

 Water-sautéing is an alternative to pan frying. Simply heat a pan on high heat for several minutes, long enough that a few tablespoons of water added to the pan form balls and roll around before evaporating. Add your ingredients and keep adding tiny amounts of water to the pan to prevent sticking as the dish cooks. I prefer Better Than Bouillon as my vegetable base paste for its rich flavor and ease of use.

SERVES 4

sweet potato hash

MICAELA KARLSEN

This is a delicious, baked variation on traditional hash. The sweetness makes the perfect complement to Savory Tofu Scramble at Sunday brunch, but the addition of thyme makes the flavor more interesting. Purple Japanese yams can be used instead of the sweet potatoes, if you prefer a slightly drier texture. The hash is most enjoyable served warm, so if the rest of your meal isn't ready just open the oven after baking to cool the temperature and leave the hash inside until you're ready to serve it.

2 medium-large sweet potatoes, washed and the ends cut off
1 medium onion
½ teaspoon fresh thyme or a sprinkle of dried thyme
Salt and pepper

1. Preheat the oven to 425°F.
2. Shred the sweet potatoes and onion in a food processor or grate by hand.
3. Place the shredded vegetables in a large bowl and toss with ¼ cup water, thyme, and salt and pepper to taste.
4. Line a large baking sheet with parchment paper. Spread the hash mixture thinly on the covered sheet and bake in the oven until slightly browned and crispy on top, about 30 to 35 minutes. At 15 minutes and 25 minutes, remove from oven and turn/stir the hash to ensure even cooking.

SERVES 4 TO 6

159

the best waffle you'll ever have

MARK KARLSEN

I have to say, I feel pretty lucky to be married to a Cook. My job is usually that of "Executive Taster," but I've always been good at one thing—pancakes. And when we received a Belgian waffle iron from Micaela's aunt as a wedding gift I decided to branch out. Every gluten-free waffle I've ever eaten in a restaurant has given me the impression of potato-flavored rubber, so I spent many days and nights experimenting and, finally, I think I've got it—the last waffle you'll ever have! Moist on the inside but with a crispy outside and a melt-in-your-mouth sensation, they're not only completely delicious, they're also as "whole food" as a waffle can be.

1½ cups oat flour

½ cup chickpea flour

½ cup hazelnut meal

½ cup cornmeal

1 tablespoon ground flaxseed

1 tablespoon baking powder

¼ to ½ teaspoon salt

2 teaspoons vanilla

2¼ cups soy milk or other plant milk

2 tablespoons maple syrup

1. Mix dry ingredients in a medium bowl.
2. Mix wet ingredients plus 3 tablespoons water in a separate medium bowl.
3. Add the dry ingredients to the wet mixture and whisk to stir, but don't overmix.
4. Cook the batter in your waffle iron according to instructions.

You can create your own oat flour (as well as your own nut meal) in a high-powdered blender. However, if you make your own nut meal, be sure to mix the nuts with the flour prior to grinding them; otherwise, you will get nut butter.

MAKES 4 8-INCH WAFFLES

ONGOING SUCCESS

breakfast sunshine salad

JULIEANNA HEVER, MS, RD, CPT

Yes, salad for breakfast! Bring fresh to your morning with this crunchy and simple dish, infused with sweetness and zest. You can throw this salad together in five minutes, and it is a great way to start your day with all of those fruits and veggies. This would also make a great dessert.

3 to 4 medium carrots, shredded
½ cup raisins or currants
2 tablespoons unsweetened shredded coconut
1 banana, cut into disks
1 orange, halved

1. In a medium bowl, combine the carrots, raisins, coconut, and banana. Squeeze the juice from half of the orange over the salad, and stir to combine.
2. Peel the remaining orange half, then chop it up into small pieces and add to the salad. Serve immediately or store in an airtight container in the refrigerator for 2 to 3 days.

SERVES 2 TO 4

breakfast rice pudding

JULIEANNA HEVER, MS, RD, CPT

Knowing this cozy and enticing pudding is on the menu, you'll love waking up on a cold day. The cinnamon undertones are warming, while the crunch of the smooth almonds balanced with the chewiness of the raisins makes this dish hearty.

2 cups cooked brown rice
1 cup raisins
½ cup slivered raw almonds
¼ cup maple syrup
1 tablespoon vanilla extract
1 tablespoon ground cinnamon
3 cups unsweetened soy milk

1. Combine all ingredients in a medium saucepan, and cook over medium heat.
2. Bring mixture to a boil, and reduce heat to low. Simmer over low heat, stirring occasionally, for 20 minutes or until pudding thickens.
3. Serve hot, or refrigerate to serve chilled.

 This is the perfect dish to use up your leftover rice. Or in a pinch, microwave single-ingredient ready-cooked brown rice packets to use instead.

MAKES 6 CUPS

162

florentine frittata

MICAELA KARLSEN

Why use eggs or even tofu? This easy chickpea-and-quinoa frittata started out as an attempted omelet recipe with the goal of using canned beans instead of chickpea flour, but the consistency is much better suited to making a frittata. You can use leftover cooked rice (a more traditional frittata choice) instead of quinoa, but the quinoa cooks quickly inside the batter, making it exceptionally well suited for times when you haven't planned ahead. Plus, you can make this dish your own by using any of your favorite veggies. Serve with Jacked-Up Fruity Appetizers and the Best Waffle You'll Ever Have for a luxurious Sunday brunch.

1 cup frozen leaf spinach, thawed and finely chopped

2 15-ounce cans chickpeas, undrained

2 tablespoons ground flaxseed or chia seed

2 teaspoons vegetable base paste

1 teaspoon white miso paste

¾ cup uncooked quinoa

2 garlic cloves, minced

1 medium onion, finely chopped

½ large red bell pepper, finely chopped

2 medium tomatoes, thinly sliced

1. Preheat the oven to 375°F.
2. Allow the frozen spinach to thaw while preparing the other ingredients.
3. In a blender or in a medium bowl with an immersion blender, blend the chickpeas, flaxseed, vegetable base paste, and miso paste on high speed until smooth.
4. In a large bowl, combine the quinoa (or leftover rice, if you prefer), garlic, onion, bell pepper, and chopped spinach. Pour the chickpea mixture into the quinoa mixture, and stir until evenly distributed.
5. Pour the mixture into a 9×13–inch glass pan. Arrange the tomato slices evenly over the top to cover. Bake for 55 minutes or until lightly browned on top. Cool for 10 to 20 minutes or until the frittata is set before serving.

 If you bake this in a glass dish, there is no need to oil the pan to prevent sticking.

SERVES 6 TO 8

SNACKS

speedy spinach-artichoke dip with snack stick buffet

MICAELA KARLSEN

The majority of the difficulty in eating cut vegetables as a snack is taking the time in the moment to wash them, cut them, and organize them into cute little compartments. But how many times have you said to yourself at a party with veggie hors d'oeuvres, "Oh, no, I just couldn't take time to put those carrot sticks on my napkin . . ."? Make every day a party in your refrigerator and cut up your veggies ahead of time! All cut vegetables pair nicely with this great, no-cook variation on oven-baked artichoke dip. It's a great snack option for kids, too, since they love to eat food with their hands; just keep veggie dippers in a tray at their level for easy access.

1 15-ounce can cannellini beans or other white beans
1 tablespoon fresh lemon juice
3 to 4 tablespoons frozen spinach
½ cup frozen artichoke hearts
3 dates, pitted
3 tablespoons nutritional yeast
1 teaspoon white miso paste
selection of vegetables

1. Place the beans, lemon juice, spinach, artichokes, dates, nutritional yeast, and miso paste in a blender. Blend on medium speed for 10 to 15 seconds or until mixture reaches desired creaminess. Refrigerate and/or freeze some dip for later.

2. Serve with your choice of veggies, such as finger-length sticks of carrots, celery, bell peppers, and zucchini, cucumber slices, or radishes.

 Frozen spinach often comes in one big piece in the bag. Use a cutting board and knife to remove tablespoon-sized pieces. And yes, you can pop them into the blender frozen. Ditto the artichoke hearts.

MAKES 16 (3-TABLESPOON) SERVINGS

167

teatime cornmeal muffins

MICAELA KARLSEN

Grab these low-fat, staple snack foods on the way out the door, or sit down at the table and eat them toasted with a cup of tea. Best of all is right out of the oven. This recipe is delicious with spelt flour, but feel free to substitute with a gluten-free flour mix, such as Bob's Red Mill gluten-free all-purpose baking flour. Serve them with sweet or savory accompaniments—a honey or apple butter pairing makes a sweet snack for afternoon tea, while serving with The Best Bean Chili forms a hearty dinner.

1½ cups finely ground cornmeal

1¼ cups whole spelt or other whole-grain flour

2 tablespoons baking powder

¼ teaspoon salt

1½ cups almond milk or soy milk

½ cup applesauce

⅓ cup maple syrup

1. Preheat the oven to 375°F and prepare a 16-cup muffin tray with non-stick muffin cups.
2. In a large bowl, stir together the cornmeal, spelt, baking powder, and salt.
3. Stir together the almond milk, applesauce, and maple syrup.
4. Make a well in the center of the cornmeal mixture and add the wet ingredients to the well. Stir until the dry ingredients are just moistened; do not overmix.
5. Spoon the batter into the prepared cups, filling two-thirds of each cup. Bake 22 to 26 minutes or until the tops are just browned.
6. Cool in the pan on a wire rack for 10 minutes before removing the muffins.

MAKES 16 MUFFINS

oatmeal bars

KATHY POLLARD

If I have oatmeal bars on hand, they are what the whole family will grab—even the teenagers! These bars can be a filling and satisfying portable breakfast or a perfect snack to stash at the office. They also freeze well. My friend Lesley makes batches of these all the time and pops them in the freezer. Then each morning she takes out a bar for her late-day snack at work. This recipe has saved many people from afternoon chocolate.

3 cups thick rolled oats (not quick or instant)

½ cup whole wheat or spelt flour

2 teaspoons baking powder

1 tablespoon egg replacer (optional)

1 teaspoon cinnamon

¼ teaspoon salt (optional)

½ cup applesauce

1 teaspoon vanilla

1 cup soy milk or other plant milk

¼ cup maple syrup or dates, pitted and soaked

⅓ cup raisins

SUGGESTED TOPPINGS

⅓ cup dried cranberries or dried fruit

⅓ cup walnuts

½ cup chopped apple

⅓ cup peanut butter

⅓ cup dried, shredded coconut

1. Preheat the oven to 350°F.

2. In a large bowl, mix oats, flour, baking powder, egg replacer (if desired), cinnamon, and salt (if desired). Add maple syrup, applesauce, vanilla, soy milk, raisins, and any additional optional ingredients desired, and mix just until uniform.

3. Spread out in a 9×13–inch pan. (Glass works well, as it tends not to stick.)

4. Bake 25 to 35 minutes, until a toothpick comes up clean.

5. Cool and cut into rectangles.

I always have a box of Ener-G egg replacer in my pantry.

MAKES 16 BARS

carrot cake smoothie

AL DAVIS

Micaela invited me to share this recipe after she tried it at a potluck in Boston, which is no surprise as it has always been a favorite among my potlucking circle. Everyone who tries it says something along the lines of, "Wow, that really does taste like carrot cake!"

1 cup almond milk

4 to 5 carrots, peeled and cut into 1½-inch chunks

½ frozen banana, cut into 1-inch pieces

1 heaping tablespoon walnuts

1 tablespoon raw agave, or to taste

2 to 3 cloves, or ⅛ rounded teaspoon clove powder

⅛ rounded teaspoon ginger

⅛ rounded teaspoon cardamom

⅛ rounded teaspoon freshly ground nutmeg

1. If you have a high-powered blender, put everything into it and blend until smooth. If you have a lower-grade blender, soak the walnuts in water for a few hours, use powdered cloves, and grate the carrots prior to blending the ingredients; this will ensure that everything blends properly and no chunks remain. You may need to blend for several minutes more than for a fruit smoothie.

2. Add small amounts of water until it reaches the desired consistency.

MAKES 2 TO 4 CUPS

unlimited baked corn chips

MICAELA KARLSEN

One of the more frustrating aspects of grocery shopping is that you really can't find crunchy chips that are free of added fat and salt. Even the "baked" chips are made with a lot of oil and salt. Fortunately, it is easy to make your own healthy and tasty baked corn chips, and they are an extremely satisfying vessel for all kinds of delicious dips and spreads. The crunch is what's most important. The great thing about baked corn chips is that if you eat them all, there's no need to stop—you can simply bake some more and keep going.

1 package small soft corn tortillas

1. Preheat the oven to 350°F.
2. Cut each tortilla symmetrically into 6 or 8 triangular pieces.
3. Arrange pieces on a metal cooling rack so they are not touching and bake for 12 to 15 minutes or until the chips are stiff and just starting to brown.
4. Serve with Use-Me-All-the-Time Hummus (page 231), salsa, or guacamole, or use as a garnish for soups and stews.

 A cooling rack is useful because the mesh permits hot air in the oven to circulate, allowing the chips to brown evenly. You can also use a baking sheet covered with parchment paper. The chips just may need another minute or two in the oven, and you may want to turn them halfway through.

MAKES 48 OR 64 CHIPS

pumpkin-oatmeal-raisin-carrot cookies (aka porccs)

NATALIE HUNTER

For Christmas one year my mother-in-law gave me a 50-pound bag of rolled oats, and coming up with ways to use such a versatile ingredient was both fun and delicious. These "cookies" are tasty treats for anytime—breakfast on the go, an afternoon snack, or with banana ice cream for a healthy dessert. After my husband cut his finger carving a pumpkin, he ate lots of these cookies while his wound was healing. However, we now use canned pumpkin to avoid any cuts!

1 tablespoon ground flaxseed

2 very ripe bananas, mashed

1 15-ounce can pumpkin

1 teaspoon molasses

1 teaspoon cinnamon

3 cups rolled oats

1 carrot, shredded

1 cup raisins

1. Preheat the oven to 350°F.

2. In a small bowl, let flaxseed sit in 3 tablespoons water.

3. In a large bowl, mix mashed bananas, pumpkin, molasses, and cinnamon until well combined.

4. Add the flaxseed mixture, oats, shredded carrot, and raisins and mix with the banana mixture until it comes together as a ball of dough.

5. Form dough into cookies and bake on a baking stone or nonstick cookie sheet for 18 to 20 minutes. When done, cool on a wire rack.

6. Enjoy a hot pumpkin cookie (or two) with a glass of cold almond milk!

MAKES ABOUT 30 2-INCH COOKIES

fresh fruit snacks

MICAELA KARLSEN

All the interesting and flavorful dishes out there can sometimes make us forget that the simplest foods are the most important. I often take four or more pieces of fruit with me in the morning to eat throughout the day, and I'm always happy I did. This "recipe" is, in fact, a schedule for fruit snacking. I find these simple reminders often help me stay on track. Keep eating fruit!

SUGGESTED SELECTIONS
- 1 apple
- 1 pear
- 1 banana
- 1 peach
- 1 cup berries
- 1 cup pineapple chunks
- 1 cup melon chunks
- 1 cup mango slices

1. Pack four pieces of fruit before you leave home in the morning. If space or weight is an issue, it is okay to use some dried fruit, if you avoid added sugar. Better than dried fruit, however, is stopping by a corner store or cafeteria and loading up on fresh fruit just before you get to the office—and definitely before you get hungry.
2. Schedule your fruit eating for times during the day when you know you hit a lull in your energy or ability to concentrate, or for times when you tend to think about going to a vending machine, office candy dispenser, or deli. The times I suggest are: 10:30 A.M., 2:30 P.M., 4:00 P.M., and 5:30 P.M.
3. Enjoy your freshly replenished energy!

MAKES 4 HEALTHY SNACKS

APPETIZERS

oyster mushroom ceviche and bitter orange-lime sauce

MATTHEW KENNEY

The chewy oyster mushrooms are treated in the same way that a traditional ceviche recipe for marinating fish or shellfish does—"cooking" with the acidic component of citrus fruit while absorbing the flavors it sits with. I love marinated oyster mushrooms and find their flavor more pleasant than raw shiitake, which sometimes have a musty taste I don't care for.

¼ cup red onion, finely chopped

½ cup fresh plum tomatoes, peeled, seeded, and diced

½ medium habanero chili, seeds and ribs removed, finely chopped

¾ cup freshly squeezed orange juice, strained

¼ cup freshly squeezed lime juice, strained

Pinch salt

2 cups oyster mushrooms, torn into thirds lengthwise

1 large avocado, peeled and cut into medium chunks

4 orange wedges

4 lime wedges

Cilantro leaves, chopped

1. In a bowl, mix the onion, tomatoes, habanero chili, orange juice, lime juice, and salt. Add the oyster mushrooms and mix.

2. Cover very tightly with plastic wrap and refrigerate 2 hours.

3. Add the avocado and mix carefully so it doesn't fall apart.

4. Serve in medium-size martini glasses garnished with an orange wedge, lime wedge, and chopped cilantro.

SERVES 4

177

cape cod delights

CRAIG COCHRAN | TERRI

This is my favorite recipe for parties. These mushrooms are awesome ambassadors of vegan cooking. The hearts of palm make a very good crab substitute because of their shredded texture, and the richness of the cashew cream will satisfy any omnivore. Our fish-less filet at Terri is based on this recipe, and none of the customers can believe it's housemade.

1 cup Cashew Cream (page 226)

1 15-ounce can hearts of palm, finely chopped lengthwise

1 pinch cayenne

¼ teaspoon thyme

1 teaspoon Old Bay seasoning

25 cremini (baby bella) mushrooms, stems removed

2 tablespoons tamari to sprinkle on mushrooms (optional)

1. Preheat the oven to 350°F.
2. Mix the Cashew Cream, hearts of palm, cayenne, thyme, and Old Bay seasoning. If desired, sprinkle each mushroom with a few drops of tamari.
3. Stuff each mushroom with about 1 tablespoon of the mixture.
4. Bake for about 20 minutes. Serve warm or cool.

MAKES 25

tasty corn cakes

KATHY POLLARD

These savory cakes are filling as well as versatile—serve them plain for a traditional American side dish or top them with salsa for a Mexican flavor or with dill dressing for a Southwestern ranch style. This recipe is such a simple kid-pleaser that it became a regular in my home. The key to gently frying these cakes without oil is a nonstick skillet, a lower heat than you would typically use for pancakes, and a bit of patience. I use a ceramic-coated skillet.

1 cup cornmeal
2½ teaspoons baking powder
1 cup unsweetened soy milk or other plant milk
1 tablespoon miso or soy sauce
8 ounces firm tofu, drained and crumbled
⅓ cup red bell pepper, chopped
½ cup frozen corn kernels
1 green onion, chopped
Salsa (optional)

1. Place cornmeal, baking powder, soy milk, and miso in a large bowl, and mix well.
2. Add tofu, pepper, corn, and green onion gently, and gently fold until fully mixed. Do not overstir.
3. Warm a nonstick skillet to medium heat.
4. For each corn cake, drop ¼ cup batter onto the skillet.
5. Cook until browned on the bottom, 2 or 3 minutes. Lower heat to medium-low if cakes are turning dark brown before getting bubbly and solidifying.
6. When solid, flip each cake to the other side and cook until brown on the bottom.
7. Serve with salsa or your favorite topping.

MAKES ABOUT 8 3-INCH CAKES

179

summer rolls with red chili–pineapple dipping sauce

MATTHEW KENNEY

When entertaining, it is always most practical to make use of foods that are easily handled and not in danger of becoming wet or sticky. Dipping sauces are very useful, as they allow guests to apply them only when they are ready to taste, and it creates an interactive experience that adds to the pleasure of eating. I first fell in love with summer rolls at a French Vietnamese restaurant, Le Colonial, in New York City. Although summer rolls are traditionally made with rice paper, I actually prefer the use of collard greens, which add flavor.

DIPPING SAUCE:
- 2 cups fresh pineapple juice
- 1 tablespoon lime juice
- ¼ cup raw agave
- 1 teaspoon red pepper flakes
- ½ teaspoon paprika

DRESSING:
- 1 cup almond butter
- 2 Roma or plum tomatoes
- ¼ cup nama shoyu
- 3 tablespoons freshly squeezed lime juice
- 2 tablespoons maple syrup
- 1 teaspoon miso
- 1 1½–inch piece ginger
- 1 ½–inch piece lemongrass
- 3 to 4 Thai chilies
- ½ teaspoon salt

SUMMER ROLLS:

½ cup macadamia nuts, chopped

8 collard leaves, cut in half with rib removed

2 cups carrots, julienned in 3-inch strips

2 cups cucumbers, julienned in 3-inch strips

2 medium zucchini, julienned in 3-inch strips

2 cups young coconut, mango, or papaya, julienned in 3-inch strips

2 red or yellow bell peppers, julienned in 3-inch strips

2 tablespoons black sesame seeds

1. **Make the dipping sauce a day ahead:** Place the pineapple juice, lime juice, agave, red pepper flakes, and paprika in a bowl, and stir vigorously. Place bowl in a dehydrator to reduce overnight.

2. **Make the dressing:** Blend the almond butter, tomatoes, nama shoyu, lime juice, maple syrup, miso, ginger, lemongrass, chilies, and salt in a high-powered blender and whip until completely smooth, adding water as necessary to create a very thick dressing.

3. **Assemble the summer rolls:** Mix macadamia nuts with enough dressing to hold them together.

4. Place nut-dressing mixture on a collard leaf half, and top with a few of each julienned item and black sesame seeds. Roll tightly. If needed, use a dab of dressing to hold the edge of the leaf in place.

5. Serve rolls with dipping sauce.

MAKES 16

181

cowboy caviar

SUSAN BENIGAS

During the summer, this is a staple around our household. The recipe involves lots of chopping, but it's worth it! When I'm asked to bring an appetizer to a friend's home, this often fills the bill. I pair it with homemade, no-oil corn chips, and, without fail, someone requests the recipe. For added kick, just add a little more hot sauce! We'll often make a pot of quinoa, using half vegetable broth and half water. When the quinoa is cool, I mix equal parts quinoa and Cowboy Caviar, and it makes a perfect main course.

2 15-ounce cans black-eyed peas, rinsed and drained

1 15-ounce can black beans, rinsed and drained

½ to ¾ cup canned shoepeg corn (or sweet corn), rinsed and drained

⅓ to ½ cup fat-free zesty, homemade Italian salad dressing (try Classic Italian Dressing, pg 234)

⅓ cup fresh cilantro, chopped

2 garlic cloves, pressed

6 to 7 drops hot sauce, or to taste

1 large red bell pepper, seeded and chopped

1 large green bell pepper, seeded and chopped

1 large jalapeño pepper, seeded and chopped

6 scallions, finely chopped

salt and ground pepper to taste

Juice of 1 lime

1 14-ounce can diced tomatoes or three finely chopped Roma tomatoes (optional)

1 firm avocado, chopped (optional)

1. Mix all ingredients together and refrigerate for several hours to allow flavors to meld.

2. Serve with Unlimited Baked Corn Chips (page 171), and enjoy!

For the black beans, I like the S&W brand because the beans are smaller.

MAKES ABOUT 10 TO 12 CUPS

182

jacked-up fruity appetizers

ROBBY BARBARO (AKA MINDFUL DIABETIC ROBBY)

This dish can be a great appetizer for a crowd or a satisfying meal for one. It features jackfruit, which is the largest tree-borne fruit on the planet. The fruits themselves can actually be up to 100 pounds, but the ones you'll typically find at your local Asian market will be closer to around 15 pounds. The famous gum, Juicy Fruit, mimicked its flavor after this unique fruit. On the inside, you will find pods. The fleshy part on the outside of the pod is sweet and juicy; it can be eaten raw. The seeds on the inside can be cooked. Jackfruit is awesome with other tropic fruits, such as dragon fruit, lychee, mangoes, rambutan, or even just bananas. Personally, I eat a large platter of these delicious fruits all in one sitting!

½ jackfruit (about 15 to 25 pods)
2 bananas, cut into ½-inch slices
1 mango, peeled, pitted, and cut into 1-inch cubes

1. Remove the seeds from each jackfruit pod.
2. Arrange all fruit artistically on a platter, spearing pairs of fruits with a toothpick.
3. Serve to guests and watch everyone ooh and aah!

 Purchase a jackfruit that is already cut in half to ensure that it is ripe and ready to be eaten.

SERVES 1 AS A MEAL OR UP TO 25 AS AN APPETIZER

almond-crusted tempeh fingers

NATALIE HUNTER

My husband claims he hates tempeh, but he absolutely loves it like this! Dipped in healthy Homemade Ketchup, these almond-crusted bites are a fun finger food for the whole family. Tempeh fingers are my go-to recipe if children are coming over for dinner. Tempeh is made by fermenting whole soybeans, which makes the nutrients more readily digestible. I personally love tempeh and can eat it plain anytime, but this almond coating brings tempeh to an entirely new level.

- 1 8-ounce package tempeh
- 1 cup low-sodium vegetable broth
- 1 tablespoon balsamic vinegar
- 1 teaspoon soy sauce
- 4 garlic cloves, minced
- ½ cup raw almonds, whole or in pieces
- ½ cup nutritional yeast
- ½ teaspoon chili powder
- ¼ teaspoon onion powder

1. **Prepare the tempeh:** In a small sauce pan, simmer the tempeh in 1 cup of water for 10 minutes.
2. Drain the tempeh well, then cut it in the short direction into ½-inch strips.
3. **Make the marinade:** In a small bowl, mix the vegetable broth, balsamic vinegar, soy sauce, and garlic together.
4. Place the tempeh in a shallow bowl or pan and cover with the marinade. Refrigerate for at least one hour.
5. Preheat the oven to 400°F.
6. **Prep the coating:** In a high-powered blender, grind the almonds briefly into a course meal, but don't overgrind or you'll get almond butter. In a shallow bowl, combine the almond meal, nutritional yeast, chili powder, and onion powder.
7. Remove tempeh strips from marinade and roll in almond mixture to coat.
8. Bake tempeh strips in the oven for 30 minutes.
9. Serve hot with Homemade Ketchup (page 224).

 If you have extra coating, mix in some marinade to make it into a wet cake. Bake it in the oven until dry for a tasty treat.

MAKES 16

ONGOING SUCCESS

collard wraps

MICAELA KARLSEN

Collard greens are so large and lovely, and in this dish they make the perfect substitute for tortillas. The trick is to use two leaves per roll, one on top of the other perpendicularly so that the slits where the stems were removed cross each other. When collard greens are cooked they are surprisingly strong as wraps given how tender they are. Using collards instead of tortillas gives me the luxurious feeling of the summer garden harvest. You can use these leaves to wrap a variety of foods—turning them into an appetizer, snack, or side dish for dinner.

6 to 8 collard leaves

1. Prepare the collard leaves by cutting out the thickest part of the stem. You will be left with a large leaf in a V-shape.
2. Fill a large pot with about 1 inch of water. Bring the water to a roiling boil.
3. Cook collard leaves 2 at a time for approximately 2 to 3 minutes, or until they are tender but still bright green. You may need to use a cooking utensil to hold them under the surface of the water.
4. Lay one leaf on top of the other perpendicularly, so that the cut-out sliver where the stem was in each leaf is covered by the other leaf.
5. Add your desired filling, such as Use-Me-All-the-Time Hummus (page 231) or Favorite Sandwich Spread (page 228), roll, and enjoy.

MAKES 3 OR 4 WRAPS

pesto-stuffed mushrooms

KATHY POLLARD

After making this recipe, you will find that there is no need for oil in pesto and will appreciate this lighter, flavorful version. The pesto is a beautiful green and looks so elegant placed atop the mushrooms!

2 8-ounce boxes mushrooms of your choice, stems removed

1 14-ounce can artichoke hearts in water, drained

1 generous bunch basil leaves

1 garlic clove

1½ tablespoons miso

1 15-ounce can white beans (cannellini or great northern), drained

½ cup loosely packed fresh spinach leaves (optional)

1. Preheat the oven to 325°F.
2. Bake mushrooms on a baking sheet covered with parchment paper for 15 minutes.
3. Blend artichoke hearts, basil, garlic, miso, white beans, and spinach in a food processor until smooth.
4. Place baked mushrooms on a plate, cap down, and fill each with a dollop of pesto. Serve as is, or warm under the broiler for 3 minutes prior to serving.

 For a richer texture, substitute ½ cup walnuts or pine nuts for the white beans.

MAKES 30 TO 40

sweet blintzes

MICAELA KARLSEN

One of my fondest childhood memories is visiting my cousins' family party every summer. I loved connecting with relatives I didn't see very often, and the cheese blintzes that were always served were out of this world! On more than one occasion my cousin and I strategically lurked around the kitchen door waiting for them to be brought out. This recipe re-creates two possibilities for the filling—a more traditional cream-cheesy option that uses cashews, as well as a squash filling that is perfect for autumn.

TRADITIONAL FILLING:
- 1½ cups Cashew Cream (page 226)
- ½ cup firm tofu
- ½ teaspoon cinnamon
- 1 teaspoon vanilla
- Juice of ½ lemon
- ¼ cup maple syrup

SQUASH FILLING:
- 1 large or 2 small delicata squash, cut in half with seeds, center, and ends removed
- ½ cup raw cashews
- ½ teaspoon cinnamon
- 6 to 8 dates, pitted
- 1 tablespoon nutritional yeast

CREPES:
- 1 cup spelt or other whole-grain flour
- ¼ teaspoon salt or to taste
- 1 tablespoon ground flaxseed
- 1 tablespoon arrowroot powder
- ¼ cup beer or hard cider

TOPPING:
- 2 tablespoons maple syrup

187

recipe continues

1. **Make the traditional filling:** Combine the Cashew Cream, tofu, cinnamon, vanilla, lemon juice, and maple syrup in a blender and whip until smooth.

2. **Make the squash filling:** Preheat the oven to 450°F. Chop the delicata squash into 1-inch half rounds and place in a glass pan with ½ cup water. Cover the pan with aluminum foil and bake for 25 to 30 minutes, until soft. After removing the squash, turn down the oven to 400°F. While the squash is baking, soak cashews in water to soften. (If you have a high-powered blender, it is not necessary to soak the cashews.) Once the squash is cooked, put it in a blender along with the cashews, cinnamon, dates, and nutritional yeast, and whip until smooth. Add 1 to 2 tablespoons water, as needed, to create a creamy consistency.

3. **Make the crepes:** Follow steps 1 to 5 for Buckwheat Crepes with Chocolate on page 284, making sure to substitute spelt or other whole-grain flour for buckwheat.

4. **Assemble and bake the blintzes:** Spread about ¼ cup filling on each crepe, covering three-quarters of the crepe. Roll up each crepe and place the rolls next to each other in a 9×13–inch pan. Drizzle maple syrup over the top of the blintzes. Bake for 20 minutes uncovered.

5. To serve, slice each roll into six pieces and spear with a toothpick.

 Each filling option should yield about 2 cups, though the squash filling is more variable, depending on the size of your squash.

MAKES 48 BITES

188

SOUPS

corn chowder

CRAIG COCHRAN | TERRI

This soup is creamy, savory, and sweet from the corn. In fact, it's the best version of corn chowder I've ever had. I've actually eaten it many times for breakfast, as well as in the afternoon and evening. I don't think it's possible to get tired of this one.

3 cups Spanish or yellow onion, diced

2 cups carrots, diced

2 cups celery, diced

1 cup red pepper, diced

2 cups Yukon potatoes, diced

⅛ teaspoon dried thyme

1 quart corn, fresh or frozen and thawed

1 cup Cashew Cream (page 226)

⅛ teaspoon black pepper

salt to taste

1. Place the onion, carrots, and celery in a large pot with a ½ cup of water and cook on high heat until the onions turn golden or the celery turns bright green.
2. Add the remaining ingredients plus 6 cups water, bring to a boil, then simmer on medium-low heat for 25 minutes.

SERVES 6 TO 8

simple split pea comfort soup

MICAELA KARLSEN

Curl up on the sofa with a good book and a great split pea soup to stay warm. The world offers many delicious versions of split pea soup. This comfort soup is absolutely delicious as is. However, if you're feeling adventurous, you can use this as your basic starter recipe and branch out in any number of interesting directions. Soup doesn't get any simpler than this.

1 cup split peas
1 medium onion, diced
1 medium carrot, diced
1 medium celery rib, diced
1 medium potato, diced
1 tablespoon vegetable base paste
Salt and freshly ground black pepper to taste

1. Soak your split peas for 4 to 6 hours, or even longer, if possible, to ensure a shorter cooking time.
2. Drain the split peas, and place them in a large saucepan with 8 cups water. (Don't add salt.) Cook over high heat for 15 to 20 minutes or until boiling. Reduce heat to low and simmer, partially covered, for 20 minutes or until split peas are tender.
3. Add the onion, carrot, celery, potato, vegetable base paste, and salt and pepper. Turn heat to high and return to a boil. Reduce heat to low and simmer, partially covered, for 15 more minutes or until vegetables are tender. Serve with crackers and chopped fresh parsley, if desired.

 Split peas vary a lot in how long they take to cook. While the cooking time is somewhat unpredictable, it partly depends on whether you presoak the split peas and whether or not you have salt in the water when you cook them. If your water is salty, it will take longer. Rule of thumb: It should take no more than 2 hours to cook unsoaked peas and no more than 40 minutes to cook presoaked peas. Plus, it's definitely more efficient to cook the peas first, without any salt, and then, once they are cooked to your satisfaction, add everything else in the recipe.

SERVES 2 TO 4

classic borscht

KATHY POLLARD

This is my Baba Rose's recipe for borscht—a traditional Eastern European soup that is eaten chilled. The beets lend themselves to sweetness, and the deep red soup looks beautiful on any table!

SOUP:
- 3 to 4 beets, scrubbed clean, with leaves and tops cut off
- 1 medium onion, peeled and scored with an *X* on top
- 1 teaspoon rock or Kosher salt
- 2 to 3 tablespoons liquid sweetener (brown rice syrup, maple syrup, or date syrup)
- Juice of ½ to 1 lemon

"SOUR CREAM":
- Juice of ½ lemon
- 1 cup silken tofu
- 1 tablespoon vinegar
- ½ teaspoon nutritional yeast
- ½ teaspoon liquid sweetener (brown rice syrup, maple syrup, or date syrup)

1. Put the beets, onion, vegetable broth, and salt in a pot with 8 cups of water. The water should amply cover the beets, with about ½ inch to spare. Set the heat to high and bring to boil.
2. Reduce heat and simmer until beets are tender, about 1 hour. Cool to room temperature.
3. Remove beets with a slotted spoon. Pinch off the skins, grate the beets, and place them back into the pot.
4. Add liquid sweetener and lemon juice to the borscht to taste. Cool soup in fridge overnight.
5. **Make the "sour cream":** Place lemon juice, tofu, vinegar, nutritional yeast, and liquid sweetener in a food processor or blender and whip until smooth.
6. Serve chilled borscht with a dollop of "sour cream."

SERVES 4 TO 6

dr. lederman's black bean soup

MATT LEDERMAN, MD

One of the most rewarding aspects of medical practice is teaching patients to cook. This is because cooking actually empowers patients to take their health into their own hands. This easy recipe is a favorite among my patients as well as my family.

1 large onion, chopped
2 medium carrots, chopped
2 celery ribs, chopped
6 15-ounce cans black beans, rinsed and drained
1 pound frozen corn
4 15-ounce cans crushed tomatoes spiced with green chilies
2 banana peppers, chopped
1 jalapeño pepper, chopped
10 cups low-sodium vegetable broth or water (or adjust to desired thickness)
1 head kale, chopped
1 head collard greens, chopped
1 head Swiss chard, chopped
Salt and pepper to taste
½ to 1 cup of fresh cilantro

1. **Make the soup:** Add half of the onion, plus all of the carrots, celery, beans, corn, crushed tomatoes, banana peppers, jalapeño pepper, and 10 cups vegetable broth or water to a large pot. Cover, set heat to high, and bring to a boil. Reduce to low heat and simmer uncovered for 30 minutes.
2. Place the other half of the onion, plus the kale, collard greens, swiss chard, and salt and pepper as desired in a large pan and water-sauté for 10 minutes.
3. Place cooked greens and cilantro in a food processor or blender and whip until desired consistency is reached.
4. Add blended greens to soup and mix thoroughly.
5. Serve in a bowl and mix with crushed oil-free tortilla chips.

 This recipe makes a large pot of soup and freezes well, so plan to freeze lunch- or dinner-sized portions for another day.

SERVES 8 TO 10

potato-leek soup

KATHY POLLARD

This soup reminds me of Kermit the Frog for its color, and it's the soup that I make when I'm feeling a cold coming on. One bowl, followed by a good night's sleep, and I always wake up better. Plus, it's green! This is simply a lovely, creamy soup with the rich addition of nuttiness from sunflower seeds.

2 medium leeks

2 large potatoes of any kind, cut into bite-sized chunks

7 cups low-sodium vegetable broth

1½ teaspoons pepper

2 teaspoons lemon pepper (optional)

2 teaspoons dried dill, or 4 teaspoons fresh dill, or 1 teaspoon each of thyme, basil, and oregano

¼ cup sunflower seeds

1 cup soy milk

1. Wash leeks well, slicing through layers lengthwise and rinsing in between. Chop leeks into ½-inch slices.
2. Put leeks, potatoes, vegetable broth, pepper, lemon pepper (if desired), and herbs in a big pot, set to medium-high heat, and bring to a boil.
3. Once boiling, turn down to a simmer and cook, covered, until potatoes are soft, about 15 minutes.
4. In a blender or food processor, grind sunflower seeds and soy milk.
5. Add sunflower seed mixture to potato-leek soup slowly. Keep heat on low, and stir continuously to ensure that the soup doesn't boil. (If the soup does boil, the soy milk is likely to curdle, which isn't harmful but makes the soup less creamy and pretty.)
6. Use an immersion blender (or a hand blender) to pulverize the potato chunks in the pot to your liking—keeping it chunky or making it creamy.

SERVES 4 TO 6

gingery carrot soup

PRISCILLA TIMBERLAKE AND LEWIS FREEDMAN

The ginger and curry make this soup unforgettable, and the beautiful rusty orange is the perfect color for an autumn meal. When we have a good year with our garden, we love to make this with our own carrots.

1 large onion, diced

1 tablespoon fresh gingerroot, minced or grated

½ teaspoon dried ginger

½ teaspoon curry powder

10 medium carrots, peeled and cut into large chunks

2 tablespoons rice syrup (optional)

1 teaspoon sea salt

Pinch of black pepper

6 to 8 parsley sprigs

1. Place onions and 1 tablespoon of water in a medium pot and water-sauté for 2 minutes.

2. Add fresh gingerroot and dried spices. Water-sauté for about 4 minutes more, adding more water as needed to prevent sticking.

3. Add carrots, rice syrup (if desired), sea salt, black pepper, and 5 cups water. Set to medium-high heat, and bring to a boil.

4. Turn down heat to low, cover pot, and simmer. Cook until carrots are soft, about 20 minutes. Allow soup to cool.

5. Puree soup in a blender or food processer. Add more salt or rice syrup, to taste.

6. Serve soup hot or cold, as desired. Prior to serving, garnish each bowl with parsley.

SERVES 2 TO 4

lemon-rice-kale soup

KATHY POLLARD

I'm a fan of soups, and this is one of my favorites. The lemony flavor makes it light and satisfying at the same time. Plus, it's a great way to add kale to your diet.

1 small onion or 3 scallions, chopped

3 cups chopped kale

½ teaspoon garlic powder

⅛ teaspoon turmeric

⅛ teaspoon pepper

8⅓ cups low-sodium vegetable broth or water

3 cups cooked brown rice

½ cup nutritional yeast

1 tablespoon soy sauce

¼ cup lemon juice

1. In a large pot, water-sauté onion, kale, garlic powder, turmeric, and pepper in ⅓ cup broth or water for 15 minutes.
2. Add the remainder of the ingredients, set to medium-high heat, and bring to a boil, then reduce to medium-low heat and simmer for 5 minutes. Serve and enjoy.

SERVES 2 TO 4

farmshare miso soup

MAGGIE LOEB

As a member of my local Community Supported Agriculture (CSA) farm and an optician with long workdays, I often have an abundance of veggies about to turn. This recipe was inspired as a quick fix, but then it turned into a versatile way of cooking whatever goodies I need to save from the refrigerator. For a lighter soup, I sometimes simmer this very briefly at the end; if I'm going for a stew-like consistency, I cook the ingredients longer.

½ box (about 2 cups) campagnelle, or other short, whole-grain pasta
2 cups carrots, shredded
1 onion, chopped
2 cups celery, finely chopped
1 low-sodium vegetable boullion cube
1 15-ounce can lentils or 1¾ cups home-cooked lentils
2 garlic cloves, minced
1 head escarole, chopped
¼ cup mellow white miso
Salt and pepper to taste (optional)

1. Cook pasta according to the directions. Drain and set aside.
2. Steam carrots, onion, and celery until soft. Set aside.
3. In a large pot, bring 4 cups water to a boil. Once boiling, dissolve boullion cube.
4. Add steamed vegetables, lentils, and garlic to the dissolved boullion. Set heat to low and simmer for 30 minutes.
5. Add escarole and pasta and continue to simmer the soup until it reaches the desired thickness, about 10 to 20 minutes.
6. Dissolve miso in 1 cup of hot water and add to soup. Season with salt and pepper (if desired), and serve immediately or freeze for future use.

Can be used as a soup base for other vegetables, as desired.

SERVES 4 TO 6

ONGOING SUCCESS

romantic vegetable stew

KATHY POLLARD

This recipe melds together luscious flavors and scents, making it fancier than your average stew—and a fabulous choice for a romantic evening at home. The recipe itself feeds more than two, however, so if you make this for a date night, you can look forward to leftovers—and another romantic meal later in the week! Alternatively, if your household is larger than two, share the love and turn this delicious dish into a family dinner that will warm everyone's heart.

1 cup dried shiitake mushrooms, broken into bite-sized pieces

8 to 10 cups low-sodium vegetable broth or water

8 small red potatoes, chopped into 1-inch cubes

1 large onion, chopped

2 celery ribs, chopped

8 ounces cremini mushrooms, halved (and, if large, quartered as well)

2 large carrots, cut into bite-sized pieces

2 bay leaves

1 teaspoon thyme

1 teaspoon rosemary

½ teaspoon garlic powder

1 tablespoon poultry seasoning or unsalted seasoning powder

2 tablespoons soy sauce

Freshly ground pepper to taste

¼ cup millet, uncooked

¼ cup red wine (optional)

1 cup frozen peas

2 tablespoons cornstarch or arrowroot

¼ teaspoon salt, or to taste (optional)

1. Place dried shiitake mushrooms in a small pot with 1 to 2 cups water. Set heat to medium-high and bring to boil, then turn to medium-low and simmer for 10 minutes until mushrooms are reconstituted.

2. Add vegetable broth, red potatoes, onion, celery, creminis, carrots, bay leaves, thyme, rosemary, garlic powder, poultry seasoning, soy sauce, ground pepper, and millet to a 5-quart pot, and bring to a simmer over medium-low heat.

199

recipe continues

3. Add the red wine, if desired, and simmer uncovered for about 20 minutes, until the onions are cooked and the potatoes start to soften.

4. Continue to simmer until the millet is completely cooked and not hard, about 5 more minutes, then add the peas.

5. Dissolve cornstarch or arrowroot in ¼ cup cold water, and mix well. Stir the mixture into the stew and cook until it thickens slightly.

6. Taste and add more seasonings or salt, if desired.

 Mrs. Dash makes a variety of unsalted seasoning powders. The original blend works nicely for this recipe.

SERVES 5 TO 6

the *best* bean chili

SUSAN BENIGAS

Because I'm working almost every minute I'm awake, my go-to recipes are always fast and easy. It takes less than 20 minutes to combine the ingredients. Let them simmer, fill the air with a wonderful smell, and then . . . when done, enjoy! If you like it spicy, add a little extra cayenne and chili powder. This chili is amazing—a real crowd pleaser! We sometimes use it as a topper for baked sweet potatoes. I guarantee this recipe will become one of your winter favorites.

1 large green pepper, chopped

1 large sweet yellow onion, chopped

1 14.5-ounce can tomato sauce

1 6-ounce can tomato paste

2 garlic cloves, minced

1 tablespoon chili powder

¼ teaspoon cayenne pepper

1 teaspoon oregano

1 teaspoon ground cumin

1 teaspoon salt

½ teaspoon black pepper

1 15-ounce can pinto beans, rinsed and drained

1 15-ounce can chickpeas, rinsed and drained

1 15-ounce can black beans, rinsed and drained

1 15-ounce can kidney beans, rinsed and drained

1 15-ounce can yellow hominy, rinsed and drained

1. In a large pot, bring ⅓ cup water to a boil, and add green pepper and onion.

2. Water-sauté until onion is slightly translucent, about 5 minutes, adding tiny amounts of water to prevent sticking.

3. Add tomato sauce, tomato paste, 2 cups water, garlic, and all seasonings, and mix well.

4. Add all beans and hominy, mix well, and bring to a boil. Then reduce heat to low and simmer for 1½ to 2 hours.

201

recipe continues

5. Serve with guacamole or salsa and baked chips or whole-grain bread.

 Purchase an organic green pepper, if possible, since bell peppers are on the "Dirty Dozen." Also, when purchasing canned beans or veggies, read the labels. Ideally, select those that have no salt or those that are packed only in water and salt or sea salt; avoid beans and veggies with added chemicals, food colorings, and preservatives.

SERVES 6 TO 8

italian vegetable lentil soup

LAWRENCE MUSCAT | LIGHT ON THE HILL RETREAT CENTER

I consider cooking for those on retreat to be an important undertaking, as the food they eat affects their experience doing inner work on some level. This soup was developed by one of our members of the Board of Directors, and we have served it to many retreatants. The flavors are drawn from his Italian roots.

2¼ cups vegetable broth

3 onions, chopped

6 carrots, chopped

4 cups uncooked lentils

2 bay leaves

1½ teaspoons salt

Freshly ground black pepper to taste

2 to 3 teaspoons oregano

1 28-ounce can diced tomatoes

1. Place ¼ cup vegetable broth (or water, if preferred), onions, and carrots in a large pot and water-sauté over medium-high heat until the vegetables are soft, about 5 minutes. Remove with slotted spoon to a bowl.
2. Add remaining 2 cups vegetable broth plus 4 cups water to the pot, bring to a boil, and add lentils, bay leaves, salt, pepper, and oregano, and simmer for an additional 5 minutes.
3. Add sautéed onions, carrots, and diced tomatoes to the lentil mixture.
4. Simmer on low heat about 40 minutes or longer as needed to fully cook the lentils. Serve over rice with a salad or by itself with salad and thick-crusted bread.

SERVES 6 TO 8

203

SALADS AND SIDES

blackberry mango tango

ROBBY BARBARO (AKA MINDFUL DIABETIC ROBBY)

This is one of my favorite meals. It can serve many people as a side dish, but I actually eat this salad as a full meal on a regular basis. I have type 1 diabetes and have found that fueling my body with fruit not only makes me feel amazing but also increases my insulin sensitivity. The water and fiber in fruit impede my blood glucose levels from spiking and keep me energized all day. This salad is guaranteed to satisfy your natural sweet tooth. Plus, the dressing on this salad is da bomb! It hits the spot every time.

DRESSING:
  1 mango, peeled with pit removed
  2 cups spinach
  1 large heirloom tomato, cut in half
  2 scallions, chopped
  ginger to taste

SALAD:
  3 cups arugula
  1 cup romaine lettuce
  1 pint blackberries
  2 mangoes, peeled with pit removed and cut in 1-inch cubes
  3 large heirloom tomatoes, sliced

1. **Make the dressing:** Place mango, spinach, heirloom tomato, scallions, and ginger in a blender, and whip until smooth.
2. **Assemble the salad:** Place arugula, romaine lettuce, blackberries, chopped mango, and sliced tomatoes in a mixing bowl.
3. Pour the dressing on the salad and mix well. Enjoy!

SERVES 1 AS A MEAL, OR MAKES 6 TO 8 SIDE SALADS

207

colorful yams and greens

KATHY POLLARD

The colors in this simple recipe pop—and so do the flavors. You can even get the ingredients at Walmart. Say hello to quick, inexpensive, and nutritious!

3 medium yams or sweet potatoes, scrubbed and chopped into 2-inch cubes

2 tablespoons low-sodium soy sauce

2 tablespoons white wine

1 large onion, chopped

3 or more garlic cloves, chopped or crushed

1 red bell pepper, cored, seeded, and chopped

1 bunch hearty greens (like spinach, kale, collard greens, or swiss chard), thick stems removed and leaves cut into 1-inch strips

1. Steam the yams or sweet potatoes until just soft. Remove from heat.

2. In a large skillet, bring soy sauce and white wine to a simmer over medium-high heat. Add onions, garlic, red pepper, and greens and water-sauté until soft, about 10 minutes. Make sure there is enough liquid to keep vegetables from sticking. Add a splash of water if needed.

3. Turn off heat and add steamed yams or sweet potatoes to the sautéed vegetables. Mix gently.

4. Place greens in a large bowl, add potato-vegetable mixture, toss gently, and serve.

SERVES 4

potato salad with pine nuts, olives, and dill

DEL SROUFE

I like potato salad, but every now and then I like to change it up a little. In this recipe, pine nuts and olives add an unexpected Greek flair to this otherwise traditional American fare. Serve this on a bed of spinach and you have a good meal.

2 pounds red skin potatoes, cut into ½-inch cubes

1 cup Del's Basic Mayonnaise (page 227)

4 scallions, finely chopped

½ cup pine nuts, toasted

½ cup kalamata olives, pitted

¼ cup fresh dill, minced

Sea salt and black pepper to taste

1. Place the potatoes in a large pot and cover with 2 quarts of cold, salted water.
2. Bring the pot to a boil over medium-high heat. Reduce heat to medium-low and cook until the potatoes are tender, about 8 to 10 minutes.
3. Drain potatoes in a colander. Rinse under cold water until cool and drain again.
4. Put potatoes in a large bowl, add remaining ingredients, and mix well.
5. Chill until ready to serve.

SERVES 4 TO 6

209

summer strawberry salad

MICAELA KARLSEN

Why limit salad to the afternoon? This salad is so delectable I've eaten it for breakfast, as Julieanna does with her Breakfast Sunshine Salad! It can be thrown together like any salad with big leafy greens, but sometimes it's nice to cut the lettuce into smaller pieces; this makes the texture more consistent, and can be a refreshing change from those giant bites of lettuce. I never get tired of this one.

1 bunch red leaf lettuce
1 pint strawberries, hulled and sliced
2 tablespoons pecans or walnuts, toasted and chopped
¼ medium red onion, sliced thinly
Raspberry Vinaigrette (page 232)

1. Chop the lettuce into smaller, bite-sized pieces, about the size of a cut strawberry.
2. Toss the lettuce in a large bowl with the strawberries, nuts, and onions.
3. Add Raspberry Vinaigrette to taste. Serve immediately and refrigerate the remainder to save for later.

SERVES 1 TO 2

tu-no salad

CATHY FISHER

Garbanzo beans, also known as chickpeas, are an ideal substitute for canned tuna when it comes to creating a health-promoting version of tuna salad. This salad can be served by itself, on top of a green or spinach salad, in romaine or endive leaves, or in steamed corn tortillas.

DRESSING:
- ½ cup unsalted cashews
- 3 tablespoons lemon juice
- 2 teaspoons apple cider or brown rice vinegar
- 2 tablespoons Dijon or stone ground mustard
- 1 garlic clove, finely chopped
- 2 teaspoons kelp powder or granules (optional)

SALAD:
- 2 15-ounce cans garbanzo beans, drained and rinsed
- 3 celery ribs, chopped
- ¼ cup red onion, finely chopped
- 20 fresh basil leaves, finely chopped
- 1 avocado, chopped (optional)

1. **To prepare the dressing:** Place cashews, lemon juice, vinegar, mustard, garlic, kelp(if desired), and ½ cup water in a blender, and set aside for at least 15 minutes (so the cashews can soften). When the cashews have softened, blend until smooth.

2. **To prepare the salad:** Place garbanzo beans in a food processor and pulse until the beans are just broken up and still flaky. Do not overblend. Transfer the beans to a large bowl and add the celery, red onion, basil, and avocado (if desired).

3. Add the dressing to the salad, and toss well. Serve as is or try serving suggestions mentioned above.

 If you use beans cooked from dry instead of canned, use about 3 cups. Adding kelp powder or granules lends a seafood flavor to this salad. You can find kelp powder in the bulk herb section of health food stores and kelp granules in the spice aisle.

211

SERVES 4 TO 6

zesty three-bean salad

CRAIG COCHRAN | TERRI

This is a variation of one of our top-selling sides at our restaurants in NYC. Feel free to play around with this by adding different beans or adjusting the hot sauce level to your liking. This is my go-to food when I don't have a lot of time to cook at home but I want something filling, nutritious, and tasty.

1 15-ounce can pinto beans, drained and rinsed

1 15-ounce can cannellini beans, drained and rinsed

1 15-ounce can chickpeas, drained and rinsed

½ cup thawed frozen peas

½ cup thawed frozen corn

⅓ large red onion, finely chopped (optional)

Pinch sea salt, or to taste

Black pepper to taste

1 tablespoon balsamic vinegar

2 tablespoons hot sauce

2 tablespoons raw agave or maple syrup

4 to 6 parsley sprigs (optional)

1. Add all ingredients to a large bowl, and stir to evenly distribute the vinegar, hot sauce, and syrup throughout the bean mixture.
2. Garnish with parsley (if desired), and serve as a side dish or main meal.

 There are so many great hot sauces. Personally, I like Frank's Redhot Original Cayenne Pepper Sauce for this recipe.

SERVES 4 TO 6

basket of jewels
with walnut sauce

KATHY POLLARD

Sometimes the simplest food is the nicest, and it's important to remember—especially in the midst of all these beautiful recipes—that a meal can be effortless and easy. This recipe is a reminder to us all to keep steaming vegetables and eating them every day.

BASKET OF JEWELS (select your favorites, as many as you like):

Carrots	Spinach
Brussels sprouts	Peas
Broccoli	Rutabaga
Cauliflower	Yams
Green beans	Potatos
Collard greens	Squash
Swiss chard	Snap Peas

WALNUT SAUCE:

½ cup walnuts

1 to 2 garlic cloves

2 to 4 tablespoons tamari, soy sauce, or miso

1 tablespoon nutritional yeast (optional)

2 to 3 tablespoons of fresh herbs of choice, (such as dill, parsley, chives, or cilantro (optional)

1. **Make the Basket of Jewels:** Prepare the selected vegetables by rinsing and cutting into bite-sized chunks. Place about 2 inches of water in a large pot or bottom of double boiler and bring to a simmer. In a steamer basket or in the top of a double boiler, add the hardest vegetables first, (potatoes, carrots, root vegetables), and steam for 10 minutes. Add the other vegetables (brussels sprouts, broccoli, collard greens, and so forth) to the steamer and steam about 5 minutes more, until the vegetables are soft and the greens are bright. Transfer all vegetables to a large serving bowl.

2. **Make the Walnut Sauce:** Place walnuts, garlic, tamari, and nutritional

213

recipe continues

yeast (if desired) in a blender. Add ½ cup warm water. Blend until smooth, adding additional water to achieve desired thickness.

3. Drizzle Walnut Sauce onto vegetables, add your favorite fresh herbs if desired, and serve.

SERVES 2 TO 4

colorful crudités

MICAELA KARLSEN

I have vivid memories of my friend Meghan and I learning to cook as adults, and we just couldn't stop eating blanched red cabbage and kale! Eventually we got a little tired of so much vigorous chewing and learned to cook with other techniques, so blanched red cabbage and kale moved to the back burner. Later, while I was living in France (and very homesick for both Ithaca, New York, and Meghan) I made some blanched vegetables and was surprised to hear Monique, the mother of my French host family, off-handedly mention that I had made crudités. With that encouragement, I ressurected the practice. Blanching is very brief cooking in boiling water. It doesn't make the vegetables very soft; it simply softens the cell walls a bit and releases the pigments enough to give them a brilliant color. Blanching is a great method to lend variety to serving raw, crunchy vegetables in salads.

Red cabbage (optional)
Kale (optional)
Broccoli (optional)
Cauliflower (optional)
Romanesco broccoli (optional)
Carrots, orange and purple (optional)
Radishes (optional)
Escarole (optional)

1. Wash and roughly chop the vegetables into pieces sized according to your preference.
2. Bring a medium pot of water to a boil. Add vegetables 1 to 2 cups at a time and boil for approximately 30 seconds to 1 minute, or until the color brightens. Remove vegetables from the water and transfer to a colander.
3. Run the vegetables under cold water to stop the cooking process and prevent the color from eventually turning brown.
4. Use crudités in salads or as the base for side dishes.

SERVING SIZE VARIES

RECIPES FOR EVERYONE

salade niçoise

MICAELA KARLSEN

This traditional French salad typically centers on anchovies and hard-boiled eggs. In this recipe, hearts of palm, potato, and avocado take center stage, but it still has certain classic elements, including the green beans, cucumber, tomatoes, and olives. I like to chop my greens to make them easier to eat and mix with the dressing.

1 20-ounce package mixed greens, chopped into small pieces

2 tablespoons capers

4 tablespoons Dijon or yellow mustard

5 tablespoons brown rice syrup or maple syrup

5 tablespoons red wine vinegar or apple cider vinegar

1 14-ounce jar hearts of palm, drained, rinsed, and sliced

1 cup green beans, steamed

½ medium cucumber, peeled and sliced

2 medium red potatoes, boiled and cut in 2-inch cubes

½ avocado, pitted and sliced

1 cup cherry tomatoes, sliced in half

1 14-ounce can artichoke hearts

¼ cup kalamata olives, pitted and sliced

3½ ounces smoked tofu (optional)

Salt and pepper to taste

1. In a large bowl, toss the mixed greens and capers with the mustard, rice syrup, and vinegar.
2. Arrange the rest of the ingredients on top of the bed of greens in sections. The final product is a beautiful plate of colors.
3. Salt and pepper to taste and enjoy.

SERVES 2 FOR DINNER, OR 6 TO 8 AS A SIDE SALAD

skinny red smashed potatoes

MICAELA KARLSEN

Mashed potatoes are one of my favorite comfort foods. They also really helped me transition away from cheese because they satisfied my cravings for something warm and soft in my mouth. This recipe is the perfect addition to any holiday or any weekday dinner. I love leaving the skins on because it adds texture, contrast, and more flavor. For maximum enjoyment, serve with Mushroom Gravy.

6 to 8 medium-large red potatoes, chopped in large pieces
1 cup plant milk (such as cashew milk, almond milk, oat milk, or soy milk)
2 tablespoons nutritional yeast
Salt and pepper to taste

1. Place the potatoes in a large pot and add enough water to cover them. Cover pot and bring to a boil. Uncover pot, and continue to boil for approximately 15 minutes or until the potatoes are soft enough to pierce with a fork. The smaller the potatoes are chopped, the more quickly they will cook.
2. Drain the potatoes and add the plant milk, nutritional yeast, and salt and pepper. Smash by hand with a potato masher. Serve with Mushroom Gravy (pg 223).

SERVES 4

217

flexible fennel salad

STACY BLONDIN

I eat some version of this salad nearly every day! It combines all the flavors and textures you could want into a single, delicious bowl personalized for your own enjoyment! I like to combine baby spring mix and romaine for the perfect combo of dark green and crunch. My favorite add-ins are quinoa, chickpeas, slivered almonds, and raisins, but I encourage you to mix and match until you find your own!

SALAD BASICS:

    5 to 8 ounces leafy greens of choice

    ½ to 1 cup fresh fennel, sliced or shaved

    3 tablespoons nutritional yeast flakes

    Balsamic vinegar to taste

SUGGESTED ADD-INS:

    ½ cup whole grain of choice (optional)

    ½ cup legume of choice (optional)

    ¼ cup nuts or seeds of choice, or 1/4 of an avocado (optional)

    1 tablespoon dried fruit of choice (optional)

1. Put the basic salad ingredients in a large bowl.

2. Sprinkle on your favorite add-ins and toss—simple as that!

SERVES 1 AS A MEAL, OR 2 TO 4 AS A SIDE SALAD

arame, red onion, and pine nuts

PRISCILLA TIMBERLAKE AND LEWIS FREEDMAN

Summer in upstate New York brings sunshine, rain, friends, and an abundance of vegetables. The lemon juice in this dish brings out the pink of the onions, which reminds us of the color of the sunset over our back deck. The taste of arame is very mild, so this salad is a gentle introduction to sea vegetables for someone who is just learning to like them.

> 1 packed cup dry arame
> 1 tablespoon wheat-free or regular tamari
> 1 large red onion
> Juice of ½ lemon
> 1 to 2 tablespoons raw pine nuts

1. Put arame in a pot or pan. Add ¾ cup water and allow arame to soak for 45 minutes.
2. Transfer pot or pan to the stove and turn heat to medium-low. Add tamari and simmer mixture for 15 to 20 minutes. Remove from heat and leave uncovered to allow evaporation of excess water.
3. Cut onion in half from top to bottom. Continue slicing in the same orientation to create half-moon slivers.
4. Place onions in a new pan, cover with water, and bring to a boil. Boil for 1 minute. Remove onions from water and place in a large bowl. Add lemon juice to onions.
5. Toast pine nuts in pan on stove top over medium heat for 3 to 5 minutes, stirring constantly to prevent burning.
6. Add arame to onions and mix together. Sprinkle with pine nuts and serve.

Arame is a seaweed used especially in Japanese and macrobiotic cuisine. It can be purchased online, from the bulk section of natural food stores, and in certain Asian food stores.

SERVES 2 TO 4

219

guacamole salad

MICAELA KARLSEN

This is the salad version of fresh guacamole. Using two lemons makes the dressing wetter, more lemony, and less sweet than if you were going for a more solid, stand-alone guacamole, so the optional syrup can temper that a bit if you're looking for a more balanced flavor. I actually enjoy the strong flavor of lemon— it is refreshing and kind of zesty. You have to try this for dinner!

1 20-ounce package mixed greens
1 bunch parsley
1 ripe avocado, pitted
Juice of 2 lemons
1 tablespoon brown rice syrup or maple syrup (optional)
1 bunch cilantro, chopped
¼ red onion, minced
2 medium tomatoes, chopped

1. Chop the greens and parsley together, either by pulsing in the food processor or by hand. Chopping the greens into small bits helps create a more even mixture with the sauce, as well as making the salad a denser meal. Transfer to a large bowl.
2. In a small bowl, mash the avocado with the lemon juice and then mix in the rice syrup (if desired) as well as the cilantro, onion, and tomatoes.
3. Toss the avocado mixture in the greens, coating evenly. Garnish with Unlimited Baked Corn Chips (page 171) for some crunch.

SERVES 2 FOR DINNER, OR 6 TO 8 AS A SIDE SALAD

SAUCES, SPREADS, AND DRESSINGS

mushroom gravy

MICAELA KARLSEN

No one should have to live without gravy! The mushroom base in this delightful sauce creates a rich flavor that is perfect for mashed potatoes, tempeh, and grain and vegetable dishes, or even as a garnish to soup.

1 large onion, chopped

2 garlic cloves or 1 elephant garlic clove, finely chopped

1 tablespoon arrowroot powder

1½ tablespoons whole-grain flour

1 10-ounce package cremini mushrooms, stems trimmed and caps and stems chopped

½ cup red wine

2 teaspoons tamari

2 teaspoons vegetable base paste

1. In a large pan over high heat, water-sauté the onion and garlic starting with 1 to 2 tablespoons of water and adding more water as needed to prevent them from sticking to the pan. Cook for approximately 7 to 10 minutes, until the onions are translucent.

2. In a small bowl, mix the arrowroot powder and whole-grain flour. Add ½ cup hot water and stir until dissolved.

3. Add the dissolved arrowroot, flour, mushrooms, red wine, tamari, and vegetable base paste to the onion and garlic mixture. Continue to cook on high heat for about 15 minutes, stirring and adding more water as necessary to prevent sticking to the pan.

4. When the majority of the liquid has evaporated, add about ½ cup of water to liquidize the mixture. Continue to cook about 5 more minutes.

5. Add ½ cup of water and blend with an immersion blender or in a blender until smooth (or leave slightly chunky, if desired). Serve atop Skinny Red Smashed Potatoes (page 217), baked potatoes, or any side vegetable dish.

MAKES 2 CUPS

homemade ketchup

Try this salt-free ketchup with oil-free, baked French fries, on veggie burgers, or on your morning potato scramble. It has no added salt or refined sugar, and will keep for up to 10 days in the refrigerator.

> 1 6-ounce can tomato paste
> ½ apple, diced (skin on or off)
> 1 tablespoon lemon juice
> ¼ teaspoon garlic powder
> ¼ teaspoon dried oregano

1. Place tomato paste, apple, lemon juice, garlic powder, and oregano in a blender or food processor.
2. Add ¾ cup water and blend until smooth.

MAKES 1 CUP

quick sun-dried tomato marinara

CHEF AJ

This sauce takes minutes to make but tastes like it was slow-simmered for hours. The best part is, there are no pots to clean or vegetables to cut up.

- 1 cup oil-free sun-dried tomatoes
- 3 to 4 fresh Roma tomatoes
- 1 red bell pepper, seeded
- 1 to 2 garlic cloves, peeled
- 3 to 4 dates, pitted
- 1 shallot or 1/8 cup red onion
- 1 tablespoon sun-dried tomato powder
- 3 to 4 fresh basil leaves

1. Soak the sun-dried tomatoes in water for about 30 minutes to soften them.
2. Place all ingredients in a high-powered blender and whip until smooth. If you prefer chunkier consistency, use a food processor fitted with the S blade and process until the desired consistency is reached.
3. Serve over your favorite healthy noodles such as those made from rice, tofu, sea vegetables, or zucchini.

 To make zucchini noodles, peel zucchini, then make "noodles" using a Spiralizer, Saladacco spiral slicer, or vegetable peeler.

MAKES ABOUT 3 CUPS

225

cashew cream

CRAIG COCHRAN | TERRI

Micaela is always inspiring me to use less oil, so I started substituting this cashew cream for vegan mayonnaise in potato salad and a few other dishes. I have to say it tastes better than the vegan mayo! Cashews have a mild, neutral flavor, so this recipe is highly versatile: Add salt and pepper and it's a great base for rich, savory sauces; add a little maple syrup or date paste and use it for sweeter purposes, such as frostings and desserts.

CASHEW CREAM:
>1 cup raw cashews (whole or pieces)

SUGGESTED SAVORY VARIATION:
>1 teaspoon salt, or to taste (optional)
>⅛ teaspoon pepper, or to taste (optional)

SUGGESTED SWEET VARIATION:
>3 tablespoons maple syrup (optional)
>3 to 5 dates, pitted (optional)

1. Place cashews in a small bowl, cover with water, and soak for 2 hours. Alternatively, place cashews in a small pot, cover with water, and boil for 5 to 10 minutes, until they are soft.
2. Remove softened cashews from water with a slotted spoon and transfer to a blender. Add ⅓ cup water and whip until smooth.
3. Add savory or sweet seasonings, depending upon intended use. Refrigerate for up to 1 week.

 If you have a high-powered blender, like a Vitamix, you don't need to soak the cashews.

MAKES 1 CUP

226

del's basic mayonnaise

DEL SROUFE

This versatile recipe has two options for the base. I like to make my mayonnaise with cauliflower puree instead of tofu, not only because I have a mild allergy to soy but because I prefer the taste—and cauliflower has no fat. But whether you use tofu or cauliflower, this recipe will keep refrigerated for 7 days.

1 12-ounce package organic silken tofu or 1½ cups cooked, pureed cauliflower
2 tablespoons red wine vinegar
½ teaspoon sea salt, or to taste

1. Place tofu or cauliflower in a food processor or blender. Add vinegar and puree until smooth and creamy.
2. Add salt to taste.

Mori-Nu organic silken tofu works wonderfully in this recipe.

MAKES 1½ CUPS

favorite sandwich spread

MICAELA KARLSEN

Once I got the hang of making this spread, it became a staple that I always wanted to have on hand. I didn't grow up eating wraps or sandwiches (except for bread and butter!), but I've certainly discovered the pleasure of them as an adult. This spread is incredibly enjoyable in a whole-grain wrap with fresh greens, tomato, and avocado slices. Whenever I make this quick and tasty treat, it kind of feels like I took myself out to lunch at a good plant-based deli.

¼ medium onion, cut into large chunks

2 small carrots, cut into large chunks

4 cornichons plus 1 tablespoon juice from the cornichons jar

1 to 2 tablespoons mellow white miso

1 tablespoon mustard

1 tablespoon maple syrup

2 tablespoons nutritional yeast

1 16-ounce package firm tofu, drained, or 1 15-ounce can chickpeas, drained

¼ bunch fresh parsley, chopped (optional)

1. Add onion, carrots, cornichons, miso, mustard, maple syrup, and nutritional yeast to the food processor and puree until everything is chopped in small bits and evenly mixed. This recipe doesn't yield high volume, so you may need to stop the food processor, scrape the sides down, and puree again once or twice before the consistency is to your satisfaction.

2. Add the tofu or chickpeas and parsley (if desired), and pulse to achieve a textured spread, or puree for a smoother spread.

3. Refrigerate until ready to use. This spread will keep for up to 5 days refrigerated.

MAKES ABOUT 2 CUPS

walnut-mushroom pâté

KATHY POLLARD

So easy, yet so flavorful! Use this savory pâté as a filling for wraps or sand-wiches, as a topping for rice snaps or oil-free whole-grain crackers, or as a spread on a whole-grain bagel. Experiment with spices like sage or basil; add chopped celery or peppers to add crunch.

1 8-ounce package cremini mushrooms, stems trimmed and caps and stems chopped

1 onion, chopped

2 tablespoons low-sodium soy sauce or water

Pepper to taste

1 cup walnuts

2 tablespoons miso

1 teaspoon sage or basil leaves, chopped (optional)

½ cup celery or sweet peppers, finely chopped (optional)

1. Place mushrooms, onion, and soy sauce or water in a skillet and water-sauté for 8 minutes. Add pepper as desired.
2. Add a splash of water if needed toward the end of the water-sauté process to keep the ingredients from sticking or burning.
3. Place cooked mushrooms and onions in a food processor or blender. Add walnuts and miso and blend until smooth.
4. Transfer pâté to a small bowl. If desired, add herbs or chopped vegetables. Refrigerated, this will keep for 4 to 5 days.
5. Serve with pita wedges, lettuce, cucumbers, and chopped tomato, or as variations suggested above.

MAKES 3 CUPS

surefire pesto

MICAH RISK | LIGHTER

Fresh basil is often out of stock at the store. (It's just that popular!) But no worries. If you're out of basil, an equal measure of another fresh herb—like cilantro or parsley—can make this pesto just as delicious. No mixed nuts? Any other nuts will do!

    2 cups fresh spinach
    1 cup fresh basil
    ¼ cup mixed nuts (plain or salted)
    ⅓ cup white beans
    ⅛ teaspoon apple cider vinegar
    1 garlic clove
    Salt and pepper to taste

1. Add all the ingredients with ¼ cup water to a food processor or high-powered blender.

2. Puree until you get a smooth, creamy sauce. That's it. Really!

MAKES ABOUT 1 CUP

use-me-all-the-time hummus

MICAELA KARLSEN

Hummus is another food, like granola, that is subject to food crime. Many recipes start with nice, whole chickpeas but suggest adding a ton of oil and tahini. The result is a spread so high in fat you may as well be eating butter. I actually don't even care for most kinds of commercially made hummus, because they often taste so strongly of tahini and nothing else. This wonderful recipe makes a light hummus that will go with almost anything.

2 15-ounce cans chickpeas, rinsed and drained
1 medium garlic clove, or ½ elephant garlic clove
1 small red bell pepper, seeds and stem removed
Juice of 1 lemon
2 tablespoons tahini
¼ teaspoon salt, or to taste

1. Place all ingredients in a food processor or blender.
2. Puree until you achieve the desired smoothness.

MAKES ABOUT 3 CUPS

raspberry vinaigrette dressing

MICAELA KARLSEN

I use this dressing again and again on salad. This fruity, yet tangy vinaigrette goes beautifully with light, summertime fruit and vegetable salads. The Summer Strawberry Salad is a perfect pairing, but you can also try it on combinations like spinach with apple, pecans, and red onion, or mixed greens with peach, radish, and almonds.

14 dates, pitted
1 10-ounce package frozen raspberries, thawed
2 tablespoons cider vinegar

1. Soak the dates in 2 cups hot water for 20 minutes or so, until they are soft.
2. Using a slotted spoon, transfer the dates to a blender, add raspberries, vinegar, and ⅓ cup water, and puree until smooth.

 If you have a high-powered blender, it may not be necessary to soak the dates.

MAKES 2 CUPS

peanut-lime dressing

KATHY POLLARD

This rich and satisfying dressing has a distinct Thai flavor from the peanut and curry combination. Note that it is a higher-fat dressing, but is delicious on salads, as a flavoring in wraps and sandwiches, or as the major sauce on rice or vegetable dishes.

½ cup peanuts or peanut butter
Juice of 2 limes
1 tablespoon Thai curry paste
1 tablespoon soy sauce
1 teaspoon sesame seeds
1 garlic clove or ½ teaspoon powdered garlic
2 to 3 dates, pitted (optional)

1. Place all ingredients in a blender with ½ cup water. Puree until smooth.
2. Add 1 or 2 tablespoons more water and puree again, if a thinner consistency is desired.

 Dates add a touch of sweetness to this dressing. If this is desired, follow the instructions in step 1 of Raspberry Vinaigrette (page 232) to soften the dates prior to adding them to the blender.

MAKES 1½ CUPS

233

classic italian dressing

KATHY POLLARD

The tang of this delicious dressing comes from the seasonings. When we allow our taste buds to get used to the flavors of spices without a film of fat, they pop!

1 tablespoon flaxseed meal

¼ cup red wine vinegar

1 tablespoon Dijon mustard

½ tablespoon rice syrup

1 to 2 garlic cloves, crushed

1 teaspoon herbal salt or seasoning or Italian seasoning

1 teaspoon dried basil

¼ teaspoon paprika

Pepper to taste

1. Place all ingredients plus ⅓ cup water in a blender.

2. Puree until smooth.

MAKES ABOUT 1 CUP

sweet mustard dressing

KATHY POLLARD

As an alternative to a savory Dijon vinaigrette, this sweet mustard dressing is great on sandwiches and makes a delightful dipping sauce for sushi.

¼ cup yellow mustard

⅛ to ¼ cup maple syrup

¼ cup brown rice syrup

1. Place all ingredients plus 2 tablespoons water in a blender.

2. Puree until smooth.

MAKES ¾ CUP

thousand island dressing

KATHY POLLARD

A creamy American classic—perfect for barbeques and summertime.

1 12-ounce package organic silken tofu
5 tablespoons ketchup
3 to 4 tablespoons pickle relish or chopped pickles
Juice of 1 lemon
1 teaspoon onion powder
½ teaspoon salt (optional)

1. Place all ingredients in a blender or food processor.
2. Blend until creamy. Add water to achieve desired thinness.

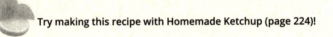 Try making this recipe with Homemade Ketchup (page 224)!

MAKES 1½ CUPS

236

QUICK BITES

emergency mini burritos

MICAELA KARLSEN

This is my true emergency food, for when I've worked too long without eating something and feel desperate and "hangry." While getting to that point is certainly not recommended, if it does happen to you, this is a meal you can whip up literally in 5 minutes.

3 6-inch soft corn tortillas
½ 15-ounce can refried beans (preferably nonfat and low sodium)
½ cup leftover rice, if you have it (optional)
3 tablespoons salsa
⅓ avocado, sliced

1. Heat the corn tortillas for 30 seconds or so in a pan on the stovetop or directly on the burner.
2. Assemble your burritos with beans, rice (if available and desired), salsa, and avocado to taste.
3. Eat right away!

You may want to microwave the tortillas, beans, and rice together if your beans and rice were refrigerated.

SERVES 1

curried chickpea salad sandwich

MICAH RISK | LIGHTER

My favorite meals feel life-giving and abundant, and are something I look forward to! This salad definitely fits the bill and makes a terrific filling for a sandwich or a wrap, or can be eaten as a dip with corn chips or crackers. If you make this salad ahead, it can be assembled quickly for lunch, making a satisfying meal even if you have only a couple of minutes. From here on out, small and boring lunch wraps need not apply!

2 tablespoons oil-free hummus (try Use-Me-All-The-Time Hummus, page 231)

1 teaspoon Dijon or yellow mustard

1 garlic clove, chopped

2 teaspoons curry powder

1 tablespoon maple syrup or other sweetener, or to taste (optional)

Salt and pepper to taste

1 15-ounce can chickpeas, rinsed and drained

¼ granny smith apple, chopped

2 celery ribs, chopped (optional)

¼ cup dry roasted or raw almonds, chopped

4 cups fresh spinach

2 slices whole-wheat bread or 1 whole-grain wrap

1. Combine the hummus, mustard, garlic, curry powder, and sweetener (if desired) in a mixing bowl. Add 2 tablespoons water and whisk or blend until evenly mixed, and a thick sauce is created. Add salt and pepper to taste.
2. Combine the chickpeas, apple, celery, and almonds in a second mixing bowl. Don't like celery? Feel free to leave it out. Add the wet mixture from step 1, and stir.
3. Enjoy the salad over a bed of spinach with a side of bread, or as a wrap or sandwich with spinach.

 Do you have a really picky pint-sized eater? Your child might love chickpeas and spinach with just a bit of hummus and salt. The salad has a nice, mild flavor on its own. You could also try feeding him or her the apple and celery on the side.

SERVES 2

ONGOING SUCCESS

rescue quinoa

MICAELA KARLSEN

When I'm not quite desperate enough for Emergency Mini Burritos but am still very hungry and wanting to make a fast and simple meal, quinoa is my go-to food because of how quickly it cooks. This particular recipe creates an Italian style flavor combo, but it can be adapted in any number of ways. The basic idea is to cook some quinoa and throw vegetables and beans into the pot while you're cooking. No one would know from eating this that you were in a hurry. This is also a great dish to bring to a potluck!

1½ cups quinoa
1 tablespoon vegetable base paste (optional)
2 tablespoons nutritional yeast (optional)
1 teaspoon Italian seasoning
½ cup frozen fava beans
1 large fresh tomato, chopped
1 medium onion, chopped
1 cup fresh basil, chopped

1. Place quinoa and 3 cups water in a large pot. Add vegetable base paste and nutritional yeast (if desired), plus seasoning, fava beans, tomato, and onion. Bring to a boil over medium-high heat, then reduce to medium-low heat.

2. Simmer until the quinoa is completely cooked, about 15 to 20 minutes.

3. Stir in the fresh basil and eat.

SERVES 2 TO 4

fresh fruit tart

LISA TENER

I had the pleasure of helping Micaela with some of the writing for this book, and in doing so I ended up eating a plant-based diet myself! This fruit tart is a quick and easy mini meal that I can whip together in just a few minutes, helping me stay focused and clear-headed while I work.

1 large sprouted-grain tortilla
3 tablespoons raw sesame tahini
1 cup fresh seaonal fruit

1. Toast the tortilla, or keep it raw.
2. Spread tahini over the entire tortilla.
3. Cover the tortilla generously with fruit.
4. Slice the tortilla, or fold it like a taco. Or—depending on how neat you are—eat it as is!

 I like Ezekiel brand sprouted-grain tortillas, but other variations work nicely as well. For instance, try a Sunfood raw vegan coconut wrap instead of the tortilla. In this case, I spread the tahini on about half of the wrap, top the tahini with fruit, and roll the wrap so the tahini and fruit are in the center.

SERVES 1

242

sprouty squash delight

LISA TENER

The first time I came up with this recipe I loved it so much I had it again the next day. The sweetness from the delicata squash is enhanced by the cinnamon, and when eaten with sprouts creates a sweet-savory combination that is delicious as well as nourishing. As I've gotten more serious about my diet I've continued to experiment with truly whole food ingredients for this dish as well as beautiful presentations. My current favorite for the leafy sprouts is a "rainbow mix" that includes sprouts of red cabbage, arugula, daikon, beet, mizuna, mustard, celery, amaranth, and kohlrabi. After cutting the squash, most of the prep time is waiting for it to bake, which means I can keep working on my writing almost up until the moment I eat.

1 small delicata squash
¼ teaspoon cinnamon
1 handful leafy sprouts

1. Preheat the oven to 400°F.
2. Cut delicata squash in half lengthwise. Bake, uncovered and face up, for 25 to 30 minutes.
3. Scoop out seeds and center, possibly leaving a few crunchy seeds if you like.
4. Sprinkle with cinnamon and stuff with a handful of green, leafy sprouts. Eat and enjoy.

I particularly like organic Ceylon cinnamon for this dish.

MAKES 2 HALF SQUASHES

five ways to sushi

MICAELA KARLSEN

Years ago I learned how easy it is to make sushi—and have been eating it several times a week as a snack ever since! Sometimes I don't have the chance to make sushi, and then I just eat a sheet or two of nori to get my seaweed fix. This recipe makes five distinct sushi rolls. You can make the rice ahead and have it on hand, so the sushi-making process doesn't have to be a big deal. You can find a bamboo sushi-rolling mat online or at a cooking supply store. And by the way, yes, pickles and peanut butter really are in the list of fillings. I learned about that combination thanks to Anita Devine, a wonderful macrobiotic chef, and I've lost count of the number of people who were won over tasting it.

SUSHI:
- 1½ cups short-grain brown rice
- ½ cup sweet brown rice
- 1 tablespoon rice vinegar
- 8 sheets nori, toasted or raw

OPTIONAL FILLINGS:
- ¼ medium sweet potato, cooked and sliced into thin strips
- ¼ avocado, sliced
- 3 cornichons or 1 dill pickle, sliced, and 1 to 2 tablespoons peanut butter
- 1½-inch strip baked tempeh, 1 leaf blanched kale, and ⅛ sliced tomato
- ¼ raw cucumber and ¼ carrot, sliced in long strips

GARNISH:
- 1 teaspoon sesame seeds

1. **Cook the rice:** Put both kinds of brown rice and 4 cups water in a medium pot. Bring to a boil and then reduce to low heat. Cook about 45 minutes—you will see tiny bubbles emerging from the surface of the rice. Add the vinegar after cooking and mix thoroughly. The sweet rice is very sticky but you don't need to use 100 percent sweet rice or it's actually too sticky and wet.

2. You can assemble the nori warm or cold, but if the rice has been in the refrigerator you might want to heat it up to soften it, either in the microwave or on the stove top with a tiny bit of water.

3. Lay a sheet of nori on the sushi mat, shiny side (the outside) down. You

will see perforated lines in the nori. Orient the nori so the lines run in the same direction you are rolling in (so that once you roll it up you would be cutting individual sushi bites along those lines).

4. Spread about ½ cup rice across about half the sheet of nori, in the half closest to you, with a rice paddle or the back of a spoon. You can dip the paddle in cold water to help prevent the rice from sticking.

5. Lay your selected filling (one of the five combinations listed) perpendicular to the perforated lines in the nori, close to the edge of the sheet. If your rice is dry, at this point you may want to wet a ½-inch strip along the opposite edge of the sheet to help it stick closed once it's rolled.

6. Fold the edge of the nori closest to you forward, so you are covering most of the rice with nori. Drag the half-rolled nori back to the closest edge of your rolling mat, then start over rolling and finish. Once the nori is completely rolled, squeeze it a few times inside the mat to help it stick.

7. Repeat steps 1 to 6 with the remaining four filling combinations.

8. Eat as is, or slice each nori roll into 8 individual sushi bites. A serrated knife dipped in cold water works best for this task. Sprinkle sushi with sesame seeds and eat.

 Sweet brown rice is a different kind of rice than short-grain brown rice, and it's what makes sushi rice sticky. For a raw sushi experience (thank you, Rebecca Michaelides!), try making a filling by pureeing carrot and jicama and then squeezing out the excess water. For totally raw sushi, make sure not to use toasted nori.

MAKES 8 ROLLS

MAIN MEALS

the esselstyns' stacked high black beans and rice

ANN ESSELSTYN

When we learned about Micaela's new book we knew just the right recipe to contribute. Our first and favorite plant-based meal was black beans and rice. We love it anytime—for dinner, for lunch, or for in between meals. It is our go-to recipe for guests because everyone adores something that's in it. And, oh, my, do they stack their plates crazily high! Some suggestions for vegetables follow below. Of course, you should feel free to be creative and use what you love.

3 15-ounce cans black beans, undrained
2 to 3 medium tomatoes, chopped
1 bunch scallions, or 1 cup Vidalia (or any another variety) onions, chopped
1 16-ounce bag frozen corn, thawed
1 to 2 medium red, yellow, or green bell peppers, chopped
1 cup carrots, grated or cut matchstick-style
1 15-ounce can water chestnuts, rinsed and drained
1 bunch fresh cilantro, chopped
1 bunch fresh arugula, chopped
½ cup salsa
½ cup guacamole (optional)
6 cups cooked brown rice

1. In a medium saucepan, cook the beans over medium heat for 10 to 15 minutes, until heated through. Transfer to a serving dish.

2. Place the tomatoes, onions, corn, bell peppers, carrots, water chestnuts, cilantro, arugula, and salsa in individual serving dishes.

3. Place cooked rice in a large serving dish.

4. Layer the rice, beans, vegetables, and herbs as desired. Top it all with salsa, guacamole (unless you are a heart disease patient!), and serve.

Feel free to experiment with different flavor combinations for the beans—the above is our basic family recipe, but there are many ways to jazz up black beans. Also, remember that if your canned beans contain salt, do drain and rinse them, then add ½ cup water back into the can before heating the beans. Any leftovers from this meal can be placed in a storage container and eaten with salad, topped by balsamic vinegar, the next day. Or try putting leftovers in a sandwich or wrap with oil-free hummus, tomato, and your favorite greens and sprouts. Delicious!

249

SERVES 6

interstellar lasagna

MICAELA KARLSEN

I finished perfecting this recipe the week that NASA's Kepler Mission found a new Earth-like planet, 452b, so I named it in honor of the discovery. This name is doubly appropriate because if I were an astronaut on a years-long space mission and could bring only one food with me, this lasagna would definitely be a top contender. Other great features of this recipe? Neither the noodles nor the filling need to be precooked—after some quick chopping, which you can do in a food processor, this dish is ready to pop in the oven.

LAYER 1:

1 medium onion

1 16-ounce package firm tofu, drained

1 teaspoon garlic powder

1½ teaspoons white miso

⅓ cup nutritional yeast

⅓ cup packed fresh basil leaves

LAYER 2:

1 medium onion

1 10-ounce package cremini mushrooms, stems trimmed

½ cup frozen spinach

¼ cup pine nuts

2 teaspoons Italian seasoning

⅛ teaspoon salt or to taste

ADDITIONAL COMPONENTS:

1 10-ounce box whole-grain lasagna noodles

3 to 4 cups of your favorite tomato sauce (or try Chef AJ's Quick Sun-Dried Tomato Marinara, page 225)

TOPPINGS:

1 medium tomato, sliced thinly

2 tablespoons nutritional yeast

Salt to taste

1. Preheat the oven to 375°F.

2. Make layer 1: Place the onion in a food processor, and pulse until it is finely chopped. Add the tofu, garlic powder, miso, and nutritional yeast and blend until everything is evenly mixed. At this point the mixture will be like a dry puree—grainy and not too wet. Add the basil leaves and pulse until the basil is chopped into small bits and evenly distributed in the mixture. Transfer the contents of layer 1 to a medium bowl.

3. Make layer 2: Place the onion in a food processor and pulse until it is finely chopped. Add the mushrooms, spinach, pine nuts, Italian seasoning, and salt and blend until everything is evenly mixed.

4. Assemble the lasagna: Divide your noodles into three equal piles, to correspond with the three noodle layers in the final dish. Cover the bottom of a 9×13–inch glass pan with ¾ cup tomato sauce and ½ cup water. Use a spoon to mix the two and evenly distribute the liquified sauce. Place one layer of lasagna noodles on top of the sauce-water mixture. Cover the noodles with 1 to 1½ cups tomato sauce, using a spoon to evenly distribute it. Add the mixture for Layer 1 to the pan. Cover the mixture with the second layer of noodles. Add the mixture for Layer 2 to the pan. Cover Layer 2 with a third layer of noodles to top it off. Cover the noodles with 1¼ to 1½ cups tomato sauce using a spoon to evenly distribute it.

5. Add the toppings: Place tomato slices on top of the sauce evenly around the pan. Sprinkle each slice with a bit of salt for added flavor, if desired, then sprinkle the nutritional yeast evenly on top of the tomatoes.

6. Cover the pan with aluminum foil and bake for 35 minutes, then remove cover and bake an additional 20 to 25 minutes or until the top surface has developed a skin.

SERVES 6 TO 8

mac and cheeze casserole

KATHY POLLARD

A healthy take on a traditional comfort food. This recipe has been kid-approved in many a household and is a great potluck dish. It reheats well, and actually tastes better the second time!

1 10-ounce package frozen spinach, thawed,
or a bunch of fresh leaves, cleaned and chopped

12 ounces whole-grain macaroni noodles

CHEEZE SAUCE:

¼ cup raw cashews

1 4-ounce jar pimentos

2 cups unsweetened soymilk or other unsweetened plant milk

1½ teaspoons salt

½ teaspoon onion powder

3 heaping tablespoons nutritional yeast flakes

¼ teaspoon garlic powder

½ teaspoon mustard powder

3 tablespoons arrowroot powder or 1½ tablespoons cornstarch

Juice from ½ lemon

TOPPING:

½ cup whole-grain bread crumbs

1. Preheat the oven to 375°F.
2. Arrange spinach evenly in the bottom of a 9×13–inch glass casserole dish.
3. Cook noodles according to instructions. Drain noodles, and place them in the casserole dish over the spinach.
4. **Make the cheeze sauce:** Place cashews, pimentos, and plant milk in a blender and blend until smooth. Add the remaining sauce ingredients and mix thoroughly. Transfer cheeze sauce to saucepan and cook on medium-low heat until thick, stirring constantly.
5. Pour sauce over noodles. Sprinkle with whole-grain breadcrumbs and cover dish with top or aluminum foil.
6. Bake covered for 10 minutes or until bubbly. Uncover dish and bake under broiler for 5 minutes, but don't burn the top.

 For a more traditional mac and cheese dish, just make the sauce and pour it over the noodles. Or add noodles to sauce and simmer on low for 10 minutes.

SERVES 4

ONGOING SUCCESS

portobello steaks

KATHY POLLARD

This is the second plant-based dinner for four on a budget mentioned in Table 3 on page 55, but these big mushrooms certainly don't have a budget for flavor. They have a meaty feel, and are very satisfying as a main course.

4 large portobello mushroom caps

¼ cup soy sauce or tamari

¼ cup balsamic vinegar

2 garlic cloves, minced

1 teaspoon pepper

1 teaspoon rosemary

¼ cup low-sodium vegetable broth or water

1. Place mushrooms, insides facing up, in a medium bowl.
2. Combine soy sauce, vinegar, garlic, pepper, and rosemary in a small bowl. Mix well and pour over mushrooms.
3. Marinate mushrooms for 30 minutes.
4. Pour water or broth in a large nonstick frying pan and set heat to medium.
5. Transfer mushrooms to the pan, keeping the insides facing up. Pour the marinade into the middle of each mushroom, divided evenly among the 4 caps.
6. Bring the liquid to a simmer. Cover the pan and cook mushrooms for 8 minutes on medium-low heat. You may need to lower the heat and add more liquid. Keep a touch of liquid in the bottom of the pan as the mushrooms cook and allow them to brown but not blacken.
7. Flip the mushrooms and cook for approximately 8 additional minutes, using the same guidelines as specified above.
8. Place on whole-grain burger buns and add your favorite condiments for a great burger, or serve with West African–Inspired Sweet Potatoes and Kale (page 265) for a meal!

SERVES 4

leftover cobbler

KATHY POLLARD

This versatile, hearty dish uses any leftover vegetables, soups, stews, bean dishes, stir-fries, potatoes, or rice that you may have on hand. The magic trick is adding a fresh and homey layer of corn bread! This dish can be a great pot-luck casserole offering.

LEFTOVERS:

Roughly 5 cups cooked vegetables, thick soup, or stew—whatever you have!

Roughly 2 cups vegetable stock or water

4 tablespoons fresh dill or parsley (optional)

2 tablespoons Italian seasoning mix, or Italian seasonings (oregano, basil, and thyme) (optional)

CORN BREAD LAYER:

1 cup cornmeal

1 cup whole-grain flour (spelt or wheat)

1 tablespoon baking powder

1 teaspoon baking soda

1 tablespoon ground flaxseed

½ teaspoon salt (optional)

1 cup unsweetened plant milk (such as soy milk)

2 teaspoons maple syrup

1 teaspoon apple cider vinegar

TOPPING:

⅛ to ¼ cup nutritional yeast (optional)

1. Preheat the oven to 425°F.

2. Combine leftover veggies, stock or water, and seasonings as desired. Altogether the mixture should measure approximately 7 cups.

3. Pour veggie mixture into a 9×13–inch baking dish. (A glass pan works especially well, but others are fine, too.)

4. Make corn bread layer: Place dry ingredients (cornmeal, flour, baking powder, baking soda, flaxseed, and salt, if desired) in a medium bowl. Add plant milk, maple syrup, and vinegar. Blend until barely mixed; do not overstir.

254

5. Spread batter on top of vegetables.

6. Bake uncovered for 25 to 30 minutes or until top is springy to the touch and lightly browned. Test by inserting a toothpick; if it comes out clean, the corn bread is cooked.

7. Sprinkle with nutritional yeast, if desired, and serve.

SERVES 6

tofu quiche with millet crust

I once fed this to someone who responded by exclaiming "I didn't know food like this existed!" You could definitely bring this dish to a party and surprise your omnivore friends—its rich flavor and creamy texture is sure to please. This dish is somewhat inspired by macrobiotic cooking, which is how I first learned to like and use millet. Millet is a good choice for any crust because when it cools after being cooked on the stove, it tends to harden, making it the perfect container for a wetter filling, like tofu quiche or pie. Feel free to experiment with vegetables other than spinach. The basic idea will work for many flavor combinations.

CRUST:
　　1 cup millet
　　½ tablespoon vegetable base paste paste

FILLING:
　　1 large onion, chopped
　　2 garlic cloves, finely chopped
　　Salt (optional)
　　½ cup frozen spinach, chopped
　　¼ cup white wine
　　1 16-ounce package firm tofu, drained
　　2 dates, pitted
　　1 teaspoon white miso
　　1 teaspoon tamari
　　2 teaspoons turmeric
　　½ cup nutritional yeast
　　2 tablespoons tahini

GARNISH:
　　¼ cup chives or scallions, chopped (optional)

1. Put the millet, vegetable base paste, and 2½ cups water in a pot and bring to a boil over medium-high heat. Reduce the heat to low and simmer until the millet is cooked all the way through, about 45 minutes. You will see little air bubbles coming through the surface, as with rice.

2. Place the onion, garlic, ¼ cup water, and a pinch of salt (if desired) in a pan over high heat. Cover the pan and water-sauté until the onions start to become translucent, about 7 to 10 minutes. The lid should keep enough water in the pan not to burn them, but check every few minutes to make sure the bottom of the pan is still wet and add small amounts of water as needed.

3. Remove the lid and add the spinach. Cook for about 5 more minutes, and once the onions have become translucent remove the lid of the pan, stirring to help the water from the spinach evaporate.

4. Add white wine and cook for about 5 more minutes, until the spinach has thawed completely and is evenly distributed, continuing to stir to help the alcohol boil off. Add tiny amounts of water if the mixture starts to stick to the bottom of the pan. Turn off the heat.

5. Combine the tofu, dates, miso, tamari, turmeric, nutritional yeast, tahini, and ¼ cup water in a food processor and blend until smooth.

6. Preheat the oven to 375°F.

7. Form the crust by pressing the cooked millet into a 9-inch glass pie pan with the back of a wooden spoon. Dip the spoon in cold water to help prevent the millet from sticking. Once the millet is spread around the pan and is cool to the touch, you can clean up the sides and edges with your fingers.

8. Pour the tofu mixture from the food processor into the pan with the cooked onions, and stir by hand.

9. Pour the filling into the crust and bake for 35 minutes.

10. Garnish with chopped chives or scallions, if desired.

SERVES 6 TO 8

best basic southwestern burgers

JEFF NOVICK, RD

When making burgers, I always make a double batch, since I never know when I'm going to need a frozen burger! If you double the recipe, feel free to switch out different beans for the second can—but for best results, make sure at least one can is kidney beans, as they seem to be the best binder with the oats. Also, the second cooked starch can be changed to almost any other cooked whole starch, such as sweet potato, quinoa, buckwheat, and so forth, but always make sure to also include the oats, as they are the best binder. This basic recipe can be a blank canvas for your favorite spices, so consider experimenting beyond cumin and chili powder. By following the basic recipe and varying the beans, starch, moisture (aka diced tomatoes), and/or spices, you can create dozens of varieties of burgers.

> 1 14-ounce can no-salt-added kidney beans, rinsed and drained well, or 1½ cups cooked kidney beans
>
> ½ cup rolled oats
>
> ½ cup cooked whole starch (such as brown rice)
>
> 2 tablespoons canned, diced, no-salt-added tomatoes
>
> ½ tablespoon cumin
>
> ½ tablespoon chili powder

1. Place kidney beans in a medium bowl and mash by hand with a potato masher. (Do not use a blender or food processer.)
2. Add the remaining ingredients and mix thoroughly.
3. Divide mixture into five equal parts and shape each part into a burger.
4. Place, uncovered, in the refrigerator for a few minutes and allow the burgers to set.
5. Grill (or broil) the burgers for 5 to 6 minutes on each side, flipping once so each side turns golden brown.

 The water content of kidney beans you cook yourself may vary according to the amount of time they were cooked, how much water was in the pot, and how long the kidney beans sat after being cooked. You may need to test the recipe a few times to make sure you get the right moisture content. As mentioned above, you can also substitue other liquids for the diced tomatoes, including vegetable broth, salsa, BBQ sauce, and so forth.

SERVES 5

ONGOING SUCCESS

cauliflower au gratin

KATHY POLLARD

I was so thrilled to create a creamy, "cheesy" casserole to satisfy even the pickiest of eaters transitioning off of cheese (namely my young daughter). The combination of nutritional yeast and soy milk gives this dish a rich and savory flavor that even a cheese-eater will love.

1 cauliflower, washed and cut into bite-size chunks

1 bunch fresh spinach leaves, washed and chopped, or 1 10-ounce bag frozen spinach

1 tablespoon whole-grain flour (such as wheat or spelt)

3 tablespoons nutritional yeast flakes

2 cups plain soy milk

¼ teaspoon salt (optional)

¼ teaspoon pepper, or to taste

¼ teaspoon coriander, or to taste

¼ teaspoon garlic powder

¼ teaspoon vinegar, either balsamic or wine

1 teaspoon soy sauce

1 cup whole-grain breadcrumbs

Paprika to shake on top (optional)

1. Preheat the oven to 375°F.
2. Steam cauliflower for 5 minutes, until just soft.
3. Place chopped spinach in the bottom of 9×13–inch glass casserole dish and add cauliflower on top of spinach.
4. Place flour, nutritional yeast, soy milk, and seasonings in a saucepan. Set heat to medium-low and cook for a minute, stirring briskly. Don't allow it to come to a boil.
5. Add vinegar and soy sauce, and turn up heat to medium. Bring almost to a boil, whisking constantly, until thickened.
6. Pour sauce over cauliflower and top with breadcrumbs.
7. Sprinkle with paprika, if desired.
8. Cover pan with top or aluminum foil and bake for 25 minutes until it starts to bubble. Remove cover and bake an additional 5 minutes.

SERVES 4

259

carrot-rice casserole

KATHY POLLARD

The unlikely pairing of peanut butter and rice lends an unbelievably rich and wholesome taste to this casserole. I have never met anyone who didn't love this dish! (You'll want to pass, of course, if peanut allergies are a concern.) This is a good recipe to bring to a dinner party.

1 10-ounce package frozen spinach, or 1 bunch fresh leaves, well washed and chopped

1 large onion, chopped

3 cups shredded carrots

1½ teaspoons garlic powder

½ teaspoon thyme

1 tablespoon salt, or to taste (optional)

¼ cup peanut butter

3 cups low-sodium vegetable broth or water

1 tablespoon soy sauce

3 cups cooked brown rice

¾ cup whole-grain breadcrumbs

1. Preheat the oven to 350°F.
2. If using frozen spinach, thaw it. Arrange spinach evenly in bottom of a 9×13–inch glass pan.
3. Place onion and carrots in a pan with a splash of water and water-sauté over medium-high heat until onions are softened, about 7 minutes.
4. Add garlic powder, thyme, and salt (if desired), then the peanut butter and broth or water.
5. Add soy sauce, rice, and bread crumbs, and warm to a simmer.
6. Pour mixture into casserole dish, on top of the spinach.
7. Cover pan with top or aluminum foil and bake for 45 minutes, until bubbly around the edges.

SERVES 4

super easy pizza

KATHY POLLARD

When you have teenage kids, life without pizza is downright weird. But pizza is usually an unhealthy combo of cheese and white flour crust, so we change all that in this version—substituting whole-grain crust and adding a simple sprinkle of nutritional yeast. Luckily, this recipe passed the "Normalcy Test," which has allowed us to hold many make-your-own-pizza parties in our home!

PIZZA:
- 2 12-inch (or 3 8-inch) whole-grain pizza crusts
- 1 15-ounce can tomato or pizza sauce
- 3 tablespoons nutritional yeast

OPTIONAL TOPPINGS:
- 1 medium onion, thinly sliced
- 1 small bell pepper of any color, thinly sliced
- ½ cup mushrooms, thinly sliced
- 2 scallions, minced
- ¼ cup fresh basil, chopped
- ½ head broccoli florets, cut to bite-size pieces
- 8 kalamata or green olives, chopped
- 1 cup fresh spinach, chopped

1. Preheat the oven to 400°F.

2. Spread each pizza crust with an equal amount of sauce.

3. Sprinkle each pizza with nutritional yeast.

4. Top each pizza with desired vegetables.

5. Place pizza crusts on baking sheets or pieces of aluminum foil.

6. Bake for 10 minutes or until crusts just start to brown.

 For crusts, I like DeLand millet flats. For sauce, I use Muir Glen organic tomato sauce, no salt added.

MAKES 2 OR 3 PIZZAS

261

pesto kasha varnishkes

KATHY POLLARD

This traditional Eastern European dish, made with buckwheat groats and bow-tie pasta, will always remind me of my roots. Baba Rose, my mom's mom, made it for us regularly, and my father thought of his grandmother every time he ate Baba's creation—such is the power of food! For my version of this dish I add veggies and pesto and use whole-grain noodles, which add nutrients and fiber as well as flavor!

PESTO:
- 1 bunch basil leaves
- 1 14-ounce can artichoke hearts, drained
- 1 large garlic clove
- Pepper to taste
- Salt to taste (optional)

KASHA VARNISHKES:
- 6 ounces whole-grain bow-tie pasta
- 1 onion, chopped or sliced
- 3 celery ribs, sliced
- 3 kale leaves, chopped
- 2 tablespoons soy sauce
- ⅔ cup buckwheat groats (kasha)
- Pepper to taste
- Salt to taste (optional)
- ½ cup pine nuts (optional)

1. **Make the pesto:** Blend basil, artichoke hearts, garlic, pepper, and salt (if desired) in a food processor until evenly mixed. Set aside.
2. Cook pasta al dente, according to directions. Drain and set aside.
3. Warm a large skillet over medium-low heat. Add onion with a splash of water and water-sauté for 4 minutes.
4. Add celery, kale, soy sauce, and kasha, and continue to water-sauté until dry, about 4 minutes.
5. Add 1⅓ cup water, pepper, and salt (if desired), and bring mixture to a boil on high heat. Reduce heat to a simmer and cook, covered, for 15 minutes or until water is absorbed.

6. Add the cooked pasta and ½ cup pesto. (If there is extra pesto, save it for later!)

7. Sprinkle each serving with pine nuts.

SERVES 4

ginger roasted vegetables and tempeh

KATHY POLLARD

This lovely, hearty dish can be modified to use up vegetables that you have around. If aiming for a gluten-free meal, make sure the tempeh does not have barley.

1 12-ounce package tempeh

1 large onion, chopped

1 medium eggplant, sliced into ½-inch rounds

1 medium green pepper, chopped

4 cups vegetables (such as carrots, yams, celery, or kale), chopped

1 teaspoon ginger powder

6 tablespoon soy sauce

3 tablespoons maple syrup

1. Preheat the oven to 400°F.
2. Slice the tempeh in half lengthwise and then cut in 1-inch rectangles in the short direction.
3. Put all veggies and tempeh in a large roasting pan.
4. Sprinkle ginger powder, soy sauce, and maple syrup on top.
5. Cover the pan with aluminum foil, and bake for 20 minutes.
6. Turn veggies and tempeh, lower the oven temperature to 375°F, and bake until tender (about 15 minutes more).
7. Remove foil, and broil for 3 minutes.

SERVES 6

west african–inspired sweet potatoes and kale

MICAH RISK | LIGHTER

This dish is the perfect mix of sweet and savory—and spicy, if you like it that way! Sweet potatoes and kale make the dish colorful and vibrant, while the quinoa makes it filling. Peanut butter, added just before serving, brings a delectable, creamy texture. This uniquely flavorful and nutrient-packed recipe will take dinner up a notch.

½ cup quinoa
2 garlic cloves, minced
1½ teaspoons fresh ginger, minced
½ teaspoon cumin
¼ teaspoon cinnamon
Salt and pepper to taste
2 sweet potatoes, cut into 1-inch cubes
1 15-ounce can diced tomatoes
½ 16-ounce package frozen kale
3 tablespoons peanut butter

1. Put quinoa and 1 cup water in a pot, and bring to a boil. Cover pot with a tight-fitting lid, reduce heat to low, and simmer for 15 to 20 minutes, until water is absorbed.
2. Heat 3 to 4 tablespoons of water in a large pot or wok over medium heat. Stir in the garlic, ginger, cumin, cinnamon, salt, and pepper until thoroughly mixed.
3. Add the sweet potatoes, tomatoes in their juices, and ¾ cup of water. Turn up the heat to high, bring the mixture to a boil, then lower the heat to medium. Cover the pot and cook at a low boil for 15 minutes, or until the potatoes are just tender. Stir occasionally.
4. Stir in the kale. Return the mixture to a boil, then reduce the heat to low, cover the pot, and simmer 5 to 10 more minutes, until the potatoes are cooked fully through, but not mushy. If the mixture gets dry, add a bit more water.

265

recipe continues

5. Stir in the peanut butter, and taste. Adjust seasonings as desired. Serve hot over quinoa.

 To save time, instead of cooking the sweet potatoes on the stove, try microwaving them. To microwave a whole sweet potato, poke a few holes in the skin and microwave it on high for 5 to 9 minutes, turning the potato over halfway through the cooking time. If you microwave, reduce the amount of water added in Step 3 to ½ cup.

SERVES 2 TO 4

hearty lentil loaf

CHEF AJ

No soy or bread crumbs in this loaf, just whole food goodness. This loaf is delicious, even without any kind of sauce or gravy, but you can also add your favorite condiments such as ketchup, mustard, or BBQ sauce. Stuff cold leftovers in pita pockets for a great lunch!

3 cups cooked lentils
1 16-ounce bag frozen carrots, defrosted and drained
1 large red onion
½ cup Italian parsley, finely chopped
2 garlic cloves, peeled
2 cups raw walnuts, chopped
2 cups uncooked oats (not instant)
2 tablespoons sundried tomato powder

1. Preheat the oven to 350°F.
2. Combine lentils, carrots, onion, parsley, 1 cup walnuts, and 1 cup oats in a food processor fitted with an S blade.
3. Process ingredients until smooth and almost paste-like.
4. Transfer mixture to a bowl, and then, by hand, stir in the second cup of oats and the second cup of chopped walnuts. Stir in the sundried tomato powder.
5. Pour mixture into a standard-size silicone loaf pan and bake, uncovered, for 50 to 55 minutes, until golden brown.
6. Remove loaf from oven and let sit at least 10 minutes.
7. Invert pan, position loaf on a serving dish, let cool another 5 minutes, and then slice.

 Delicious steamed lentils are available at Trader Joe's, and a single box is 2½ cups —almost the right amount for this loaf.

MAKES 1 LOAF

267

chilled peanut noodles

DEL SROUFE

I love anything with peanut butter—especially a spoon. Because of the fat content, however, I only eat peanut butter as a special treat, and this is the recipe for one of my favorite special treats. This dish comes together quickly. If you are cooking for one or two, you can put as much pasta as you want in a bowl, toss it with an appropriate amount of sauce, and save the rest of the sauce for later. It is especially great with veggies or other grain dishes!

1 pound whole-grain spaghetti

½ cup smooth peanut butter

¼ cup low-sodium soy sauce or tamari

2 tablespoons rice vinegar

¼ cup brown rice syrup

¾ teaspoon ground ginger

¼ teaspoon cayenne (optional)

1 cup scallions, chopped

2 tablespoons peanuts, chopped

1. Cook the spaghetti according to instructions.
2. **Make the peanut sauce:** Combine peanut butter, soy sauce, rice vinegar, brown rice syrup, ginger, and cayenne (if desired) in a bowl, and whisk well to combine.
3. Drain the noodles, rinse under cold water, and drain again.
4. Transfer the cooked spaghetti to a bowl, add ½ to ¾ cup of the peanut sauce, and toss to mix well.
5. Garnish with scallions and peanuts.
6. Store leftover sauce in the refrigerator for up to 7 days.

SERVES 4 TO 6, WITH ¼ TO ½ CUP SAUCE LEFTOVER

TREATS

rich and creamy chocolate mousse

STACY BLONDIN

This go-to dessert is for anyone looking for a rich and creamy treat in a hurry. It's a crowd-pleaser and entertainer in one—I always have fun asking friends to guess the main ingredient!

BASIC MOUSSE:

- 1 just-ripe avocado
- 1 tablespoon maple syrup, or other sweetener of choice
- 4 to 5 tablespoons cocoa powder
- 1 drop essential peppermint oil or ½ to 1 teaspoon peppermint extract (optional)

PIE VARIATION:

- 1 cup nuts
- 1 cup dates, pitted
- 2 cups (1 batch) Coconut Dream Whipped Cream (page 276)
- 2 tablespoons cocoa nibs
- 3 to 5 fresh mint sprigs

1. Puree avocado and sweetener in a blender, or with an immersion blender.
2. Add cocoa powder. (If your avocado is large or if you prefer a stronger flavor, use the larger quantity of cocoa.) Stir by hand at first (to prevent dust cloud), then blend mechanically.
3. **To make grasshopper(less) version:** Add peppermint oil or extract, and stir well.
4. Chill in fridge or freezer to harden, or eat as is. Alternatively, proceed to step 5 to make the pie variation.
5. **To make the pie variation:** Soak nuts and dates in 3 cups water in a small bowl overnight (or, for faster softening, in 3 cups hot water for 30 minutes). Transfer dates and nuts to a food processor (or use an immersion blender) and puree. Press mixture into a 9-inch pie pan, add mousse, and chill. Before serving, top pie with Coconut Dream Whipped Cream, cocoa nibs, and mint leaves.

To prevent an overt taste, err on the side of underripe when selecting your avocado. This mousse can also be used as frosting for cupcakes or cake.

SERVES 4 TO 6

carrot cake

CATHY FISHER

I make this carrot cake more than any other dessert—it's so delicious and yet so easy. It's the dessert to take to any occasion where you want to raise all the eyebrows in the room. Serve as is (it's plenty sweet). Or, for extra high eyebrows, add a decadent layer of Nutty Frosting!

CARROT CAKE:
- 1½ cups non-dairy milk
- 5 medjool or 10 deglet noor dates, pitted and quartered
- ¾ cup raisins
- ½ ripe banana, sliced
- 1¾ cups rolled oats (regular or quick), or 1¾ cups oat flour
- 2 teaspoons baking powder
- 1 teaspoon baking soda
- 2 teaspoons ground cinnamon
- 1 teaspoon ground nutmeg
- ⅛ teaspoon ground clove
- 1½ cups grated carrots
- ½ cup walnuts, chopped

NUTTY FROSTING:
- 7 medjool dates or 14 deglet dates, pitted and chopped
- ¾ cup raw, unsalted cashews
- ½ teaspoon vanilla extract

1. Preheat the oven to 350°F.
2. Place the milk, dates, ¼ cup raisins, and banana in a small bowl, and set aside.
3. Place the rolled oats into a blender (a high-speed blender works best) and process until the oats are ground into flour. Transfer ground oats to a mixing bowl, and add the baking powder, baking soda, cinnamon, nutmeg, and clove. Mix with a fork.
4. Transfer the milk, dates, raisins, and banana to the blender and whip until smooth. Add this wet mixture to the bowl of dry ingredients and mix with a wooden spoon until all dry ingredients have been incorporated. Fold in the carrots, remaining ½ cup raisins, and walnuts.

5. Transfer batter to a 8×8–inch baking pan lined with parchment paper. Bake for 40 to 45 minutes. The cake is done when the top is medium brown and has a few cracks, and when it bounces back a bit (instead of staying indented) when you press on it lightly.

6. Cool cake for 20 to 30 minutes. Serve as is or with Nutty Frosting.

7. To make Nutty Frosting: Place dates, cashews, vanilla, and 1 cup water in a blender and let sit for at least 30 minutes, so the nuts and dates can soften. Blend until smooth. Use frosting immediately, or, to thicken, chill for a couple of hours or overnight.

Deglet dates are about half as big and half as sweet as medjool, so adjust your quantities according to which variety you use.

SERVES 8

strawberry shortcakes

STACY BLONDIN

Summer would not be complete without at least one extra-large helping of strawberries and whipped cream piled high on a shortcake! Once a childhood favorite, this recipe is sophisticated enough for even the classiest of crowds.

STRAWBERRY TOPPING:
    1 to 2 pounds fresh ripe strawberries
    1 to 2 tablespoons maple syrup or honey

SHORTCAKE:
    2½ cups oat flour
    2 teaspoons baking powder
    ¼ teaspoon baking soda
    ¾ teaspoon salt
    1 tablespoon ground chia seeds
    1½ cups low-fat coconut milk
    2 teaspoons vanilla
    2 tablespoons maple syrup

WHIPPED CREAM:
    2 cups (1 batch) Coconut Dream Whipped Cream (page 276)

1. **Make the strawberry topping:** Slice, chop, and/or mash strawberries in a medium bowl according to your desired consistency. Drizzle maple syrup or honey over them and stir until well mixed. Put them in the refrigerator while making the shortcakes (for at least 30 minutes and up to several hours).
2. Preheat the oven to 400°F.
3. Combine the oat flour, baking powder, baking soda, salt, and chia seeds in a medium bowl.
4. Combine the coconut milk, vanilla, and maple syrup in a separate bowl.
5. Pour the wet mixture into the dry mixture and stir to combine.
6. Cover a baking sheet with parchment paper. Drop large spoonfuls (about ¼ cup each) of batter onto the baking sheet, evenly spaced.

7. Bake 10 to 15 minutes, or until the shortcakes are golden brown.

8. Combine shortcakes, strawberries, and whipped cream in whatever way you most enjoy. Have fun!

 If desired, 1 cup almond meal can be used instead of one of the cups of oat flour. For a sugar-free version of this dessert, simply leave out the maple syrup in the shortcake and the strawberry topping. However, be aware that the strawberries will not become juicy (macerate) without the sugar.

MAKES ABOUT 8 SHORTCAKES

coconut dream whipped cream

STACY BLONDIN

Dessert just wouldn't be the same without something to top it off! This dairy-free whipped cream is super simple to make—and appropriate for just about any dessert you can imagine. Try it on pie, waffles, crisp, or straight out of the bowl.

1 15-ounce can coconut cream
1 tablespoon maple syrup
1 teaspoon vanilla extract

1. Refrigerate the coconut cream for at least 1 hour.
2. Chill your mixing bowl and beater attachment also for at least ½ hour.
3. Open the coconut cream can from the bottom and drain the liquid, then spoon the solid cream into the chilled bowl.
4. Affix the chilled beater attachment to your mixer. Add the maple syrup and vanilla to the bowl and blend until smooth.
5. Serve immediately or refrigerate for up to a week.

 I prefer Trader Joe's coconut cream, but you can use any brand. You can also use coconut milk, but you'll be left with a lot less cream.

ABOUT 2 CUPS

pioneer gingerbread

MICAELA KARLSEN

As a child I was a big fan of Laura Ingalls Wilder's Little House on the Prairie *series, and some of my favorites parts of those books are the descriptions of what they ate. Almanzo's childhood culinary recollections in* Farmer Boy *are particularly vivid. It sort of sounds like a nonstop yearlong dinner party. A few years ago I was fortunate to come across on the Internet a letter Laura sent to a friend in 1953 (at the age of 86), enclosing her recipe for gingerbread. It's been a labor of love to create a healthier version of this pioneer treat that still does justice to the original flavor but leaves out the eggs and lard.*

3 cups whole-grain flour

1 tablespoon baking powder

1 teaspoon baking soda

1 teaspoon ginger

1 teaspoon cinnamon

1 teaspoon allspice

½ teaspoon nutmeg

½ teaspoon cloves

½ teaspoon salt

1 cup maple syrup

½ cup applesauce

¾ cup molasses

2 tablespoons white vinegar

2 cups (1 batch) Coconut Dream Whipped Cream (page 276) (optional)

1. Preheat the oven to 375°F.

2. Whisk the flour, baking powder, baking soda, ginger, cinnamon, allspice, nutmeg, cloves, and salt in a medium bowl.

3. Put maple syrup, applesauce, molasses, and white vinegar in a second medium bowl.

4. Bring a kettle of water to a boil. Once boiling, remove from heat and add 1 cup hot water to the wet ingredients, and stir.

5. Slowly add the dry ingredients to the wet ingredients while mixing, but be careful to not over-stir. The mixture should be quite thin.

6. Transfer batter to a 9×13–inch glass pan, and bake for 35 minutes.

7. Allow to cool for 10 to 15 minutes. Serve as is, or, for the traditional gingerbread experience, top with Coconut Dream Whipped Cream.

SERVES 10 TO 12

mom and me's apple thing

REBECCA MICHAELIDES

After shifting to a plant-based diet, my mom and I wanted something easy, special, and health-supporting to contribute to shared meals. After bringing this creation to a number of gatherings, requests for the "Apple Thing" were so common that, despite our attempts to call it something more lovely, the name has stuck, and it has always been known as "Apple Thing." This recipe is raw, and it is also delightful when served nut-free—simply replace the nuts with sunflower seeds.

CRUST AND TOPPING:
   2½ cups pecans or walnuts
   ¾ cup dates, pitted
   1 teaspoon ground cinnamon

FILLING:
   10 to 16 apples, cored
   6 to 8 dates, pitted
   1 tablespoon fresh lemon juice
   ½ teaspoon ground cinnamon

1. Place the nuts, dates, and cinnamon in a food processor fitted with an S blade. Chop until the mixture reaches a medium crumble. Set aside 1 cup for the topping.

2. Make the crust: Continue chopping the remaining mixture for 1 to 2 minutes, or until it starts sticking together nicely. Remove from the bowl, using a spatula to scrape down the sides. Press the mixture in the bottom of a 9×13–inch glass pan.

3. Fit the food processor with a shredder blade, and grate the apples. Transfer grated apples to a large mixing bowl.

4. Return the S blade to the food processer, and add the dates, 1 cup of the grated apples, lemon juice, and cinnamon. Chop until pureed. Stir the date-apple mixture into the grated apples until well combined. Press evenly over the crust. Sprinkle reserved topping uniformly over the top and pat down.

278

Use any variety of apples. You may substitute another spice (such as ginger, nutmeg, cloves, or allspice) for the cinnamon—or even a mixture thereof.

SERVES 8 TO 10

sweet ending baked pears

LAWRENCE MUSCAT | LIGHT ON THE HILL RETREAT CENTER

This is a universally loved and comforting dessert at the retreat center, especially during the fall and winter months. Basting the pears with fresh local apple cider graciously enhances the total flavor. Staying engaged for a full day of meditation or deep inner work can be challenging, so we are happy to serve dessert with dinner as a pleasant way to end the day.

4 pears
½ teaspoon ground cinnamon
⅛ teaspoon ground allspice
4 tablespoons raisins and/or dried cranberries
2 to 3 tablespoons maple syrup
¾ cup apple cider or other fruit juice

1. Preheat the oven to 350°F.
2. Core the pears and place in a baking dish.
3. Dust the pears, especially the interiors, with the cinnamon and allspice.
4. Fill the inner cores with the raisins and/or cranberries.
5. Drizzle the maple syrup over the pears.
6. Pour the apple cider over the pears, cover with aluminum foil, and bake for 30 minutes, or until tender. Baste with cider two or three times while cooking, as desired.
7. Cut each pear in half, and serve.

SERVES 8

two-layer vanilla-vanilla birthday cake

MICAELA KARLSEN

White cake with white frosting was a staple dessert for me growing up—especially on April 1, my birthday. After I stopped eating eggs and butter, I used to think longingly of the days when my mother would make me a white cake. I've tried a lot of cake recipes since, in an attempt to re-create that feeling. Coconut Dream Whipped Cream makes a lovely white exterior, and the creaminess and vanilla flavor succeeds in bringing me back to my childhood. This is a fairly rich and sweet dessert, so it definitely falls under the category "for special occasions." But, of course, birthdays are very special occasions!

CAKE:

- 1 cup soy milk or other plant milk
- 2 teaspoons apple cider vinegar
- 2 cups whole spelt flour
- 3 teaspoons baking powder
- 1 teaspoon baking soda
- ½ cup maple syrup
- ⅓ cup coconut cream or regular coconut milk
- 1 tablespoon vanilla extract
- ½ teaspoon salt

FILLING:

- 1 cup cashews
- 1 cup dates, pitted
- ½ cup coconut cream or regular coconut milk
- 2 vanilla beans, sliced lengthwise and scraped
- 2 teaspoons vanilla extract

FROSTING:

- 4 cups (two batches) Coconut Dream Whipped Cream (page 276), made ahead of time and refrigerated.

1. Preheat the oven to 375°F.
2. **Make the cake batter:** Combine soy milk and vinegar in a small mixing bowl and let sit for 5 to 10 minutes, until curdled. Whisk together spelt flour, baking powder, and baking soda in a medium bowl. Add the maple syrup, coconut cream, vanilla extract, and salt to the soy milk mixture. Mix thoroughly but gently, and be careful not to overstir.
3. Pour the batter evenly into two nonstick, 8-inch round springform cake pans, and quickly and gently spread the batter to cover the bottom of the pans. Try not to disturb the batter after it settles in the pan or you will lose some of the leavening action from the baking soda and the vinegar.
4. Bake cakes for 20 minutes or until a toothpick comes out clean.
5. Cool for half an hour in the pan, then remove and place on a baking rack until completely cool before frosting.
6. **Make the filling:** Place cashews, dates, coconut cream, contents of the vanilla beans, and vanilla extract in a blender. If you don't have a high-powered blender, you may want to soak the cashews and dates in water for 20 minutes before blending. (Be aware, however, that this may increase the moisture content of the frosting, which will make it less solid.) Blend on high until smooth. This make take a few minutes and require more scraping down the sides than for a smoothie.
7. **Assemble the cake:** Place one cake layer on a serving plate. Cover top generously with filling. Place second cake layer on top.
8. **Frost the cake:** The Coconut Dream Whipped Cream may be solid from being in the refrigerator. If so, rewhip with a fork or immersion blender until soft. Frost the outside of the cake and chill in the refrigerator until just before serving.

This recipe requires a double batch of Coconut Dream Whipped Cream. Make it ahead of time so it is well chilled when required for assembly.

SERVES 10 TO 12

banana ice cream

STACY BLONDIN

This dairy- and refined-sugar-free ice cream is not only nice to your taste buds but also to your wallet and waistline! The basic recipe requires only one ingredient, but my favorite version is chocolate peanut butter.

ICE CREAM:
> 2 bananas (I try to find Fair Trade bananas)
>> AND
>
> 2 tablespoons peanut butter (or nut butter of choice)
>> OR
>
> 2 tablespoons cocoa powder
>> OR
>
> 2 teaspoons instant coffee
>
> 2 tablespoons frozen berries

SUGGESTED TOPPINGS:
> 1 tablespoon cocoa nibs or shredded, unsweetened chocolate
>
> 1 tablespoon ground or slivered nuts (such as walnuts, almonds, or pecans)
>
> 1 tablespoon chia, flax, or hemp seeds
>
> 1 tablespoon sprouted, dehydrated grains (such as millet, buckwheat, or quinoa)
>
> 1 tablespoon shredded coconut, toasted
>
> 1 tablespoon unsweetened ready-to-eat cereal or rolled oats

1. Peel bananas, place in a zip-lock freezer bag or other container, and freeze until solid.
2. Remove bananas from freezer and place in blender or mixing container.
3. Add additional ingredients, as desired. (For banana-peanut butter variation, add peanut butter; for chocolate–peanut butter variation, add peanut butter and cocoa powder; for mocha variation, add cocoa powder and instant coffee.) Start with a little of each extra ingredient and add to suit your personal taste preference—because everyone has her own when it comes to ice cream!

4. Blend until smooth.

 You will need a high-powered blender (such as a Vitamix, Ninja, Blendtec, and so forth), high-wattage immersion blender, or food processor to completely puree the frozen bananas. If you don't own one of the above, let the bananas thaw a bit before blending. I recommend eating your creation immediately after blending for the creamiest ice cream; you can freeze for future consumption but the low sugar content will make for a pretty solid product (which you can thaw and blend again, if desired).

SERVES 2

buckwheat crepes with chocolate

MICAELA KARLSEN

While the tradition of buckwheat crepes is much stronger in Brittany, which is in the north, than it is in Provence-Alpes-Côte d'Azur region, which is where I lived in the south, there is a traditional southern buckwheat crepe recipe that uses just buckwheat flour and water. As you can imagine, these crepes are extremely delicate and hard to serve, so most crêperies have stopped serving them and instead use other variations that include milk, eggs, and/or beer. This version is completely plant-based, yet is delectably light and airy. The ground flaxseed and arrowroot prevent them from falling apart so they're actually pretty easy!

CREPES:

- 1 cup buckwheat flour
- ¼ teaspoon salt, or to taste
- 1 tablespoon ground flaxseed
- 1 tablespoon arrowroot powder
- ¼ cup beer or hard cider

FILLING:

- 4 ounces (about 1/2 cup grated) chocolate, chocolate chips, or raw vegan chocolate spread, for melting

1. Combine flour, salt, flaxseed, arrowroot powder, beer, and 1¾ cups water in a small bowl and whisk to mix evenly.

2. Allow mixture to set in the refrigerator at least 30 minutes but up to 3 hours before cooking. The buckwheat flour will absorb a lot more water as the batter sits, so letting it sit will ensure a creamier and more evenly thin texture. Whisk it again just before cooking to mix evenly.

3. Warm a large, nonstick pan over medium-low heat. Form a crepe by pouring ⅓ cup of batter into the pan. You can tilt the pan around to distribute the batter, but it will be hard to get the crepe thin enough without using something to spread the batter because it cooks so quickly. If you find one, a crepe-making tool is two wooden dowels connected to form a T—the top of the T is used to spread the batter.

Otherwise, the straight end of a square wooden cooking utensil will serve.

4. Spread the batter immediately upon pouring it into the pan, forming a crepe approximately 8-inches across. Continue to spread the batter as it starts to cook to fill in large air bubbles. Cook for about 1 minute, or until the surface is no longer shiny.

5. Flip crepe and cook about 30 seconds more.

6. Melt chocolate, and spread onto a hot crepe.

7. Roll up crepe, and serve.

 Buckwheat crepes are traditionally eaten even more often in Brittany as a savory dish. Try adding savory Cashew Cream (page 226), toasted walnuts, and parsley for a rich appetizer or as part of dinner. Also, for a more neutral flavor (or when making the Sweet Blintzes on page 187), substitute spelt or other whole-grain flour for buckwheat flour.

MAKES 8 8-INCH CREPES

apple crisp with almond whip

PRISCILLA TIMBERLAKE AND LEWIS FREEDMAN

We always love the smell of baking apples! This dish is one of our signature desserts with whipped topping—the whip courtesy of agar-agar, a sea vegetable used in macrobiotic cooking. We adore serving desserts that are beautifully arranged, and it's always a pleasure to top the crisp with the almond whip. A deep-dish pie pan works well, because there is a lot of filling to fit into the pan.

FILLING:

- 6 to 8 medium apples
- 1 tablespoon arrowroot
- 4 tablespoons apple juice
- ⅓ cup brown rice syrup
- 1 teaspoon cinnamon
- Pinch nutmeg
- Pinch sea salt

CRISP TOPPING:

- ⅓ cup raw walnuts
- 1⅔ cups gluten-free or regular rolled oats
- ¾ cup brown rice flour
- ⅓ teaspoon sea salt
- Pinch each of cloves, ginger, and nutmeg
- 3 tablespoons maple sugar
- ⅓ cup brown rice syrup
- 4 tablespoons unsweetened applesauce
- 2 tablespoons maple syrup
- 1 teaspoon vanilla

ALMOND WHIP:

- 1 cup unsweetened almond milk
- 4 teaspoons agar-agar flakes, or 1 teaspoon agar-agar powder
- ⅓ cup raw almonds
- ½ teaspoon almond extract
- ⅓ cup brown rice syrup
- 2 tablespoons maple syrup

1. Preheat the oven to 350°F.

2. Make the filling: Peel apples, remove core, and cut into thin slices;

place in a 9×13–inch glass baking dish. Dissolve arrowroot in 2 table-spoons of the apple juice in a small bowl and set aside. Mix remaining 2 tablespoons of apple juice, rice syrup, cinnamon, nutmeg, and salt; pour over the apple slices, and toss to make sure they are wet.

3. Cover the baking dish with aluminum foil, and bake apple mixture for 20 minutes. After removing hot apples from oven, stir in arrowroot that has been dissolved in apple juice. Do not turn off the oven.

4. **Make the crisp topping while apples are baking:** Toast walnuts in a dry pan on the stovetop over medium-high heat, or in the oven, until fragrant. Be mindful not to let walnuts burn. Cool, chop coarsely, and set walnuts aside. In a large bowl, mix together oats, rice flour, sea salt, spices, and maple sugar; stir in walnuts. In a medium bowl, whisk together rice syrup, applesauce, maple syrup, and vanilla. Pour wet mixture into dry and mix thoroughly.

5. Sprinkle crisp topping mixture over baked apples.

6. Return apples to oven and bake, covered, for 40 minutes.

7. Uncover and bake 20 minutes more.

8. **Make the almond whip:** Boil almond milk with agar-agar for 5 minutes. Pour mixture into a bowl and refrigerate for an hour or so, until it firms up. (Cooling the whip completely adds to its thickness.)

9. Blanch and remove the skins from the raw almonds. To do this, bring 1 quart of water to a boil, add almonds, let boil for 5 minutes; then replace the hot water with cold water. Squeeze the almonds between your fingers to remove the skins. Discard the skins.

10. Place the blanched almonds, almond extract, brown rice syrup, maple syrup, and cooled whip in a blender and puree until smooth. Refrigerate.

11. Serve the apple crisp. Add a spoonful of almond whip to the top of each serving.

 Agar-agar is a sea vegetable that causes gelling after dissolving in hot liquid and cooling. You can find it online, in a health food store, or in the natural section of a larger grocery store.

SERVES 6 TO 8

287

plum carpaccio with vanilla-agave syrup and ginger cream

MATTHEW KENNEY

This carpaccio may be the prettiest dish I have ever worked with. One day, I came back from the green market with the most beautiful plums but had no idea what to do with them; it soon became apparent that I needed to keep them as whole as possible. I made a quick vanilla syrup with agave and sliced the plums thin enough to have a bit of translucency to them but thick enough to have a little crunch.

VANILLA-AGAVE SYRUP:
>1 cup raw agave
>1 vanilla bean, sliced lengthwise and scraped

GINGER CREAM:
>1 cup cashews
>2 tablespoons ginger juice
>1 tablespoon raw agave
>Pinch sea salt

CARPACCIO:
>4 red plums
>4 yellow plums
>4 blue plums
>4 purple plums

GARNISH:
>4 lavender sprigs

1. **Make the vanilla-agave syrup:** Place the agave and vanilla bean in a small bowl, and mix well.
2. **Make the ginger cream:** Soak the cashews in 2 cups water for 1 to 2 hours. Drain and transfer the soaked cashews to a high-powered blender. Add ginger juice, agave, sea salt, and ½ cup water, and whip until smooth. Keep cool.

3. **Assemble the carpaccio:** Wash the plums, halve them, remove pits, and slice very thin using a mandolin or sharp knife. Distribute the plum slices among 4 plates, alternating the colors. Just before serving, pour enough vanilla-agave syrup over the plums just to coat.

4. Garnish each plate with a scoop of ginger cream and a sprig of lavender.

For more speedy preparation, start soaking the cashews ahead of time. Cashews aside, this dish is going to take you 10 minutes to make. Slicing the plums close to when they are being served is recommended.

SERVES 4

289

ONGOING SUPPORT RESOURCES

THREE WEEKS OF MEAL PLANS

The first three weeks of any dietary transition are the hardest, so that can be a good time to rely on structured meal plans to help guide your choices, remove the decision making from your to-do list, and free up your energy to focus on cooking, eating, and enjoying the food. These meal plans start on Sunday and assume you are cooking at least dinner and brunch for a family of four (though you may have to adjust the quantities for your particular situation). These meal plans are also based on the idea that you will have a bit more time on Sunday for some extra cooking to prepare for the week ahead. Try to make enough to allow for leftovers.

Dessert is suggested for Saturday only, to make the weekends a little more fun while keeping cooking time realistic. If you're feeling like sweets during the weekdays after dinner, some fresh fruit is always a good choice.

You'll recognize the names of specific recipes, which are capitalized, along with other straightforward accompaniments like wraps or side salads. Green salads are suggested with many of the dinners—try any of the oil-free dressings in the Sauces, Spreads, and Dressings section that look tasty to you, and if you don't use them up in one meal they do freeze well. Remember to drink plenty of water too!

WEEK 1

SUNDAY

- **BRUNCH:** Savory Tofu Scramble (page 157), Sweet Potato Hash (page 159), Breakfast-and-Beyond Smoothie (page 153),
- **SNACK:** apple with almond or peanut butter
- **DINNER:** Carrot-Rice Casserole (page 260) with green salad
- **SUGGESTED COOKING FOR LATER IN THE WEEK:** Almond Cinnamon Granola (page 155), Simple Split Pea Comfort Soup (page 192), Teatime Cornmeal Muffins (page 168), Tu-No Salad (page 211)

MONDAY

- **BREAKFAST:** Almond Cinnamon Granola (page 155)
- **SNACK:** banana, orange, fresh berries, or other fresh fruit
- **LUNCH:** Simple Split Pea Comfort Soup (page 192), whole-grain wrap with Tu-No Salad (page 211)
- **SNACK:** Teatime Cornmeal Muffins (page 168) with defrosted frozen strawberries
- **DINNER:** Colorful Yams and Greens (page 208), Portobello Steaks (page 253)

TUESDAY

- **BREAKFAST:** Everyday Oats (page 151), Breakfast-and-Beyond Smoothie (page 153)
- **SNACK:** grapes, kiwi, or melon
- **LUNCH:** leftover Colorful Yams and Greens, nori seaweed wraps of leftover Tu-No Salad
- **SNACK:** mixed raisins, cranberries, currents, dried apple, and walnuts
- **DINNER:** The Esselstyns' Stacked High Black Beans and Rice (page 249)

WEDNESDAY

- **BREAKFAST:** Breakfast Sunshine Salad (page 161)
- **SNACK:** Teatime Cornmeal Muffins (page 168) with apple butter
- **LUNCH:** leftover Simple Split Pea Comfort Soup
- **SNACK:** Fresh melon or other fresh fruit
- **DINNER:** Chilled Peanut Noodles (page 268) with green salad
- **COOKING FOR LATER IN THE WEEK:** Lemon-Rice-Kale Soup (page 197), make brown rice and dressing of your choice

THURSDAY

- **BREAKFAST:** Green Colada (page 156)
- **SNACK:** Almond Cinnamon Granola (page 155)

- **LUNCH:** leftover Chilled Peanut Noodles and green salad
- **SNACK:** veggies and whole-grain crackers with Mushroom Walnut Pâté (page 229)
- **DINNER:** Rescue Quinoa (page 241) and green salad

FRIDAY

- **BREAKFAST:** Breakfast Rice Pudding (page 162)
- **SNACK:** apple with almond or peanut butter
- **LUNCH:** Jacked-Up Fruity Appetizers (page 183) as a meal
- **SNACK:** dried or fresh figs and a few almonds
- **DINNER:** Five Ways to Sushi (page 244)

SATURDAY

- **BREAKFAST:** Everyday Oats (page 151)
- **SNACK:** whole-grain or spelt raisin bread with berries (fresh or defrosted)
- **LUNCH:** whole-grain pita sandwich with Walnut-Mushroom Pâté (page 229) with lettuce and tomatoes, apple or orange
- **SNACK:** Carrot Cake Smoothie (page 170)
- **DINNER:** Cauliflower au Gratin (page 259) with Colorful Crudités (page 215) and green salad
- **DESSERT:** Apple Crisp with Almond Whip (page 286)

WEEK 2

SUNDAY

- **BRUNCH:** Florentine Frittata (page 163), The Best Waffle You'll Ever Have (page 160), Morning Glorious (page 152)
- **SNACK:** banana dipped in plain, unsweetened cocoa powder
- **DINNER:** double-batch for your family of Super Easy Pizza (page 261) and Basket of Jewels with Walnut Sauce (page 213)
- **COOKING FOR LATER IN THE WEEK:** Almond Cinnamon Granola (page 155), The *Best* Bean Chili (page 201), Oatmeal Bars (page 169); make brown rice, make salad dressing of your choice

MONDAY

- **BREAKFAST:** Everyday Oats (page 151)
- **SNACK:** banana, orange, fresh berries, or other fresh fruit
- **LUNCH:** leftover Super Easy Pizza and green salad
- **SNACK:** Oatmeal Bars (page 169)
- **DINNER:** The *Best* Bean Chili (page 201) with brown rice

293

TUESDAY

- **BREAKFAST:** Everyday Oats (page 151)
- **SNACK:** apple with almond or peanut butter
- **LUNCH:** Emergency Mini Burritos (page 239) and banana
- **SNACK:** Oil-free, whole-grain crackers dipped in salad dressing of your choice
- **DINNER:** West African–Inspired Sweet Potatoes and Kale (page 265) with brown rice

WEDNESDAY

- **BREAKFAST:** Breakfast Rice Pudding (page 162)
- **SNACK:** Oatmeal Bars (page 169)
- **LUNCH:** big salad with sunflower seeds, beans and colorful veggies, with dressing of your choice
- **SNACK: defrosted frozen blueberries with shredded coconut**
- **DINNER:** Hearty Lentil Loaf (page 267), baked sweet potatoes
- **COOKING FOR LATER IN THE WEEK:** Gingery Carrot Soup (page 196), Buckwheat Crepes, without chocolate (page 284), Surefire Pesto (page 230); baked sweet potatoes

THURSDAY

- **BREAKFAST:** Everyday Oats (page 151)
- **SNACK:** cool sweet potato
- **LUNCH:** leftover Hearty Lentil Loaf in Buckwheat Crepes with lettuce and mustard or ketchup
- **SNACK:** mixed raisins, cranberries, currents, dried apple, and walnuts
- **DINNER:** Potato Leek Soup (page 195)

FRIDAY

- **BREAKFAST:** Everyday Oats (page 151)
- **SNACK:** Buckwheat Crepes with Surefire Pesto (page 230)
- **LUNCH:** canned baked beans (low-sodium and low-sweetener, such as Eden brand) on whole-grain toast with leftover baked sweet potato and green salad
- **SNACK:** banana, orange, fresh berries, or other fresh fruit
- **DINNER:** Arame, Red Onion, and Pine Nuts (page 219), Farmshare Miso Soup (page 198)

SATURDAY

- **BREAKFAST:** Breakfast Rice Pudding (page 162)
- **SNACK:** Fresh snap peas

294

- **LUNCH:** leftover Farmshare Miso Soup with whole-grain crackers
- **SNACK:** banana, orange, fresh berries, or other fresh fruit
- **DINNER:** Tasty Corn Cakes (page 179) with low-sodium salsa, Collard Wraps (page 185) filled with canned refried beans, and green salad
- **DESSERT:** Sweet Ending Baked Pears (page 279)

WEEK 3

SUNDAY

- **BRUNCH:** Savory Tofu Scramble (page 157), The Best Waffle You'll Ever Have (page 160), Morning Glorious (page 152)
- **LUNCH:** leftover Tasty Corn Cakes
- **SNACK:** sweet sliced bell peppers
- **DINNER:** Best Basic Southwestern Burgers (page 258) with whole-grain bun, Guacamole Salad (page 220)
- **COOKING FOR LATER IN THE WEEK:** Almond Cinnamon Granola (page 155), Corn Chowder (page 191), Favorite Sandwich Spread (page 228), Unlimited Baked Corn Chips (page 171)

MONDAY

- **BREAKFAST:** Everyday Oats (page 151)
- **SNACK:** banana, orange, or fresh berries
- **LUNCH:** Corn Chowder (page 191) and whole-grain wrap with Favorite Sandwich Spread (page 228)
- **SNACK:** ants on a log and wheel (aka celery and rice cakes with nut butter and raisins)
- **DINNER:** Dr. Lederman's Black Bean Soup (page 194), brown rice, and Unlimited Baked Corn Chips (page 171) and sliced avocado

TUESDAY

- **BREAKFAST:** Breakfast Rice Pudding (page 162)
- **SNACK:** banana, orange, fresh berries, or other fresh fruit
- **LUNCH:** Best Basic Southwestern Burgers (page 258) with whole-grain buns and raw veggies
- **SNACK:** Favorite Sandwich Spread (page 228) with Unlimited Baked Corn Chips (page 171)
- **DINNER:** Romantic Vegetable Stew (page 199)

WEDNESDAY

- **BREAKFAST:** Everyday Oats (page 151), Breakfast-and-Beyond Smoothie (page 153)
- **SNACK:** nectarines, peaches or sliced melon
- **LUNCH:** leftover Romantic Vegetable Stew with Unlimited Baked Corn Chips (page 171)
- **SNACK:** rice-less nori seaweed wrap of low-sodium dill pickles and peanut butter
- **DINNER:** Summer Strawberry Salad (page 210) with Raspberry Vinaigrette Dressing (page 232)
- **COOKING FOR LATER IN THE WEEK:** Classic Borscht (page 193) Use-Me-All-the-Time Hummus (page 231), Oatmeal Bars (page 169)

THURSDAY

- **BREAKFAST:** Breakfast-and-Beyond Smoothie (page 153)
- **SNACK:** Oatmeal Bars (page 169)
- **LUNCH:** whole-grain wrap with Use-Me-All-the-Time Hummus (page 231) and veggies, Classic Borscht (page 193)
- **SNACK:** banana, orange, fresh berries, or other fresh fruit
- **DINNER:** Ginger Roasted Vegetables and Tempeh (page 264), Skinny Smashed Potatoes (page 217), Mushroom Gravy (page 223)

FRIDAY

- **BREAKFAST:** Everyday Oats (page 151)
- **SNACK:** Oatmeal Bars (page 169)
- **LUNCH:** Curried Chickpea Salad Sandwich (page 240), Classic Borscht (page 193)
- **SNACK:** apple with almond or peanut butter
- **DINNER:** Interstellar Lasagna (page 250)

SATURDAY

- **BREAKFAST:** Breakfast Sunshine Salad, (page 161) Morning Glorious (page 152)
- **SNACK:** cut veggies with Use-Me-All-the-Time Hummus (page 231)
- **LUNCH:** Interstellar Lasagna (page 250) and Zesty Three-Bean Salad (page 212)
- **SNACK:** banana, orange, fresh berries, or other fresh fruit
- **DINNER:** Zesty Three–Bean Salad (page 212), Potato Salad with Pine Nuts, Olives, and Dill (page 209), and green salad
- **DESSERT:** Pioneer Gingerbread (page 277) with Coconut Dream Whipped Cream (page 276)

BOOKS

FOR FURTHER NUTRITION EDUCATION

The China Study by T. Colin Campbell, PhD (BenBella Books, 2005)

Whole by T. Colin Campbell, PhD (BenBella Books, 2014)

The Low-Carb Fraud by T. Colin Campbell, PhD (BenBella Books, 2014)

Prevent and Reverse Heart Disease by Caldwell B. Esselstyn Jr., MD (Avery, 2007)

The Pleasure Trap by Douglas J. Lisle, PhD, and Alan Goldhamer, DC (Healthy Living Publications, 2003)

Dr. Neal Barnard's Program for Reversing Diabetes by Neal D. Barnard, MD (Rodale Books, 2008)

Breaking the Food Seduction by Neal D. Barnard, MD (St. Martin's Press, 2003)

The Vegiterranean Diet by Julieanna Hever, MS, RD (Da Capo Lifelong Books, 2014)

The Complete Idiot's Guide to Plant-Based Nutrition by Julieanna Hever, MS, RD (Alpha, 2011)

The Starch Solution by John McDougall, MD, and Mary McDougall (Rodale Books, 2013)

Dr. McDougall's Digestive Tune-Up by John A. McDougall, MD (Book Pub. Co., 2006)

Food over Medicine by Pamela A. Popper, ND (BenBella Books, 2014)

Dr. Dean Ornish's Program for Reversing Heart Disease by Dean Ornish, MD (Ivy Books, 1995)

Salt Sugar Fat by Michael Moss (Random House, 2013)

Becoming Vegan (Express or Comprehensive Editions) by Brenda Davis, RD, and Vesanto Melina, MS, RD (Book Pub. Co., 2013)

How Not to Die by Michael Greger, MD (Flatiron Books, 2015)

Building Bone Vitality by Amy Joy Lanou, PhD, and Michael Castleman (McGraw-Hill Education, 2009)

FOR BROADER EDUCATION

Willpower by Roy F. Baumeister, PhD, and John Tierney (Penguin Press HC, 2011)

The End of Overeating by David A. Kessler, MD (Rodale Books, 2009)

Connected by Nicholas A. Christakis, MD, PhD and James H. Fowler, PhD (Back Bay Books, 2011)

Food Politics by Marion Nestle, PhD (University of California Press, 2013)

Food and Addiction by Kelly D. Brownell, PhD, and Mark S. Gold, MD (Oxford University Press, 2014)

FOR PRACTICAL SUPPORT

The Forks over Knives Plan by Alona Pulde, MD, and Matthew Lederman, MD (Touchstone, 2014)

The Campbell Plan by Thomas Campbell, MD (Rodale Books, 2015)

Thrive Fitness by Brendan Brazier (Penguin Canada, 2008)

The Plant-Based Journey by Lani Muelrath (BenBella Books, 2015)

COOKBOOKS

Forks over Knives: The Plant-Based Way to Health edited by Gene Stone (The Experiment, 2011)

The China Study Cookbook by LeAnne Campbell, PhD (BenBella Books, 2013)

The Prevent and Reverse Heart Disease Cookbook by Ann Crile Esselstyn and Jane Esselstyn (Avery, 2014)

Forks over Knives: The Cookbook by Del Sroufe (The Experiment, 2012)

The China Study Quick and Easy Cookbook by Del Sroufe (BenBella Books, 2015)

Bravo! by Ramses Bravo (Book Pub. Co., 2012)

The Health Promoting Cookbook by Alan Goldhamer, DC (Book Pub. Co., 1997)

Engine 2 Diet by Rip Esselstyn (Grand Central Life & Style, 2009)

Unprocessed by Chef AJ and Glen Merzer (CreateSpace Independent Publishing Platform, 2011)

Appetite for Reduction by Isa Chandra Moskowitz (Da Capo Lifelong Books, 2010)

Fresh from the Vegan Slow Cooker by Robin Robertson (Harvard Common Press, 2012)

Plant-Powered Families by Dreena Burton (BenBella Books, 2015)

The Happy Herbivore by Lindsay Nixon (BenBella Books, 2011)

The Great Life Cookbook by Priscilla Timberlake and Lewis Freedman, RD (Coddington Valley Publishing, 2014)

The Candle Café Cookbook by Joy Pierson, Bart Potenza, and Barbara Scott-Goodman (Clarkson Potter, 2003)

Vegan Family Meals by Ann Gentry (Andrews McMeel Publishing, 2011)

The Angelica Home Kitchen by Leslie McEachern (Ten Speed Press, 2003)

The McDougall Quick and Easy Cookbook by John A. McDougall, MD, and Mary McDougall (Plume, 1999)

WEBSITES

FOR FURTHER NUTRITION EDUCATION

plantbasedresearch.org
nutritionstudies.org
nutritionfacts.org
dresselstyn.com
jeffnovick.com
drmcdougall.com
plantbaseddietitian.com
wellnessforum.com

RECIPES

StraightUpFood.com
blog.fatfreevegan.com
happyherbivore.com
plantpoweredkitchen.com
forksoverknives.com/recipes/

PLANT-BASED MEAL DELIVERY

22daysnutrition.com
veestro.com
forksoverknives.com/forksfreshmeals
thepurplecarrot.com
thevegangarden.com
veginout.com

macro-mediterranean.com
kitchentherapy.nyc

MEAL PLANS AND/OR GROCERY DELIVERY

thrivemarket.com
lighterculture.com
instacart.com
peapod.com
shop.rochebros.com
shop.safeway.com
freshdirect.com
hellofresh.com

PLANT-BASED OR PLANT-FRIENDLY HEALTHCARE CONFERENCES

International Plant-Based Nutrition Healthcare Conference (pbnhc.com)
Plant-based Prevention of Disease Conference (P-POD; preventionofdisease.org)
American College of Lifestyle Medicine Conference (lifestylemedicine.org)

LIVE LOCAL CONNECTIONS

vegan.meetup.com
vegetarian.meetup.com
plantpurenation.com/plantpure-pods

VEGGIE/VEGAN/GREEN DATING SITES

vegandating.org
veggiedate.org
veganpassions.com
veggiematchmakers.com
greensingles.com
veggieromance.com

ONLINE DISCUSSION FORUMS

drmcdougall.com/forums/

TO FIND COMMUNITY SUPPORTED FARMS AND FARM FRESH FOOD

localharvest.org/csa/
farmigo.com

TO FIND A PLANT-FRIENDLY PHYSICIAN

plantbaseddocs.com

TO FIND A COGNITIVE BEHAVIORAL THERAPIST

findcbt.org/xFAT/

VIDEOS

Forks over Knives
Forks over Knives: The Extended Interviews
PlantPure Nation
Planeat

May I Be Frank
The Future of Food

COOKING INSTRUCTION

Rouxbe Plant-Based Cooking Certification
Forks over Knives Online Cooking Course
Matthew Kenney Culinary
The School of Natural Cookery

GETTING STARTED GUIDES

The Plantrician Project Quick Start Guide (plantricianproject.org/quickstartguide)
PCRM's 21 Day Kick Start (pcrm.org/kickstartHome)
HabitsofHealth.support

RESIDENTIAL PROGRAMS

RESIDENTIAL MEDICAL PROGRAMS

TrueNorth Health Center
Complete Health Improvement Program (CHIP)
Total Health Immersions
Dr. McDougall's Residential Programs

RETREATS FOR REFLECTION AND PERSONAL GROWTH

Light on the Hill Retreat Center
Omega Institute for Holistic Studies
Kripalu Center for Yoga & Health Esalen Institute
Oh-An Zendo Meditation Center

ESSENTIAL SOCIAL MEDIA TO FOLLOW ON FACEBOOK, TWITTER, OR YOUTUBE

Forks over Knives
Plant-Based Dietitian /Julieanna Hever
T. Colin Campbell Center for Nutrition Studies
PlantPureNation
FatFreeVegan
NutritionFacts
Happy Herbivore
Dr. Caldwell B. Esselstyn Jr.
Dr. John McDougall
Micaela Karlsen, PlantbasedResearch.org

ACKNOWLEDGMENTS

There are so many important people who have helped in some way to make this book possible, either by inspiring or teaching me, by working directly on the book chapters with me, or by supporting me personally. I'm truly grateful and feel so much love for all of you.

First, and most importantly, thank you to my wonderful husband, Mark—for your love and support, your help on this project, and your trust and belief in me. Thank you to my parents—for your love and support my whole life. And thank you to my wonderful friends—for making it feel as if everywhere I go, I'm among family.

To my amazing editors at AMACOM—thank you to Bob Nirkind, for his patience and skill with this project, even as he was on the brink of retiring, and then into his retirement, as well as to Stephen S. Power, Barry Richardson, and Alison Hagge. To my wonderful agent, Linda Konner— thank you for believing in this book and taking a chance on working with me. And to Lisa Tener—thank you for guiding me from a fresh idea to an actual manuscript, and helping me with the writing many times over.

To all the recipe contributors in this book—thank you for sharing a piece of yourself in this project and being living examples of the many beautiful ways there are to eat a plant-based diet.

To my colleagues, collaborators, friends, and mentors from the plant-based nutrition community—thank you for the work you do, the lives you save, and the societal change you are making possible. We are building a new world, and I couldn't be happier than to be doing it with you.

To Kathy Pollard—thank you for being my friend and collaborator, as well as for all your feedback on this manuscript. To Megan Mueller—thank you for your crucial assistance in identifying some of the important research to share around behavior change. To Meghan Murphy—thank you for being my partner in crime for so many years, and for the memories we made together.

To Alice McDowell—thank you for showing me how to follow the wisdom of my heart. To my dearest friends and community through Light on the Hill—thank you for being on this spiritual path together and holding a space for all of us to live in alignment with our highest purpose.

To the inspiring people who have been generous enough to share their stories in this book—thank you for modeling what is possible when you take control of your health and showing others that they can do it too.

To my academic mentors—especially Dr. Nicola McKeown and Dr. Sara Folta—thank you for giving me the opportunity to investigate the questions that keep me up at night, and thank you for your guidance and training as I strive to practice evidence-based thinking and unbiased investigation.

Finally, to Dr. T. Colin Campbell and his incredible wife, Karen Campbell—thank you for living and teaching the true meaning of integrity. Because of you, some surprising research results from decades ago that would otherwise have been brushed aside made their way into research funding, into active investigation, and into the kitchen. None of us can thank you enough.

RECIPE CONTRIBUTORS

Robby Barbaro has been a type 1 diabetic for over 15 years and has found a fruit-based diet to be ideal for his blood glucose management and energy levels. He has been eating raw fruits and vegetables for over 9 years, with HbA1c numbers in the 5.9–6.4 range. Robby started the Mindful Diabetic website to share the benefits of whole food, planted-based eating for diabetics, with an emphasis on the benefits of fruits. Robby also serves as the operations manager for Forks over Knives, where he has been an integral team member since 2010. [mindfuldiabetic.com]

Susan Benigas, while president of a worksite wellness company, had the paradigm shift leading to her life's passion: questioning the status quo approach to "wellness"—all too often to diagnose and medicate—as opposed to a primary focus on identifying and eradicating the cause of disease. She has a BS in Communications from the University of Tulsa and a Certificate in Plant-Based Nutrition from eCornell and the T. Colin Campbell Center for Nutrition Studies. Susan's passion for reaching the gatekeepers of dietary recommendations—our nation's physicians and healthcare practitioners—led to her founding The Plantrician Project and co-founding the International Plant-Based Nutrition Healthcare Conference, showcasing the efficacy of whole food, plant-based nutrition in its ability to prevent, suspend, and often even reverse much of the chronic, degenerative disease afflicting our world. In addition to her work with The Plantrician Project, Susan serves as executive director of the American College of Lifestyle Medicine. [plantricianproject.org]

Stacy Blondin, MSPH is a PhD candidate at Tufts Friedman School of Nutrition Science and Policy, studying the health, economic, social, and environmental impact of dietary patterns and behavior. Her dissertation research focuses on food waste and plant-based meals in the National School Meal programs, with the goal of informing policies that promote long-term health and food system sustainability.

Kris Carr is a *New York Times* bestselling author, as well as a speaker and wellness activist. She is the subject and director of the documentary *Crazy Sexy Cancer*, which premiered at the SXSW Film Festival in 2007 and has aired on TLC, The Discovery Channel, and The Oprah Winfrey Network. Kris is also the author of the award-winning Crazy Sexy book series, including *Crazy Sexy Diet* and *Crazy Sexy Kitchen*. Kris regularly lectures at hospitals, wellness centers, corporations such as Whole Foods, and Harvard University. As an irreverent foot soldier in the fight against disease, she inspires countless people to take charge of their health and happiness by adopting a plant-passionate diet and self-care practices, and learning to live and love like they really mean it. "Morning Glorious" and "Green Colada" recipes are adapted from *Crazy Sexy Kitchen* by Kris Carr, published by Hay House, Inc., 2012. Used with permission. [kriscarr.com]

Chef AJ has been devoted to a plant-based diet for almost 40 years. She is the host of the television series *Healthy Living with Chef AJ*, which airs on Foody TV. A chef, culinary instructor, and professional speaker, she is author of the popular book *Unprocessed: How to Achieve Vibrant Health and Your Ideal Weight*, which chronicles her journey from a junk-food vegan faced with a diagnosis of precancerous polyps, to learning how to create foods that nourish and heal the body. She is the creator of *The Ultimate Weight Loss Program*, was the executive pastry chef at Sante La Brea Restaurant in Los Angeles, and creator of *Healthy Taste of LA* and the YouTube cooking show *The Chef and the Dietitian*. Chef AJ holds a Certificate in Plant-Based Nutrition from eCornell and is a member of the American College of Lifestyle Medicine. [eatunprocessed.com]

Craig Cochran has been a tour-de-force in the New York City vegan scene with over 10 years of opening and running notable restaurants around town. Starting in 2003, Craig opened Candle 79 and managed the restaurant until he went on to Angelica Kitchen in 2006. After that, Craig opened Blossom Cafe and acted as general manager there, eventually opening two off-shoots for the company, until he decided he had a calling of his own. In 2010, he and partner Mike Pease co-founded Terri and opened the first location in Chelsea, opening branches in the financial district in 2013 and midtown east in 2015. Craig is also the co-founder of Blackbird Seitan, which has been distributing seitan to New York City and Philadelphia restaurants since 2013. [terrinyc.com]

Al Davis has been cooking for over 60 years and lives in Belmont, MA. He became almost 100 percent vegan over three years ago and enjoys cooking for himself and others. He enjoys helping others overcome both their weight problems and health challenges stemming from diet. [curbthose cravings.com]

Ann Crile Esselstyn is a relentlessly energetic and creative advocate for the plant-based, whole food way of life. She has devoted herself to inventing recipes to prevent and reverse heart disease in support of the research of her husband, Dr. Caldwell Esselstyn, Jr. Ann never stops looking for ways to bring that important agenda to delicious life, devising ever more practical and powerful ways to shop, cook, and engage even the most reluctant eaters in the plant-perfect diet. She is the author of the recipe section of Dr. Esselstyn's bestselling book, *Prevent and Reverse Heart Disease*, and co-author of *The Prevent and Reverse Heart Disease Cookbook* with her daughter, Jane Esselstyn. When not in the kitchen, Ann counsels patients and lectures around the world on how to prepare and eat plant-based foods. [www. dresselstyn.com]

Cathy Fisher is a chef and teacher whose passion is creating health-promoting recipes that avoid all animal foods, as well as any added salt, oil, or sugar. Sixteen years ago, she sought out a plant-based diet in an effort to find substitutions for dairy foods, which had always given her terrible stomachaches. The results were so immediate and exciting that a few years later she began pursuing a career in the field of plant-based cooking. Cathy teaches cooking classes to patients at TrueNorth Health Center and the McDougall Program, both located in Santa Rosa, California, and is also the creator of the popular recipe blog Straight Up Food, offering recipes and information on eating a whole foods, plant-based diet free of added salt, oil, and sugar. [straightupfood.com]

Julieanna Hever, MS, RD, CPT is the host of Veria Living Network's *What Would Julieanna Do?*, author of the bestselling book *The Complete Idiot's Guide to Plant-Based Nutrition* as well as *The Vegiterranean Diet*, and the nutrition columnist for *VegNews Magazine*. She is the co-author of *The Complete Idiot's Guide to Gluten-Free Vegan Cooking*. Julieanna was also a special consultant for the bestselling documentary *Forks over Knives* and has contributed recipes to both *Forks over Knives* books. Her recent work as the executive director of EarthSave, International, provided an opportunity for Julieanna to bring whole food, plant-based nutrition to the forefront of efforts to improve the current global health crisis. Julieanna received her BA from UCLA and Masters of Science in Nutrition at California State University, Northridge, where she also completed her dietetic internship. [plantbaseddietitian.com]

Mark Karlsen is an avid environmentalist and animal lover, as well as a musician. A long-time vegetarian, Mark took the next step to being animal-free in 2006 thanks to his wife, Micaela, and reading *The China Study*. His cooking specialty is breakfast: smoothies, potatoes, pancakes, and, of course, waffles. [journeywestmusic.com]

Micaela Karlsen, MSPH is a contributor to the *New York Times* best-seller *Forks over Knives: The Plant-Based Way to Health*. Micaela was one of the two founding employees of the T. Colin Campbell Foundation (now the T. Colin Campbell Center for Nutrition Studies), where she served as the foundation's executive director and played a critical role in launching the Certificate Program in Plant-Based Nutrition with eCornell, before leaving the organization to focus on her doctoral studies. Micaela holds an MSPH in Human Nutrition from Johns Hopkins Bloomberg School of Public Health and a BA in Psychology from Cornell University. She is a PhD candidate in Nutritional Epidemiology at the Tufts Friedman School of Nutrition Science and Policy. She serves on the board of directors for the nonprofits, Plant-Based Prevention of Disease (P-POD) and Light on the Hill Retreat Center. With her partner, Kathy Pollard, Micaela co-created Habits of Health. In 2013 she created Plant-Based Research.org, a free online data-base of original, peer-reviewed research studies relevant to plant-based nutrition. [plantbasedresearch.org and mikaelakarlsen.com]

Matthew Kenney graduated from the French Culinary Institute and, after working in upscale New York City kitchens, opened a number of his own highly regarded restaurants in New York and along the East Coast. He has earned several awards, including being named one of America's Best New Chefs by *Food and Wine Magazine*, and was twice nominated as a Rising Star

Chef in America by the James Beard Foundation. Kenney has appeared on numerous food and talk shows, and regularly lectures on the subject of food and health. In 2009, Kenney founded the world's first classically structured raw food culinary academy, Matthew Kenney Academy. Along with operating his namesake academy and restaurant brand, Kenny is involved in raw food chef and plant-based projects around the world, and travels extensively to forward his mission to show others that food can be delicious and vibrant, while still healthful. [matthewkenneycuisine.com]

Matthew Lederman, MD is a board-certified internal medicine physician with an avid interest in the field of nutrition and lifestyle medicine. Dr. Lederman seeks to change the way chronic illness is treated, with an emphasis on medication elimination and disease reversal through diet and lifestyle change. He has participated in projects such as lecturing for the eCornell Certificate Program in Plant-Based Nutrition and films such as *Healing Cancer* and *Forks over Knives*. With his wife, Dr. Alona Pulde, Dr. Lederman coauthored *Keep It Simple, Keep It Whole: Your Guide to Optimum Health* as well as *The Forks over Knives Plan*. [transitiontohealth.com]

Maggie Loeb is a lover of gardening, fresh veggies, and good wine. She is an optician in central Pennsylvania and appreciates all aspects of health. Her pleasure in plant-based foods goes back many years, and she continues to enjoy developing new recipes.

Rebecca Michaelides, MS holds an MS in Applied Clinical Nutrition from the New York Chiropractic College and a BS in Environmental Science with a focus on sustainable development and pesticide use issues from SUNY College of Environmental Science and Forestry. The focus of her work and education has been the interactions between food, people, the environment, and health: how food is grown, marketed, prepared, and eaten; how it energizes the body and supports well-being, and how social and environmental issues challenge food security. She is the former instructor team coordinator for the Certificate Program in Plant-Based Nutrition through the T. Colin Campbell Center for Nutrition Studies and eCornell.

Lawrence Muscat co-founded Light on the Hill Retreat Center in upstate New York together with his wife, Dr. Alice McDowell. He is an ordained minister and student of the Mysteries, both ancient and modern. Lawrence manages the buildings and ground maintenance at the retreat center, as well as overseeing the cooking for both individual and group retreats. [lightonthehill.org]

Jeff Novick, RD has over 24 years of experience in nutrition, health, fitness, and natural living as a registered dietitian and nutritionist. Jeff serves as vice president of health promotion for Executive Health Exams International and lectures at the McDougall Program in Santa Rosa, California and at the Engine 2 Immersion program in Austin, Texas. He is also the director of nutrition for the Meals for Health community project, which is helping empower low-income families to achieve optimal health. Jeff has also created and taught the Nutrition Education Initiative, a preventive medicine curriculum for medical doctors, residents, and medical students. He has also appeared in the documentary *Processed People* and the movie *Fatboy*. [jeffnovick.com]

Natalie Obermeyer Hunter, MS, MPH first experienced the benefits of plant-based eating in high school while cross-country ski racing in Colorado. Her love of health and nutrition followed her to New Hampshire, where she studied biology and ran on the endurance racing team at Dartmouth College. Afterwards, Natalie continued her education at Tufts University, where she pursued a Master of Public Health and a Master of Science in Nutrition Communication. She currently lives in Boston with her husband, Matt, and is the nutrition science lead for Lighter, which creates customized meal plans paired with home delivery of the groceries.

Kathy Pollard, MS is an instructor for the renowned T. Colin Campbell Center for Nutrition Studies, offering the Certificate in Plant-Based Nutrition through eCornell. She holds a Master's degree in Applied Clinical Nutrition from New York Chiropractic College. Previously, Kathy's interest in teaching others led her to open The Wellness Forum Health at State College in 2010, empowering her community to take control of personal health through an understanding of evidence-based nutrition. Her extensive experience with those interested in making change has inspired her to develop, along with founder and partner Micaela Karlsen, MSPH, Habits of Health, a distance-based support program helping individuals to successfully transition to a more whole food, plant-based diet. She presently serves on the board of directors for the nonprofit Plant-Based Prevention of Disease (P-POD), speaks on the power of plant-based diets to groups, and

308

continues her research and education in plant-based nutrition. [habitsof health.support]

Micah Risk, MS is the co-founder of Lighter, a nutrition-tech company that creates customized meal plans making plant-based eating easy. She holds an MS in Food Policy and Applied Nutrition with a specialization in Nutrition Interventions from the Tufts University Friedman School of Nutrition Science and Policy and a BS in Exercise Science with a concentration in Community Health Education from Virginia Commonwealth University. As a mom and an ultra marathoner, food is essential for keeping her family happy and healthy and her legs running fast. She emphasizes easy-to-cook ingredients dressed up with no-frill blends of delicious spices and flavors in her plant-based recipes. [lighterculture.com]

Del Sroufe is the co-owner and executive chef at the Wellness Forum Health. He is the author of *Forks over Knives: The Cookbook*, which appeared on the *New York Times* bestseller list for 33 weeks, *Better than Vegan*, and *The China Study Quick* and *Easy Cookbook*. He joined Wellness Forum Health in 2006, where he has developed delicious ready-to-eat meals, low-fat sauces and dressings, a popular line of In-the-Bag quick mixes, catering, and cooking classes. He has also developed an international reputation as a speaker; his talks focus not only on how to make fabulous and healthy dishes, but also on his own health improvement journey, which includes losing over 240 pounds. [wellnessforum.com]

Lisa Tener became a vegan and embraced a whole foods, plant-based diet while working with Micaela Karlsen on *A Plant-Based Life*, as Micaela's book coach. Lisa serves on the faculty of the Harvard Medical School, teaching a continuing education course on writing and publishing books. As she's changed her diet, she's enjoyed developing new recipes that use truly whole food ingredients to replace the sugary foods that used to be her go-to snacks. [lisatener.com]

Priscilla Timberlake and **Lewis Freedman, RD** have been hosting weekly macrobiotic community dinners in their home in the Ithaca area for nearly 20 years. Priscilla is a wellness instructor at Cornell University and also teaches cooking classes at her local cooperative market. Lewis is an instructor for the Certificate Program in Plant-Based Nutrition through the T. Colin Campbell Center for Nutrition Studies and eCornell,

309

allowing him to be directly involved with the growing global movement toward embracing a whole food plant-based diet. He is also a registered dietitian and teaches yoga and stress management at Cornell University. [thegreatlifecookbook.com]

NOTES

INTRODUCTION

1. Barnard ND, Cohen J, Jenkins DJ, et al. "A low-fat vegan diet and a conventional diabetes diet in the treatment of type 2 diabetes: a randomized, controlled, 74-wk clinical trial." *American Journal of Clinical Nutrition.* 2009: 1588S–96S.

    Barnard ND, Cohen J, Jenkins DJ, et al. "A low-fat vegan diet improves glycemic control and cardiovascular risk factors in a randomized clinical trial in individuals with type 2 diabetes." *Diabetes Care.* 2006: 1777–83.

    Barnard ND, Katcher HI, Jenkins DJ, Cohen J, Turner-McGrievy G. "Vegetarian and vegan diets in type 2 diabetes management." *Nutrition Reviews.* 2009: 255–63.

    Barnard ND, Scialli AR, Turner-McGrievy G, Lanou AJ, Glass J. "The effects of a low-fat, plant-based dietary intervention on body weight, metabolism, and insulin sensitivity. *American Journal of Medicine.* 2005: 991–7.

2. Esselstyn CB, Jr. "Is the present therapy for coronary artery disease the radical mastectomy of the twenty-first century?" *American Journal of Cardiology.* 2010: 902–4.

    Esselstyn CB, Jr. "Updating a 12-year experience with arrest and reversal therapy for coronary heart disease (an overdue requiem for palliative cardiology)." *American Journal of Cardiology.* 1999: 339–41, A338.

    Esselstyn CB, Jr. "Changing the treatment paradigm for coronary artery disease." *American Journal of Cardiology.* 1998: 2T–4T.

    Esselstyn CB, Jr., Ellis SG, Medendorp SV, Crowe TD. "A strategy to arrest and reverse coronary artery disease: a 5-year longitudinal study of a single physician's practice." *Journal of Family Practice.* 1995: 560–68.

    Esselstyn CB, Jr., Gendy G, Doyle J, Golubic M, Roizen MF. "A way to reverse CAD?" *"Journal of Family Practice.* 2014: 356–64b.

    Ornish D, Scherwitz LW, Billings JH, et al. "Intensive lifestyle changes for reversal of coronary heart disease." *Journal of the American Medical Association.* 1998: 2001–07.

3. Swank RL, Dugan BB. Effect of low saturated fat diet in early and late cases of multiple sclerosis. *Lancet.* 1990:37–39.

    Lauer K. "Diet and multiple sclerosis." *Neurology.* 1997: S55–61.

4. Burkitt, DP. "Epidemiology of cancer of the colon and rectum." *Nutrition Reviews.* 1987: 212–14.

Armstrong B, Doll R. "Environmental factors and cancer incidence and mortality in different countries, with special reference to dietary practices." *International Journal of Cancer.* 1975: 617–31.

Burkitt DP. "Cancer of the colon and rectum. Epidemiology and possible causative factors." *Minnesota Medicine.* 1972: 779–83.

Burkitt DP. "Epidemiology of cancer of the colon and rectum." *Cancer.* 1971: 3–13.

Doll R, Peto R. "The causes of cancer: quantitative estimates of avoidable risks of cancer in the United States today." *Journal of the National Cancer Institute.* 1981: 1191–308.

Key TJ, Chen J, Wang DY, Pike MC, Boreham J. "Sex hormones in women in rural China and in Britain." *British Journal of Cancer.* 1990: 631–36.

Li JY, Liu BQ, Li GY, Chen ZJ, Sun XI, Rong SD. "Atlas of cancer mortality in the People's Republic of China." An aid for cancer control and research. *International Journal of Epidemiology.* 1981: 127–33.

Wu AH, Pike MC, Stram DO. "Meta-analysis: Dietary fat intake, serum estrogen levels, and the risk of breast cancer." *Journal of the National Cancer Institute.* 1999: 529–34.

HOW TO USE THIS BOOK

1. Blanchard CM, Fisher J, Sparling PB, et al. "Understanding adherence to 5 servings of fruits and vegetables per day: a theory of planned behavior perspective." *Journal of Nutrition Education and Behavior* 41, no. 1 (Jan-Feb 2009): 3–10.

   Teixeira PJ, Silva MN, Mata J, Palmeira AL, Markland D. "Motivation, self-determination, and long-term weight control." *International Journal of Behavioral Nutrition and Physical Activity* 9 (2012): 22.

2. Wilson K, Senay I, Durantini M, et al. "When it comes to lifestyle recommendations, more is sometimes less: a meta-analysis of theoretical assumptions underlying the effectiveness of interventions promoting multiple behavior domain change." *Psychological Bulletin* 141, no. 2 (Mar 2015): 474–509.

3. See note 1 above.

4. Fortuna JL. "The obesity epidemic and food addiction: clinical similarities to drug dependence." *Journal of Psychoactive Drugs* 44, no. 1 (Jan-Mar 2012): 56–63.

5. Feng J, Glass TA, Curriero FC, Stewart WF, Schwartz BS. "The built environment and obesity: a systematic review of the epidemiologic evidence." *Health & Place* 16, no. 2 (Mar 2010): 175–90.

   Mayne SL, Auchincloss AH, Michael YL. "Impact of policy and built environment changes on obesity-related outcomes: a systematic review of naturally occurring experiments." *Obesity Reviews* 16, no. 5 (May 2015): 362–75.

6. Shay LE. "A concept analysis: adherence and weight loss." *Nursing Forum* 43, no. 1 (Jan-Mar 2008): 42–52.

7. See note 5 above.

8. Hedley AA, Ogden CL, Johnson CL, Carroll MD, Curtin LR, Flegal KM. "Prevalence of overweight and obesity among US children, adolescents, and adults, 1999–2002." *Journal of the American Medical Association* 291, no. 23 (Jun 16 2004): 2847–50.

9. French SA, Story M, Jeffery RW. "Environmental influences on eating and physical activity." *Annual Review of Public Health* 22 (2001): 309–35.

10. See note 6 above.

Rothman AJ, Sheeran P, Wood W. "Reflective and automatic processes in the initiation and maintenance of dietary change." *Annals of Behavioral Medicine* 38 Suppl 1 (Dec 2009): S4–17.

Privitera GJ, Zuraikat FM. "Proximity of foods in a competitive food environment influences consumption of a low calorie and a high calorie food." *Appetite* 76 (May 2014): 175–79.

11. Gearhardt AN, Davis C, Kuschner R, Brownell KD. "The addiction potential of hyperpalatable foods." *Current Drug Abuse Reviews* 4, no. 3 (Sep 2011): 140–45.

12. van't Riet J, Sijtsema SJ, Dagevos H, De Bruijn GJ. "The importance of habits in eating behaviour. An overview and recommendations for future research." *Appetite* 57, no. 3 (Dec 2011): 585–96.

13. See note 12 above.

14. See note 2 above.

STEP ONE: FIND YOUR MOTIVATING FORCE

1. Cushman K. "The Motivation Equation." Next Generation Press, www.howyouthlearn.org/educator_resources_motivationequation.html. Accessed June 2, 2015.

2. Laba TL, Essue B, Kimman M, Jan S. "Understanding patient preferences in medication nonadherence: A review of stated preference data." *Patient* 8, no. 5 (Oct 2014): 385–95.

Polonsky WH. "Poor medication adherence in diabetes: what's the problem?" *Journal of Diabetes* 7, no. 6 (Nov 30 2015): 777–78.

3. Lam RW, Michalak EE, Bond DJ, Tam EM, Axler A, Yatham LN. "Which depressive symptoms and medication side effects are perceived by patients as interfering most with occupational functioning?" *Depression Research and Treatment* 2012 (2012): 630206.

Martel MO, Finan PH, Dolman AJ, et al. "Self-reports of medication side effects and pain-related activity interference in patients with chronic pain: a longitudinal cohort study." *Pain* 156, no. 6 (Jun 2015): 1092–1100.

Meehan T, Stedman T, Wallace J. "Consumer strategies for coping with antipsychotic medication side effects." *Australasian Psychiatry* 19, no. 1 (Feb 2011): 74–77.

Sheltawy AA, Criseno S, Gittoes NJ, Crowley RK. "Fear of medication side effects is a barrier to optimal osteoporosis care." *Osteoporos International* 26, no. 2 (Feb 2015): 843–44.

4. Orlich MJ, Fraser GE. "Vegetarian diets in the Adventist Health Study 2: a review of initial published findings." *American Journal of Clinical Nutrition* 100 Suppl 1 (Jul 2014): 353S–58S.

5. Macknin M, Kong T, Weier A, et al. "Plant-based, no-added-fat or American Heart Association diets: impact on cardiovascular risk in obese children with hypercholesterolemia and their parents." *Journal of Pediatrics* 166, no. 4 (Apr 2015): 953–59, e953.

Turner-McGrievy GM, Davidson CR, Wingard EE, Wilcox S, Frongillo EA. "Comparative effectiveness of plant-based diets for weight loss: a randomized controlled trial of five different diets." *Nutrition* 31, no. 2 (Feb 2015): 350–58.

6. Bodai BI, Tuso P. "Breast cancer survivorship: a comprehensive review of long-term medical issues and lifestyle recommendations." *Permanente Journal* 19, no. 2 (Spring 2015): 48–79.

Tuso PJ, Ismail MH, Ha BP, Bartolotto C. "Nutritional update for physicians: plant-based diets." *Permanente Journal* 17, no. 2 (Spring 2013): 61–66.

7. See note 4 above.

313

Wang Y, Beydoun MA. "Meat consumption is associated with obesity and central obesity among US adults." *International Journal of Obesity (London)* 33, no. 6 (Jun 2009): 621–28.

8. Japas C, Knutsen S, Dehom S, Dos Santos H, Tonstad S. "Body mass index gain between ages 20 and 40 years and lifestyle characteristics of men at ages 40–60 years: the Adventist Health Study-2." *Obesity Research & Clinical Practice* 8, no. 6 (Nov–Dec 2014): e549-557.

9. See note 5 above.

10. Barnard ND, Scialli AR, Turner-McGrievy G, Lanou AJ, Glass J. "The effects of a low-fat, plant-based dietary intervention on body weight, metabolism, and insulin sensitivity." *American Journal of Medicine* 118, no. 9 (Sep 2005): 991–97.

11. See note 5 above.

12. Yang L, Colditz GA. "Prevalence of overweight and obesity in the United States, 2007–2012." *JAMA Internal Medicine,* 175, no. 8 (Aug 2015): 1412–13.

13. Singh GK, Kogan MD, van Dyck PC. "Changes in state-specific childhood obesity and overweight prevalence in the United States from 2003 to 2007." *Archives of Pediatric & Adolescent Medicine* 164, no. 7 (Jul 2010): 598–607.

14. Ng M, Fleming T, Robinson M, et al. "Global, regional, and national prevalence of overweight and obesity in children and adults during 1980–2013: a systematic analysis for the Global Burden of Disease Study 2013." *Lancet* 384, no. 9945 (Aug 30 2014): 766–81.

15. Williamson DF, Kahn HS, Byers T. "The 10-y incidence of obesity and major weight gain in black and white US women aged 30–55 y." *American Journal of Clinical Nutrition* 53, no. 6 Suppl (Jun 1991): 1515S–18S.

16. Kopelman PG. "Obesity as a medical problem." *Nature* 404, no. 6778 (Apr 6 2000): 635–43.

Martin-Rodriguez E, Guillen-Grima F, Marti A, Brugos-Larumbe A. "Comorbidity associated with obesity in a large population: the APNA study." *Obesity Research & Clinical Practice* 9, no. 5 (Sept-Oct 2015): 435–47.

17. US Department of Agriculture, Agricultural Research Service, Nutrient Data Laboratory. USDA National Nutrient Database for Standard Reference, Release 28. Version Current: September 2015. Internet: http://www.ars.usda.gov/nea/bhnrc/ndl

18. Thomas DM, Bouchard C, Church T, et al. "Why do individuals not lose more weight from an exercise intervention at a defined dose? An energy balance analysis." *Obesity Reviews* 13, no. 10 (Oct 2012): 835–47.

19. Blair SN. "Evidence for success of exercise in weight loss and control." *Annals of Internal Medicine* 119, no. 7 Pt 2 (Oct 1 1993): 702–6.

20. Katan MB, Ludwig DS. "Extra calories cause weight gain—but how much?". *Journal of the American Medical Association* 303, no. 1 (Jan 6 2010): 65–66.

21. Yokoyama Y, Nishimura K, Barnard ND, et al. "Vegetarian diets and blood pressure: a meta-analysis." *JAMA Internal Medicine* 174, no. 4 (Apr 2014): 577–87.

22. Pettersen BJ, Anousheh R, Fan J, Jaceldo-Siegl K, Fraser GE. "Vegetarian diets and blood pressure among white subjects: results from the Adventist Health Study-2 (AHS-2)." *Public Health Nutrition* 15, no. 10 (Oct 2012): 1909–16.

23. Key TJ, Fraser GE, Thorogood M, et al. "Mortality in vegetarians and nonvegetarians: detailed findings from a collaborative analysis of 5 prospective studies." *American Journal of Clinical Nutrition* 70, no. 3 Suppl (Sep 1999): 516S–24S.

24. Esselstyn CB, Jr., Ellis SG, Medendorp SV, Crowe TD. "A strategy to arrest and reverse coronary artery disease: a 5-year longitudinal study of a single physician's practice." *Journal of Family Practice* 41, no. 6 (Dec 1995): 560–68.

Esselstyn CB, Jr., Favaloro RG. "More than coronary artery disease." *American Journal of Cardiology* 82, no. 10B (Nov 26 1998): 5T–9T.

Esselstyn CB, Jr. "Changing the treatment paradigm for coronary artery disease." *American Journal of Cardiology* 82, no. 10B (Nov 26 1998): 2T–4T.

Esselstyn CB, Jr. "Updating a 12-year experience with arrest and reversal therapy for coronary heart disease (an overdue requiem for palliative cardiology)." *American Journal of Cardiology* 84, no. 3 (Aug 1 1999): 339–41, A338.

Esselstyn CB, Jr. "In cholesterol lowering, moderation kills." *Cleveland Clinic Journal of Medicine* 67, no. 8 (Aug 2000): 560–64.

Esselstyn CB, Jr. "Resolving the coronary artery disease epidemic through plant-based nutrition." *Preventive Cardiology* 4, no. 4 (Autumn 2001): 171–77.

Esselstyn CB, Jr. "Is the present therapy for coronary artery disease the radical mastectomy of the twenty-first century?" *American Journal of Cardiology* 106, no. 6 (Sep 15 2010): 902–4.

Ornish D, Scherwitz LW, Billings JH, et al. "Intensive lifestyle changes for reversal of coronary heart disease." *Journal of the American Medical Association* 280, no. 23 (Dec 16 1998): 2001–7.

25. Mozaffarian D, Benjamin EJ, Go AS, et al. "Heart disease and stroke statistics—2015 update: a report from the American Heart Association." *Circulation* 131, no. 4 (Jan 27 2015): e29–322.

26. "National diabetes fact sheet: national estimates and general information on diabetes and prediabetes in the United States, 2011." U.S. Department of Health and Human Services, Centers for Disease Control and Prevention, www.cdc.gov/diabetes/pubs/pdf/ndfs_2011.pdf. Accessed May 21, 2015.

27. "Heart disease fact sheet." Centers for Disease Control and Prevention, www.cdc.gov/dhdsp/data_statistics/fact_sheets/fs_heart_disease.htm. Accessed July 16, 2015.

28. "National diabetes statistics report." National Center for Chronic Disease Prevention and Health Promotion, www.cdc.gov/diabetes/pubs/statsreport14/national-diabetes-report-web.pdf. Accessed July 16, 2015.

29. See note 26 above.

30. Miner M, Kim ED. "Cardiovascular disease and male sexual dysfunction." *Asian Journal of Andrology* 17, no. 1 (Jan–Feb 2015): 3-4.

31. American Diabetes Association. "Standards of medical care in diabetes—2014." *Diabetes Care* 37 Suppl 1 (Jan 2014): S14–80.

32. West KM, Kalbfleisch JM. "Influence of nutritional factors on prevalence of diabetes." *Diabetes* 20, no. 2 (Feb 1971): 99–108.

Snowdon DA, Phillips RL. "Does a vegetarian diet reduce the occurrence of diabetes?" *American Journal of Public Health* 75, no. 5 (May 1985): 507–12.

Fraser GE. "Associations between diet and cancer, ischemic heart disease, and all-cause mortality in non-Hispanic white California Seventh-day Adventists." *American Journal of Clinical Nutrition* 70, no. 3 Suppl (Sep 1999): 532S–38S.

33. Wu L, Parhofer KG. "Diabetic dyslipidemia." *Metabolism* 63, no. 12 (Dec 2014): 1469–79.

34. See note 10 above.

Barnard ND, Cohen J, Jenkins DJ, et al. "A low-fat vegan diet and a conventional diabetes diet in the treatment of type 2 diabetes: a randomized, controlled, 74-wk clinical trial." *American Journal of Clinical Nutrition* 89, no. 5 (May 2009): 1588S–96S.

Barnard ND, Cohen J, Jenkins DJ, et al. "A low-fat vegan diet improves glycemic control and cardiovascular risk factors in a randomized clinical trial in individuals with type 2 diabetes." *Diabetes Care* 29, no. 8 (Aug 2006): 1777–83.

Barnard ND, Katcher HI, Jenkins DJ, Cohen J, Turner-McGrievy G. "Vegetarian and vegan diets in type 2 diabetes management." *Nutrition Reviews* 67, no. 5 (May 2009): 255–63.

Barnard ND, Noble EP, Ritchie T, et al. "D2 dopamine receptor Taq1A polymorphism, body weight, and dietary intake in type 2 diabetes." *Nutrition* 25, no. 1 (Jan 2009): 58–65.

35. Riboli E. "The role of metabolic carcinogenesis in cancer causation and prevention: evidence from the European Prospective Investigation into Cancer and Nutrition." *Cancer Treatment and Research* 159 (2014): 3–20.

Bertram JS, Kolonel LN, Meyskens FL, Jr. "Rationale and strategies for chemoprevention of cancer in humans." *Cancer Research* 47, no. 11 (Jun 1 1987): 3012–31.

Yu S, Yang CS, Li J, et al. "Cancer prevention research in China." *Cancer Prevention Research (Philadelphia)* 8, no. 8 (Aug 2015): 662–74.

36. Li JY, Liu BQ, Li GY, Chen ZJ, Sun XI, Rong SD. "Atlas of cancer mortality in the People's Republic of China. An aid for cancer control and research." *International Journal of Epidemiology* 10, no. 2 (Jun 1981): 127-133.

Chen J CT, Li J, Peto R. *Diet, life-style, and mortality in China. A study of the characteristics of 65 Chinese counties.* Oxford, UK; Ithaca, NY; Beijing, PRC: Oxford University Press; Cornell University Press; People's Medical Publishing House, 1990.

Doll R, Peto R. "The causes of cancer: quantitative estimates of avoidable risks of cancer in the United States today." *Journal of the National Cancer Institute* 66, no. 6 (Jun 1981): 1191–308.

Armstrong B, Doll R. "Environmental factors and cancer incidence and mortality in different countries, with special reference to dietary practices." *International Journal of Cancer* 15, no. 4 (Apr 15 1975): 617–31.

Key TJ, Chen J, Wang DY, Pike MC, Boreham J. "Sex hormones in women in rural China and in Britain." *British Journal of Cancer* 62, no. 4 (Oct 1990): 631–36.

Wu AH, Pike MC, Stram DO. "Meta-analysis: dietary fat intake, serum estrogen levels, and the risk of breast cancer." *Journal of the National Cancer Institute* 91, no. 6 (Mar 17 1999): 529–34.

Burkitt DP. "Epidemiology of cancer of the colon and rectum." *Cancer* 28, no. 1 (Jul 1971): 3–13.

37. Campbell TC, Junshi C. "Diet and chronic degenerative diseases: perspectives from China." *American Journal of Clinical Nutrition* 59, no. 5 Suppl (May 1994): 1153S–61S.

38. Madhavan TV, Gopalan C. "The effect of dietary protein on carcinogenesis of aflatoxin." *Archives of Pathology* 85, no. 2 (Feb 1968): 133–37.

Campbell TC, Chen JS, Liu CB, Li JY, Parpia B. "Nonassociation of aflatoxin with primary liver cancer in a cross-sectional ecological survey in the People's Republic of China." *Cancer Research* 50, no. 21 (Nov 1 1990): 6882–93.

Hayes JR, Mgbodile MU, Campbell TC. "Effect of protein deficiency on the inducibility of the hepatic microsomal drug-metabolizing enzyme system. I. Effect on substrate interaction with cytochrome P-450." *Biochemical Pharmacology* 22, no. 9 (May 1 1973): 1005–14.

Nerurkar LS, Hayes JR, Campbell TC. "The reconstitution of hepatic microsomal mixed function oxidase activity with fractions derived from weanling rats fed different levels of protein." *Journal of Nutrition* 108, no. 4 (Apr 1978): 678–86.

Adekunle AA, Hayes JR, Campbell TC. "Interrelationships of dietary protein level, aflatoxin B metabolism, and hepatic microsomal epoxide hydrase activity." *Life Sciences* 21, no. 12 (Dec 15 1977): 1785–92.

Youngman LD, Campbell TC. "High protein intake promotes the growth of hepatic

316

preneoplastic foci in Fischer #344 rats: evidence that early remodeled foci retain the potential for future growth." *Journal of Nutrition* 121, no. 9 (Sep 1991): 1454–61.

Youngman LD, Campbell TC. "Inhibition of aflatoxin B1-induced gamma-glutamyltranspeptidase positive (GGT+) hepatic preneoplastic foci and tumors by low protein diets: evidence that altered GGT+ foci indicate neoplastic potential." *Carcinogenesis* 13, no. 9 (Sep 1992): 1607–13.

Dunaif GE, Campbell TC. "Dietary protein level and aflatoxin B1-induced preneoplastic hepatic lesions in the rat." *Journal of Nutrition* 117, no. 7 (Jul 1987): 1298–302.

Schulsinger DA, Root MM, Campbell TC. "Effect of dietary protein quality on development of aflatoxin B1-induced hepatic preneoplastic lesions." *Journal of the National Cancer Institute* 81, no. 16 (Aug 16 1989): 1241–45.

Cheng Z, Hu J, King J, Jay G, Campbell TC. "Inhibition of hepatocellular carcinoma development in hepatitis B virus transfected mice by low dietary casein." *Hepatology* 26, no. 5 (Nov 1997): 1351–54.

Hu JF, Cheng Z, Chisari FV, Vu TH, Hoffman AR, Campbell TC. "Repression of hepatitis B virus (HBV) transgene and HBV-induced liver injury by low protein diet." *Oncogene* 15, no. 23 (Dec 4 1997): 2795–801.

39. Levine ME, Suarez JA, Brandhorst S, et al. "Low protein intake is associated with a major reduction in IGF-1, cancer, and overall mortality in the 65 and younger but not older population." *Cell Metabolism* 19, no. 3 (Mar 4 2014): 407–17.

40. See note 6 above.

41. Frattaroli J, Weidner G, Dnistrian AM, et al. "Clinical events in prostate cancer lifestyle trial: results from two years of follow-up." *Urology* 72, no. 6 (Dec 2008): 1319–23.

Ornish DM, Lee KL, Fair WR, Pettengill EB, Carroll PR. "Dietary trial in prostate cancer: Early experience and implications for clinical trial design." *Urology* 57, no. 4 Suppl 1 (Apr 2001): 200–01.

42. Kris-Etherton P, Eckel RH, Howard BV, et al. "AHA science advisory: Lyon Diet Heart Study: benefits of a Mediterranean-style, National Cholesterol Education Program/American Heart Association step I dietary pattern on cardiovascular disease." *Circulation* 103, no. 13 (Apr 3 2001): 1823–25.

Rees K, Hartley L, Flowers N, et al. "'Mediterranean' dietary pattern for the primary prevention of cardiovascular disease." *Cochrane Database of Systematic Reviews* 8 (2013): CD009825.

43. Willcox DC, Scapagnini G, Willcox BJ. "Healthy aging diets other than the Mediterranean: a focus on the Okinawan diet." *Mechanisms of Ageing and Development* 136-137 (Mar-Apr 2014): 148–62.

44. Cerqueira MT, Fry MM, Connor WE. "The food and nutrient intakes of the Tarahumara Indians of Mexico." *American Journal of Clinical Nutrition* 32, no. 4 (Apr 1979): 905–15.

McMurry MP, Cerqueira MT, Connor SL, Connor WE. "Changes in lipid and lipoprotein levels and body weight in Tarahumara Indians after consumption of an affluent diet." *New England Journal of Medicine* 325, no. 24 (Dec 12 1991): 1704–8.

45. *U.S. Department of Health and Human Services and U.S. Department of Agriculture. 2015 – 2020 Dietary Guidelines for Americans. 8th Edition. December 2015. Available at http:// health.gov/dietaryguidelines/2015/guidelines/*

46. Bjelakovic G, Nikolova D, Gluud LL, Simonetti RG, Gluud C. "Antioxidant supplements for prevention of mortality in healthy participants and patients with various diseases." *Sao Paulo Medical Journal* 133, no. 2 (Mar–Apr 2015): 164–65.

Dolara P, Bigagli E, Collins A. "Antioxidant vitamins and mineral supplementa-

317

tion, life span expansion and cancer incidence: a critical commentary." *European Journal of Nutrition* 51, no. 7 (Oct 2012): 769–81.

Hooper L, Thompson RL, Harrison RA, et al. "Risks and benefits of omega 3 fats for mortality, cardiovascular disease, and cancer: systematic review." *BMJ* 332, no. 7544 (Apr 1 2006): 752–60.

Marik PE, Flemmer M. "Do dietary supplements have beneficial health effects in industrialized nations: what is the evidence?" *Journal of Parenteral and Enteral Nutrition* 36, no. 2 (Mar 2012): 159–68.

47. van't Riet J, Sijtsema SJ, Dagevos H, De Bruijn GJ. "The importance of habits in eating behaviour. An overview and recommendations for future research." *Appetite* 57, no. 3 (Dec 2011): 585–96.

48. Rothman AJ, Sheeran P, Wood W. "Reflective and automatic processes in the initiation and maintenance of dietary change." *Annals Behavioral Medicine* 38 Suppl 1 (Dec 2009): S4–17.

49. Jackson RE. "Preference for the nearer of otherwise equivalent navigational goals quantifies behavioral motivation and natural selection." *PLoS One* 8, no. 1 (2013): e54725.

STEP TWO: ADD PLANT-BASED FOODS TO YOUR DIET

1. Davis C. "From passive overeating to 'food addiction': a spectrum of compulsion and severity." *International Scholarly Research Network Obesity* 2013 (2013): 435027.

2. Javaras KN, Laird NM, Reichborn-Kjennerud T, Bulik CM, Pope HG, Jr., Hudson JI. "Familiality and heritability of binge eating disorder: results of a case-control family study and a twin study." *International Journal of Eating Disorders* 41, no. 2 (Mar 2008): 174–79.

3. Maki KC, Nieman KM, Schild AL, et al. "Sugar-sweetened product consumption alters glucose homeostasis compared with dairy product consumption in men and women at risk of type 2 diabetes mellitus." *Journal of Nutrition* 145, no. 3 (Mar 2015): 459–66.

Rippe JM, Angelopoulos TJ. "Fructose-containing sugars and cardiovascular disease." *Advances in Nutrition* 6, no. 4 (Jul 2015): 430–39.

4. *Modern Nutrition in Health and Disease (10th ed.).* Baltimore, MD: Lippincott Williams & Wilkins, 2006.

5. See note 4 above.

6. LeBlanc JG, Milani C, de Giori GS, Sesma F, van Sinderen D, Ventura M. "Bacteria as vitamin suppliers to their host: a gut microbiota perspective." *Current Opinion in Biotechnology* 24, no. 2 (Apr 2013): 160–68.

7. Schwarz J, Dschietzig T, Schwarz J, et al. "The influence of a whole food vegan diet with Nori algae and wild mushrooms on selected blood parameters." *Clinical Laboratory* 60, no. 12 (2014): 2039–50.

8. Watanabe F, Yabuta Y, Bito T, Teng F. "Vitamin B_{12}-containing plant food sources for vegetarians." *Nutrients* 6, no. 5 (May 2014): 1861–73.

9. "Vitamin D: fact sheet for professionals." National Institutes of Health, Office of Dietary Supplements, 2014.

10. See note 4 above.

Holick MF. "Sunlight and vitamin D for bone health and prevention of autoimmune diseases, cancers, and cardiovascular disease." *American Journal of Clinical Nutrition* 80, no. 6 Suppl (Dec 2004): 1678S–88S.

Wacker M, Holick MF. "Sunlight and vitamin D: a global perspective for health." *Dermatoendocrinology* 5, no. 1 (Jan 1 2013): 51–108.

11. See note 10 above.

12. See note 9 above.

13. Ross AC, Manson JE, Abrams SA, et al. "The 2011 report on dietary reference intakes for calcium and vitamin D from the Institute of Medicine: what clinicians need to know." *Journal of Clinical Endocrinology & Metababolism* 96, no. 1 (Jan 2011): 53–58.

14. See note 10 above.

15. See note 4 above.

16. See note 4 above

17. Fleming JA, Kris-Etherton PM. "The evidence for alpha-linolenic acid and cardio-vascular disease benefits: comparisons with eicosapentaenoic acid and docosahex-aenoic acid." *Advances in Nutrition* 5, no. 6 (Nov 2014): 863S–76S.

18. Byelashov OA, Sinclair AJ, Kaur G. "Dietary sources, current intakes, and nutritional role of omega-3 docosapentaenoic acid." *Lipid Technology* 27, no. 4 (Apr 2015): 79–82.

19. U.S. Department of Health and Human Services and U.S. Department of Agriculture. 2015 – 2020 Dietary Guidelines for Americans. 8th Edition. December 2015. Available at http://health.gov/dietaryguidelines/2015/guidelines/

20. Shao KT. "Marine biodiversity and fishery sustainability." *Asian Pacific Journal of Clinical Nutrition* 18, no. 4 (2009): 527–31.

21. Goyens PL, Spilker ME, Zock PL, Katan MB, Mensink RP. "Conversion of alpha-linolenic acid in humans is influenced by the absolute amounts of alpha-linolenic acid and linoleic acid in the diet and not by their ratio." *American Journal of Clinical Nutrition* 84, no. 1 (Jul 2006): 44–53.

22. See note 21 above.

23. Harris WS. "Achieving optimal n-3 fatty acid status: the vegetarian's challenge... or not." *American Journal of Clinical Nutrition* 100 Suppl 1 (Jul 2014): 449S–52S.

24. See note 23 above.

25. Tal A, Wansink B. "Fattening fasting: hungry grocery shoppers buy more calories, not more food." *JAMA Internal Medicine* 173, no. 12 (Jun 24 2013): 1146–48.

26. Ramey VA. "Time spent in home production in the twentieth-century United States: New estimates from old data." *Journal of Economic History* 69, no. 01 (2009): 1–47.

27. Smith LP, Ng SW, Popkin BM. "Trends in US home food preparation and consumption: analysis of national nutrition surveys and time use studies from 1965–1966 to 2007–2008." *Nutrition Journal* 12 (2013): 45.

28. Martin-Biggers J, Spaccarotella K, Berhaupt-Glickstein A, Hongu N, Worobey J, Byrd-Bredbenner C. "Come and get it! A discussion of family mealtime literature and factors affecting obesity risk." *Advances in Nutrition* 5, no. 3 (May 2014): 235–47.

29. Kant AK, Whitley MI, Graubard BI. "Away from home meals: Associations with biomarkers of chronic disease and dietary intake in American adults, NHANES 2005–2010." *International Journal of Obesity (London)* 39, no. 5 (May 2015): 820–27.

30. Cynthia J, Zalilah MS, Lim MY. "Relationship between family meals away from home and nutritional status of adolescents." *Malaysian Journal of Nutrition* 19, no. 1 (Apr 2013): 25–35.

31. Schlundt DG, Hill JO, Sbrocco T, Pope-Cordle J, Kasser T. "Obesity: A biogenetic or biobehavioral problem." *International Journal of Obesity* 14, no. 9 (Sep 1990): 815–28.

    Granner ML, Mburia-Mwalili A. "Correlates of television viewing among African American and Caucasian women." *Women & Health* 50, no. 8 (Dec 2010): 783–94.

32. Wood D. "Teaching the young child: some relationships between social interaction, language and thought." *Lev Vygotsky: Critical Assessments* 3 (1999): 259–75.

33. Birch LL. "Development of food preferences." *Annual Review of Nutrition* 19 (1999): 41–62.

   Birch LL. "Child feeding practices and the etiology of obesity." *Obesity (Silver Spring)* 14, no. 3 (Mar 2006): 343–44.

   Cornwell TB, McAlister AR. "Alternative thinking about starting points of obesity. Development of child taste preferences." *Appetite* 56, no. 2 (Apr 2011): 428–39.

STEP THREE: CHOOSE HEALTH OVER HABIT

1. Joyner MA, Gearhardt AN, White MA. "Food craving as a mediator between addictive-like eating and problematic eating outcomes." *Eating Behaviors* 19 (Aug 4 2015): 98–101.

2. Kurihara K. "Umami the Fifth Basic Taste: History of Studies on Receptor Mechanisms and Role as a Food Flavor." *BioMed Research International* 2015 (2015): 189402.

3. Ahmed SH, Guillem K, Vandaele Y. "Sugar addiction: pushing the drug-sugar analogy to the limit." *Current Opinion in Clinical Nutrition and Metabolic Care* 16, no. 4 (Jul 2013): 434–39.

4. Gearhardt AN, Davis C, Kuschner R, Brownell KD. "The addiction potential of hyperpalatable foods." *Current Drug Abuse Reviews* 4, no. 3 (Sep 2011): 140–45.

5. Brownell KK, Gold, MS. *Food and Addiction.* New York, NY: Oxford University Press, 2012.

6. Moubarac JC, Martins APB, Claro RM, Levy RB, Cannon G, Monteiro CA. "Consumption of ultra-processed foods and likely impact on human health. Evidence from Canada." *Public Health Nutrition* 16, no. 12 (Dec 2013): 2240–48.

7. Henningfield JE, Keenan RM. "Nicotine delivery kinetics and abuse liability." *Journal of Consulting and Clinical Psychology* 61, no. 5 (Oct 1993): 743–50.

   Davis, C. "From passive overeating to 'food addiction': a spectrum of compulsion and severity." *International Scholarly Research Network Obesity* 2013 (2013): 435027.

   Breslin PA. "An evolutionary perspective on food and human taste." *Current Biology* 23, no. 9 (May 6 2013): R409–18.

8. Cassady BA, Mattes RD. "Taste sensation: influences on human ingestive behavior." In *Nutrition Guide for Physicians.* Edited by Wilson T, Temple NJ, Bray GA, Struble MB. 2010. doi:10.1007/978-1-60327-431-9_14.

9. Grieve FG, Vander MW. "Desire to eat high- and low-fat foods following a low-fat dietary intervention." *Journal of Nutrition Education and Behavior* 35, no. 2 (Mar-Apr 2003): 98–104.

   Ledikwe JH, Ello-Martin J, Pelkman CL, Birch LL, Mannino ML, Rolls BJ. "A reliable, valid questionnaire indicates that preference for dietary fat declines when following a reduced-fat diet." *Appetite* 49, no. 1 (Jul 2007): 74-83.

10. Little TJ, Feinle-Bisset C. "Effects of dietary fat on appetite and energy intake in health and obesity — oral and gastrointestinal sensory contributions." *Physiology & Behavior* 104, no. 4 (Sep 2011): 613--20.

   Louis-Sylvestre J. "Perception and food behaviour: the specific case of fats." *OCL —Oilseeds & Fats Crops and Lipids* 6, no. 4 (Jul-Aug 1999): 311–15.

11. See note 7 above.

12. See note 8 above.

   Stubenitsky K, Aaron JI, Catt SL, Mela DJ. "Effect of information and extended use on the acceptance of reduced-fat products." *Food Quality and Preference* 10, no. 4–5 (Jul–Sep 1999): 367–76.

13. Robinson E. "Relationships between expected, online and remembered enjoyment for food products." *Appetite* 74 (Mar 2014): 55–60.

14. See notes 4 and 5 above.

15. See note 7 above.

16. See notes 1, 4, and 7 above.

17. See note 7 above.

18. See notes 8, 9, 10, and 12 above.

19. See note 13 above.

20. U.S. Department of Health and Human Services and U.S. Department of Agriculture. 2015 – 2020 Dietary Guidelines for Americans. 8th Edition. December 2015. Available at http://health.gov/dietaryguidelines/2015/guidelines/.

21. "Dietary reference intakes (DRIs): estimated average requirements." Food and Nutrition Board, Institute of Medicine, National Academies, 2011.

22. See note 20 above.

23. Maalouf J, Cogswell ME, Yuan K, et al. "Top sources of dietary sodium from birth to age 24 mo, United States, 2003-2010." *American Journal of Clinical Nutrition* 101, no. 5 (May 2015): 1021–28.

   Van Horn L. "Dietary sodium and blood pressure: how low should we go?" *Progress in Cardiovascular Diseases* 58, no. 1 (Jul-Aug 2015): 61–68.

   Gillespie C, Maalouf J, Yuan K, et al. "Sodium content in major brands of US packaged foods, 2009." *American Journal of Clinical Nutrition* 101, no. 2 (Feb 2015): 344–53.

24. See note 7 above.

25. Revedin A, Aranguren B, Becattini R, et al. "Thirty thousand-year-old evidence of plant food processing." *Proceedings of the National Academy of the Sciences of the United States of America* 107, no. 44 (Nov 2 2010): 18815–19.

26. See note 7 above.

27. Sayers K, Lovejoy CO. "Blood, bulbs, and bunodonts: on evolutionary ecology and the diets of *Ardipithecus*, *Australopithecus*, and early *Homo*." *Quarterly Review of Biology* 89, no. 4 (Dec 2014): 319–57.

28. US Department of Agriculture, Agricultural Research Service, Nutrient Data Laboratory. USDA National Nutrient Database for Standard Reference, Release 28. Version Current: September 2015. Internet: http://www.ars.usda.gov/nea/bhnrc/ndl.

29. Faith MS, Keller KL, Johnson SL, et al. "Familial aggregation of energy intake in children." *The American Journal of Clinical Nutrition* 79, no. 5 (May 2004): 844–50.

   Kral TV, Allison DB, Birch LL, Stallings VA, Moore RH, Faith MS. "Caloric compensation and eating in the absence of hunger in 5- to 12-y-old weight-discordant siblings." *American Journal of Clinical Nutrition* 96, no. 3 (Sep 2012): 574–83.

30. Wansink B. "From mindless eating to mindlessly eating better." *Physiology & Behavior* 100, no. 5 (Jul 14 2010): 454–63.

   Wansink B, Shimizu M. "Eating behaviors and the number of buffet trips: an observational study at all-you-can-eat Chinese restaurants." *American Journal of Preventive Medicine* 44, no. 4 (Apr 2013): e49–50.

31. Flood-Obbagy JE, Rolls BJ. "The effect of fruit in different forms on energy intake and satiety at a meal." *Appetite* 52, no. 2 (Apr 2009): 416–22.

   Haber GB, Heaton KW, Murphy D, Burroughs LF. "Depletion and disruption of dietary fibre. Effects on satiety, plasma-glucose, and serum-insulin." *Lancet* 2, no. 8040 (Oct 1 1977): 679–82.

32. Stein LJ, Cowart BJ, Beauchamp GK. "The development of salty taste acceptance is related to dietary experience in human infants: a prospective study." *American Journal of Clinical Nutrition* 95, no. 1 (Jan 2012): 123–29.

NOTES

33. Birch LL. "Development of food preferences." *Annual Review of Nutrition* 19 (1999): 41–62.

   Birch LL. "Child feeding practices and the etiology of obesity." *Obesity (Silver Spring)* 14, no. 3 (Mar 2006): 343–44.

   Cornwell TB, McAlister AR. "Alternative thinking about starting points of obesity. Development of child taste preferences." *Appetite* 56, no. 2 (Apr 2011): 428–39.

   Harris G. "Development of taste and food preferences in children." *Current Opinion in Clinical Nutrition and Metabolic Care* 11, no. 3 (May 2008): 315–19.

   Hendricks K, Briefel R, Novak T, Ziegler P. "Maternal and child characteristics associated with infant and toddler feeding practices." *Journal of the American Dietetic Association* 106, no. 1 Suppl 1 (Jan 2006): S135–48.

34. Ayya N, Beauchamp GK. "Short-term effects of diet on salt taste preference." *Appetite* 18, no. 1 (Feb 1992): 77–82.

35. See note 5 above.

36. See note 5 above.

37. See note 5 above.

STEP FOUR: MAKE YOUR FOOD ENVIRONMENT MATCH YOUR BIOLOGY

1. Hofmann W, Baumeister RF, Forster G, Vohs KD. "Everyday temptations: an experience sampling study of desire, conflict, and self-control." *Journal of Personality and Social Psychology* 102, no. 6 (Jun 2012): 1318–35.

2. Gailliot MT, Baumeister RF. "The physiology of willpower: linking blood glucose to self-control." *Personality and Social Psychology Review* 11, no. 4 (Nov 2007): 303–27.

   Masicampo EJ, Baumeister RF. "Toward a physiology of dual-process reasoning and judgment: lemonade, willpower, and expensive rule-based analysis." *Psychological Science* 19, no. 3 (Mar 2008): 255–60.

3. Gailliot MT, Baumeister RF, DeWall CN, et al. "Self-control relies on glucose as a limited energy source: willpower is more than a metaphor." *Journal of Personality and Social Psychology* 92, no. 2 (Feb 2007): 325–36.

4. Lu L, Grimm JW, Hope BT, Shaham Y. "Incubation of cocaine craving after withdrawal: a review of preclinical data." *Neuropharmacology* 47 Suppl 1 (2004): 214–26.

5. Lisle DJ, and Alan Goldhamer. The Pleasure Trap: Mastering the Hidden Force That Undermines Health & Happiness. Summertown, TN: Healthy Living Publ., 2006.

   Fortuna JL. "The obesity epidemic and food addiction: clinical similarities to drug dependence." Journal of Pxsychoactive Drugs 44, no. 1 (Jan-Mar 2012): 56-63.

   Gearhardt AN, Davis C, Kuschner R, Brownell KD. "The addiction potential of hyperpalatable foods." Current Drug Abuse Reviews 4, no. 3 (Sep 2011): 140-145.

6. Wansink B, Sobal J. "Mindless eating: The 200 daily food decisions we overlook." *Environment and Behavior*, no. 39 (2007): 106–23.

7. Mattes R, Foster GD. "Research issues: the food environment and obesity." *American Journal of Clinical Nutrition* 100, no. 6 (Dec 2014): 1663–65.

8. Kant AK, Graubard BI. "40-year trends in meal and snack eating behaviors of American adults." *Journal of the Academy of Nutrition and Dietetics* 115, no. 1 (Jan 2015): 50–63.

   Tropp D, Ragland E, Barham J. "The dynamics of change in the US food marketing environment." USDA, Agricultural Marketing Service, Transportation and Marketing Program. Accessed March 30, 2015.

9. Jiao J, Moudon AV, Ulmer J, Hurvitz PM, Drewnowski A. "How to identify food deserts: measuring physical and economic access to supermarkets in King County, Washington." *American Journal of Public Health* 102, no. 10 (Oct 2012): e32–39.

Smith C, Morton LW. "Rural food deserts: low-income perspectives on food access in Minnesota and Iowa." *Journal of Nutrition Education and Behavior* 41, no. 3 (May-Jun 2009): 176–87.

Walker RE, Keane CR, Burke JG. "Disparities and access to healthy food in the United States: a review of food deserts literature." *Health & Place* 16, no. 5 (Sep 2010): 876–84.

10. Baumeister RF, Bratslavsky E, Muraven M, Tice DM. "Ego depletion: is the active self a limited resource?" *Journal of Personality and Social Psychology* 74, no. 5 (May 1998): 1252–65.

11. Mattes RD. "Fat preference and adherence to a reduced-fat diet." *American Journal of Clinical Nutrition* 57, no. 3 (Mar 1993): 373–81.

Bertino M, Beauchamp GK, Engelman K. "Long-term reduction in dietary sodium alters the taste of salt." *American Journal of Clinical Nutrition* 36, no. 6 (Dec 1982): 1134–44.

Bolhuis DP, Lakemond CM, de Wijk RA, Luning PA, de Graaf C. "Effect of salt intensity on ad libitum intake of tomato soup similar in palatability and on salt preference after consumption." *Chemical Senses* 35, no. 9 (Nov 2010): 789–99.

12. Michels N, Sioen I, Braet C, et al. "Stress, emotional eating behaviour and dietary patterns in children." *Appetite* 59, no. 3 (Dec 2012): 762–69.

13. Al'Absi M, Nakajima M, Hooker S, Wittmers L, Cragin T. "Exposure to acute stress is associated with attenuated sweet taste." *Psychophysiology* 49, no. 1 (Jan 2012): 96–103.

STEP FIVE CULTIVATE CONNECTION FOR THE LONG HAUL

1. Brunstrom JM. "Associative learning and the control of human dietary behavior." *Appetite* 49, no. 1 (Jul 2007): 268–71.

2. Higgs S. "Social norms and their influence on eating behaviours." *Appetite* 86 (Mar 2015): 38–44.

3. See note 2 above.

Leone T, Pliner P, Peter Herman C. "Influence of clear versus ambiguous normative information on food intake." *Appetite* 49, no. 1 (Jul 2007): 58–65.

4. de la Haye K, Robins G, Mohr P, Wilson C. "Adolescents' intake of junk food: processes and mechanisms driving consumption similarities among friends." *Journal of Research on Adolescence* 23, no. 3 (Sep 2013): 524–36.

5. Christakis NA, Fowler JH. "Social contagion theory: examining dynamic social networks and human behavior." *Statistics in Medicine* 32, no. 4 (Feb 2013): 556–77.

6. Christakis NA, Fowler JH. *Connected: The Surprising Power of our Social Networks and How They Shape Our Lives.* New York: Little Brown and Co., 2009.

7. Rancourt D, Leahey TM, LaRose JG, Crowther JH. "Effects of weight-focused social comparisons on diet and activity outcomes in overweight and obese young women." *Obesity* 23, no. 1 (Jan 2015): 85–89.

8. Barclay KJ, Edling C, Rydgren J. "Peer clustering of exercise and eating behaviours among young adults in Sweden: a cross-sectional study of egocentric network data." *BMC Public Health* 13 (Aug 2013).

9. Conklin AI, Forouhi NG, Surtees P, Khaw KT, Wareham NJ, Monsivais P. "Social relationships and healthful dietary behaviour: evidence from over-50s in the EPIC cohort, UK." *Social Science & Medicine* 100 (Jan 2014): 167–75.

10. Morisky DE, DeMuth NM, Field-Fass M, Green LW, Levine DM. "Evaluation of family health education to build social support for long-term control of high blood pressure." *Health Education Quarterly* 12, no. 1 (Spring 1985): 35-50.

323

Gomes-Villas Boas LC, Foss MC, Freitas MC, Pace AE. "Relationship among social support, treatment adherence and metabolic control of diabetes mellitus patients." *Revista Latino-Americana de Enfermagem* 20, no. 1 (Jan–Feb 2012): 52–58.

11. Barrera M, Jr., Toobert DJ, Angell KL, Glasgow RE, Mackinnon DP. "Social support and social-ecological resources as mediators of lifestyle intervention effects for type 2 diabetes." *Journal of Health Psychology* 11, no. 3 (May 2006): 483–95.

12. Gleeson-Kreig J. "Social support and physical activity in type 2 diabetes: a social-ecologic approach." *Diabetes Education* 34, no. 6 (Nov–Dec 2008): 1037–44.

13. Gruber KJ. "Social support for exercise and dietary habits among college students." *Adolescence* 43, no. 171 (2008): 557–75.

14. Pachucki MA, Jacques PF, Christakis NA. "Social network concordance in food choice among spouses, friends, and siblings." *American Journal of Public Health* 101, no. 11 (Nov 2011): 2170–77.

15. Jackson SE, Steptoe A, Wardle J. "The influence of partner's behavior on health behavior change—the English longitudinal study of ageing." *JAMA Internal Medicine* 175, no. 3 (Mar 2015): 385–92.

INDEX

329